Reforming the Austr

Reforming
the Australian
welfare state

Edited by
Peter Saunders

Australian Institute
of Family Studies

Australian Institute of Family Studies
300 Queen Street, Melbourne 3000 Australia
Phone (03) 9214 7888; Fax (03) 9214 7839
Internet www.aifs.org.au/

The Australian Institute of Family Studies is committed to the
creation and dissemination of research-based information on family
functioning and wellbeing. Views expressed in its publications are
those of individual authors and may not reflect Institute policy or
the opinions of the Editor or the Institute's Board of Management.

National Library of Australia
Cataloguing-in-Publication Data

Reforming the Australian welfare state.

Bibliography.
Includes index.
ISBN 0 642 39474 1.

1. Public welfare - Australia. 2.Family - Australia. 3. Family
policy - Australia. 4. Welfare recipients - Australia. 5. Labour
market - Australia. 6. Public welfare. 7. Australia - Social
policy. I. Saunders, Peter, 1950-. II. Australian Institute of
Family Studies.

361.60994.

Cover photograph by International Picture Library
Designed by Double Jay Graphic Design
Printed by Impact Printing

Contents

Preface

This book is published at a time when Australia, in common with a number of other western countries, is reassessing its welfare system. The book brings together Australian and international authors representing a variety of different interests and perspectives in the welfare field. Its aim is to contribute to the Australian debate over welfare reform by clarifying the issues that are at stake and presenting relevant and up-to-date evidence which bears upon the core arguments.

The Australian Institute of Family Studies has a particular interest in the issue of welfare reform because any change to the welfare state has important implications for Australian family life. In many ways, the modern welfare state and the family can be seen as functional substitutes for each other. Obviously the state cannot supply the affection that we look for in family life, any more than the family can supply the range of services and level of support that the state can provide. But in general, the more the state welfare system does, the less the family is likely to be required to do, and vice versa. This is why welfare policy and family policy are so closely linked – change in one will normally imply change in the other.

In December 1999, the Institute began to explore these links by publishing a special issue of its research magazine, *Family Matters*, devoted to 'Families, welfare and social policy'. The feedback on this special issue was extremely positive, and this prompted us to commission a number of essays from leading figures in the welfare field in order to explore in more depth some of the main issues which lie at the heart of the current welfare debate. The current volume is the result.

Most of the essays published here were specially written or revised for this volume. Earlier versions of chapter 2, by Lawrence Mead, chapter 3, by Frank Field, and chapter 4, by Alan Buckingham, originally appeared in the December 1999 special issue of *Family Matters* (no. 54). However, the Mead and Buckingham essays have subsequently been revised, developed and updated for this book, and only Field's essay remains essentially unchanged.

Two of the chapters are based on articles which have been published elsewhere. Anna Yeatman's essay on mutual obligation in chapter 8 is a substantially revised version of a paper first published in the *Proceedings* of the 1999 National Social Policy Conference. Peter Dawkins' discussion in chapter 11 of issues considered in the Reference Group's *Interim Report* is an edited version of an article which appeared in the April 2000 issue of the *Melbourne Institute Quarterly Bulletin of Economic Trends*.

The *Family Matters* December 1999 special issue contained articles by Noel Pearson and Lucy Sullivan, who both also contribute chapters to this book (chapter 7 and chapter 9 respectively), but in both cases these authors have chosen to produce entirely new pieces for inclusion here. The chapters by Frances McCoull and Jocelyn Pech (chapter 5), Don Siemon and Fiona MacDonald (chapter 10), Michael Raper (chapter 12), and Wendy Stone and myself (chapter 6) are all also published here for the first time, as is my introductory essay (chapter 1).

This is the first time I have edited a book of essays. Folk wisdom has it that such a task should be avoided if at all possible, for an edited book moves at the glacial pace of the slowest contributor, and even when all the essays are submitted, the editor still ends up spending weeks and even months having to mould them all into a common style while negotiating with authors reluctant to rework their material.

Such, however, was not my experience here. I am enormously grateful, therefore, to all of the contributors to this book for producing such excellent material under exceedingly tight deadlines, and for the alacrity with which they responded to subsequent editorial queries.

I should also like to thank David Stanton, the Director of the Australian Institute of Family Studies, and Peter Whiteford, of the OECD in Paris, for their very helpful comments on an earlier draft of the whole manuscript. I acknowledge and thank Alan Fettling, the Director of IP Communications, for his interest and initial encouragement of the project, and I appreciate Meredith Michie's professionalism, as the Institute's editor, in steering the book through to final publication.

Welfare policy is a contentious area of public debate and governance, and the issues being addressed in this book often stir strong passions. In homage to the Popperian spirit of open and critical argument, the book brings together contributors representing different positions in the debate who have been allowed as much freedom as is practicable to develop and express their own arguments in whichever way they believe is most appropriate. It is therefore the case that none of the opinions and arguments expressed in the chapters that follow should be taken to represent the views of the Australian Institute of Family Studies.

Peter Saunders
Australian Institute of Family Studies
May 2000

Notes on the contributors

Alan Buckingham is Lecturer in Sociology in the School of Social Sciences at the University of Sussex, England. Brought up by his divorced and jobless mother on a Local Authority housing estate in South East England, he recently completed a doctoral thesis on the underclass in Britain, and the main findings from this work have been published in the *British Journal of Sociology*. He is currently writing a book with Peter Saunders about quantitative research methods.

Peter Dawkins has, since 1996, been the Ronald Henderson Professor and Director of the Melbourne Institute of Applied Economic and Social Research at the University of Melbourne. He is well known for research in the areas of labour economics, social economics and industrial relations, and has published extensively in these areas. He has been prominent in policy debates about unemployment and the tax and welfare system. In August 1997 he addressed a special meeting of the Federal Cabinet on the subject of unemployment, and in October 1998 he was one of five economists who sent a letter to the Prime Minister outlining a plan for reducing unemployment. In October 1999 he was appointed to the Reference Group on Welfare Reform set up by the Minister for Family and Community Services.

Frank Field is a Labour Member of Parliament in the United Kingdom and was formerly Director of the Child Poverty Action Group. In the House of Commons he has been Labour's front bench spokesman on education and social security, he has chaired the Social Security Select Committee and, from 1997 to 1998, he was Minister for Welfare Reform, Department of Social Security, in the Blair government. He has published extensively, including two recent titles on welfare reform, both published by the Social Market Foundation (*Reforming Welfare* in 1997, and *Reflections on Welfare Reform* in 1998). He has been awarded an Honorary Doctorate of Law from Warwick University, and a Doctorate of Science from Southampton University.

Fiona MacDonald is a research and policy worker with the Social Action and Research directorate of the Brotherhood of St Laurence which she joined as a member of the Future of Work project team in the mid 1990s. The Brotherhood of St Laurence provides a range of services for people with low incomes and works for an Australia free of poverty through community education, research, social action and advocacy. Her work there has been mainly in the areas of employment and unemployment, industrial relations and wages, young people and labour market disadvantage, and on the longitudinal study of the life chances of children. She holds a B.Sc, a Grad. Dip in Couns. Psych. and a M.SocSci.

Frances McCoull is a Project Officer working in the Strategic Policy and Analysis Branch in the Commonwealth Department of Family and Community Services in Canberra. She has eight years experience in policy development and research related to income support. She is currently working on a project investigating trans-generational income support dependence in Australia.

Lawrence Mead is Professor of Politics at New York University, where he teaches public policy and American government. He has been a visiting professor at Harvard, Princeton, and the University of Wisconsin. Professor Mead is an expert on the problems of poverty and welfare in the United States, and the politics of these issues. His works include *Beyond Entitlement* (1986), *The New Politics of Poverty* (1992), *The New Paternalism* (1997), and *From Welfare to Work: Lessons from America* (1997). These books set out much of the theory and practice for recent welfare reform in the United States.

Noel Pearson is a history and law graduate of the University of Sydney, and his thesis on his home town of Hope Vale has recently been published in *Maps Dreams History* by the History Department of the University. He was part of the indigenous negotiating team during the drafting of the *Native Title Act* in 1993, and was the Executive Director of the Cape York Land Council until July 1996 when he was elected its Chairman. He resigned as Chairman at the end of 1997, but he remains an adviser to the Cape York Land Council, as well as to a number of other indigenous organisations in the Cape York region of Queensland.

Jocelyn Pech is Director of Participation Projects in the Commonwealth Department of Family and Community Services, and is currently seconded to the Department's Welfare Review team. In her usual role, she is responsible for a team undertaking applied policy research on emerging issues of concern to government and the community – including the current project on trans-generational income support dependence.

Michael Raper was elected President of the Australian Council of Social Service (ACOSS) in November 1997 and was re-elected in 1999. (ACOSS is the national peak council for the community welfare sector and brings together through its membership the major national charities and church groups, consumer groups, social justice groups, community service organisations and State and Territory Councils of Social Service.) The position of ACOSS President is an honorary one and he combines this with his employment as Director of the New South Wales Welfare Rights Centre, a position he has held since 1990. The Welfare Rights Centre specialises in Social Security law, policy and administration, and deals with over 4000 low income and disadvantaged clients each year. He has recently completed the 3rd edition of the *Independent Social Security Handbook*.

Peter Saunders is Professor of Sociology at the University of Sussex and is currently on secondment as Research Manager at the Australian Institute of Family Studies. His books include *Social Theory and the Urban Question* (1986), *Social Class and Stratification* (1990), *A Nation of Home Owners* (1990), *Privatization and Popular Capitalism* (1994), *Capitalism: A*

Social Audit (1995) and *Unequal But Fair?* (1996). He has held visiting academic positions at the University of Bremen (Germany), Brown University (USA), the University of Canterbury (New Zealand), the University of Melbourne, and the Australian National University, and he is a member of the Board of the Institute for the Study of Civil Society in London.

Don Siemon is Acting Director of Social Action and Research at the Brotherhood of St Laurence. His policy and research interests include poverty measurement; child care; social security policies – particularly those affecting families and young people; tax and budget policies; provision and pricing of essential services; and the restructuring of human services. He holds a B.E and M.EngSci and has worked for community sector organisations in the overseas aid, environment, consumer, welfare and publishing fields prior to joining the Brotherhood of St Laurence in 1992. Past directorships include the Renewable Energy Authority of Victoria (Energy Victoria), Community Technology Ltd, and Australian Society Publishing Company Ltd.

Wendy Stone is a Research Fellow at the Australian Institute of Family Studies where she has been working on studies of housing, social polarisation and, most recently, the importance of 'social capital' in understanding patterns of family engagement in economic, community and political life. She is author of numerous Institute reports and publications and is currently a doctoral candidate in the Sociology Program at the University of Melbourne, where she is undertaking research investigating social exclusion and labour market inequalities and the role of social networks in mediating poverty.

Lucy Sullivan has an Honours Degree in English and a Doctorate in Psychology. Specialising initially in cognitive psychology and learning theory, her more recent work has been on policy issues relating to parenting, child rearing and family wellbeing. She is currently a Research Fellow working in the Taking Children Seriously program of the Centre for

Independent Studies, where her major publications have included *State of the Nation* and *Rising Crime in Australia.* She is working on a study of taxation policy as it affects the family, and a series of analyses of family welfare issues is in preparation. She has previously published articles in Australian and international journals including *The British Journal of Sociology, The Journal of Medicine and Law, The Australian Journal of Social Issues* and *The Medical Journal of Australia.*

Anna Yeatman is Professor of Sociology at Macquarie University in Sydney. She is the author of *Bureaucrats, Technocrats, Femocrats* (1990) and *Postmodern Revisionings of the Political* (1994), and her new book, *The Politics of Individuality*, is to be published by Routledge. She is also editor or co-editor of a number of collections including *Activism and the Policy Process* (1998), *The New Contractualism* (1997), and *Justice and Identity* (1995).

Chapter 1

Issues in Australian welfare reform

Peter Saunders

On 29 September 1999, the Minister for Family and Community Services, Senator Jocelyn Newman, announced the Federal government's intention to reform the Australian welfare system. Pointing to the ever-increasing numbers of Australians claiming welfare support, she argued that rising rates of welfare dependency were not only placing an increasing burden on government expenditure, but were also damaging the self-esteem and future life chances of many of the recipients themselves. She made clear her view that, in most circumstances, it was better for people to be active than to be idle, and she emphasised her government's commitment to reversing the trend of increasing welfare dependency by encouraging people wherever possible to be more self-reliant.

At the close of her speech, the Minister announced the establishment of a Reference Group of welfare experts to advise her on the various options for reform. The Group was to report by June 2000, following which she would bring forward a Green Paper setting out specific proposals for change. The Reference Group was required to develop proposals for reform which were efficient, equitable and consistent with the principle of 'mutual obligation'.

In essence, the idea of mutual obligation is that individuals who receive financial support from the welfare system should normally be expected to do something in return. This principle is already embedded in Australia's Work for the Dole policy, under which people under the age of 35 who have been unemployed for a year or more can be required to work on community projects or attend literacy and numeracy classes as a condition of receiving their benefits. It is also a feature of the Youth Allowance system, under which young people are required to work or participate in education or training schemes as a condition of receiving financial support. The Minister's intention in launching her welfare reform initiative was that this principle of mutual obligation should be extended as far as possible throughout the welfare support system, encompassing groups such as lone parents and those on Disability Support Pension, and excluding only those past retirement age.

The Minister's announcement of her intention to reform the welfare system provoked widespread comment, and within weeks of its establishment, the Welfare Reform Reference Group, chaired by the Chief Executive of Mission Australia, Patrick McClure, had received submissions from more than 360 organisations and individuals throughout Australia. In March 2000, the Group produced an *Interim Report* in which it responded to some of these submissions and outlined some of its own ideas for reform (Reference Group on Welfare Reform 2000).

The *Interim Report* called for a fundamental change to the welfare system. One of its key proposals was that the current complex and fragmented system of pensions, benefits and allowances targeted at different categories of claimants should, over time, be replaced by a single Participation Support payment. The value of this payment could vary according to the needs and circumstances of different individuals, but the distinctions between different categories of claimants (job-seekers, those on disability pension, lone parents etc.) would disappear. The payment would normally be conditional upon some agreed form of 'economic participation' (such as paid work, education, training) or 'social participation' (such as child-rearing, care for an elderly relative, community work) on the part of the recipient, although some claimants (such as those with severe disabilities) would be exempted from any expectation of reciprocity. Peter Dawkins, a member of the Reference Group, discusses the rationale for this proposal, as well as some of the other ideas canvassed in the *Interim Report*, in chapter 11 of this volume.

The Reference Group's final report, due to be completed in June 2000, should be followed in due course by a Green Paper setting out the government's detailed reform proposals. The publication of both the final report and the Green Paper is certain to generate much comment and controversy, for welfare policy is an area that stirs the emotions on all sides of politics. In this debate, however, it is important that there should be light as well as heat, for the issues are often complex, and there are strong and persuasive arguments both for and against the sorts of changes that are now being proposed.

The main aim of this book is to contribute to the debate by clarifying some of the core issues which lie at the heart of contemporary arguments and disputes about welfare reform in Australia. To this end, essays have been solicited from a wide range of contributors – academics, politicians, those working in the voluntary sector, and those employed within the public service – who represent different interests and perspectives in the welfare field and who end up arguing for very different positions in the debate. The book includes both advocates of reform and opponents – those who believe that the welfare system has swollen to a point where it must be rethought, and those who believe that it is still doing too little to help people who are least fortunate.

Such divergent views can, of course, be evaluated against each other in terms of their factual accuracy and the logical consistency of their arguments, but the fundamental principles from which they derive, and the basic axioms upon which they stand, often turn out to be irreconcilable. Rather than trying to effect some spurious synthesis between competing positions, this book sets out to inform and contribute to the debate by mapping and clarifying some of the main arguments and evidential claims which bear upon it, identifying common ground where it exists. It is then for the reader to weigh the evidence, evaluate the arguments, and come to an informed conclusion.

Some chapters present detailed empirical evidence to support their position, while others adopt a more discursive approach. Most of the chapters deal specifically with the Australian welfare system, but some focus on what has been happening in the United States and the United Kingdom, for many of the problems being confronted in Australian public policy are also being addressed outside Australia, and there are some striking similarities in the issues and debates currently taking place across all of the English-speaking 'Anglo' countries.

With the exception of Peter Dawkins in chapter 11, the various contributors do not discuss specific reform proposals in any detail, for it is not the intention of this book to engage with the particular ideas put forward by the welfare reform reference group. Rather, the book seeks to address some broader questions about how the present welfare system is working, whether and why it may need changing, and how it impacts on different aspects of family and community life in Australia.

In this opening chapter, I review some of main themes running through the various contributions that follow. I begin by addressing the crucial ethical question of whether it can ever be right to reduce welfare payments to people deemed to be in need of them, for opponents of current reform proposals often base their arguments in the moral claim that it is 'wrong' to reduce the level of payments or to try to push welfare claimants into jobs. I then go on to consider three crucial issues raised by the current debate: the recurring problem in the Anglo countries of how to prevent people from abusing the welfare system; the argument that provision of welfare may have encouraged people to abandon self-sufficiency; and the possibility that long-term reliance on welfare support fosters a 'culture of dependency'. Finally, the chapter considers whether Australia has anything to learn from recent changes to welfare systems in other parts of the world such as the United States where dramatic policy shifts seem to have produced dramatic reductions in the numbers of people claiming government support.

Is it 'immoral' to reduce the size of the welfare state?

The *Interim Report* of the Welfare Reform Reference Group makes a point which has often been made before in discussions of social policy – namely, that the modern welfare state not only helps meet the material needs of individuals and their families, but also expresses and contributes to the overall cohesion of Australian society. Drawing on the contemporary language of 'social capital' (see Winter 2000 for a review), the Report suggests that, properly organised, the welfare system can help combat social inequality, crime and social disadvantage, and can thereby help to foster the bonds of trust and reciprocity that are essential for the development of strong communities.

This idea of the welfare state as a cohesive social force has a long pedigree. Perhaps the most influential example of it is found in T. H. Marshall's essay, 'Citizenship and social class', published in Britain in 1950. Marshall argued that the 'social rights' of welfare entitlement which evolved through the nineteenth and twentieth centuries were, together with earlier legal and political rights, one of the three defining elements in the modern idea of citizenship. In his view, the capitalist market system fragments society by emphasising individual self-interest, but the welfare state unifies it by granting equal rights of entitlement to everybody. Seen in this way, the welfare state functions as a form of social cement, tempering the individualism of the market with a good strong dose of social altruism.

This image of the welfare state as the human face of the capitalist market system is crucial to understanding the nature of popular support for it in countries like Australia and Britain, as well as the unease which often surrounds attempts to reform it. These are individualistic and acquisitive cultures, wedded to the principles of private property, competitiveness and market exchange, yet in both countries we also find widespread popular support for the collectivistic principles of the welfare state. It seems that most people feel that the collectivity has a duty to support those who cannot support themselves in the marketplace, and the idea of withdrawing such support and telling people to fend for themselves (such as has happened to some extent in the United States in recent years) is generally seen as callous and uncaring.

The welfare state thus has a moral dimension underlying it – it is seen by many as a necessary feature of a decent and compassionate society, and in Australia it is strongly associated with the idea that everybody deserves 'a fair go'. Indeed, in chapter 9, Lucy Sullivan suggests that the welfare system is an integral part of Australia's very sense of nationhood.

It is, of course, open to argument whether the welfare state can really be seen as 'moral' when it involves individuals delegating their duty to help others to a third party – the state – acting notionally in their name. Hayek (1967), for example, believes that morality depends upon the exercise of free choice by individuals, in which case the compulsory levying of taxes to pay for the support of the poor and needy cannot be deemed moral. Indeed, to the extent that state welfare crowds out voluntary and charitable activity by individuals, it could be argued that it weakens rather than strengthens social morality (Saunders 1993). Nevertheless, those who argue for an expansion of welfare provision coupled with increased spending have traditionally justified their demands by tapping into the idea that state welfare provision is an ethical as much as a practical imperative.

In the 1960s and 1970s, this expansionist lobby held the initiative. Studies were published to show that the welfare system was falling short of its moral imperative and purpose – it was not redistributing income and wealth as radically as it should, 'poverty' (variously defined) was still widespread, and middle-income groups were benefiting more from tax breaks than were the poor from receipt of benefits and state services. Governments in Britain and the United States, as well as in Australia, responded by increasing welfare spending and introducing a raft of new welfare rights aimed at eliminating deprivation and enhancing 'social justice'.

With the advance of the so-called New Right in the 1980s, however, socialists and social democrats were forced to switch from attacking the welfare state for its inadequacies to defending it against those who sought to reduce its scope and influence. There is still a vociferous lobby in support of increasing the size and generosity of the welfare system in Australia, but it is no longer setting the reform agenda, and through the Keating and Howard years of the 1990s, it has become increasingly re-active rather than pro-active.

In chapter 10, for example, Fiona MacDonald and Don Siemon of the Brotherhood of St. Laurence respond to the current reform initiative by arguing that, rather than looking to expand Work for the Dole policies, the government should be reforming the welfare system with the aim of eradicating poverty and strengthening community life through enhanced provision of health, housing and education facilities. They think it shameful that the level of welfare benefits in Australia is still so low that up to a half of all children living in households where nobody is employed are living in poverty. Similarly, Michael Raper of the Australian Council of Social Service argues in chapter 12 that more than 60 per cent of the unemployed are living below the poverty line and that attempts to extend or tighten up Work for the Dole requirements are 'morally repugnant'. In both of these chapters, the argument is essentially that the main thrust of the current reform agenda is misplaced. Rather than focusing on the need to make welfare recipients 'participate' in some way in return for their payments, these authors believe there is a much more pressing need to raise the level of the payments themselves.

Notwithstanding such demands, few people expect the government's review of the Australian welfare system to result in a significant expansion of provision. Rather, despite Ministers' assurances to the contrary, fears have been expressed that the review may end up cutting back welfare support to those in need. Arguments in support of expanding the welfare system have today been marginalised as a result of the continuing influence of a 'neo-liberal' critique of welfare which emerged in all of the Anglo countries during the 1980s and which has to varying degrees come to influence the social agendas of parties of the left as well as parties of the right ever since.

This neo-liberal attack on welfare rested on two main arguments. The first was that the cost of modern welfare state systems was spiralling and that radical cuts would be needed to prevent social security and other welfare budgets from absorbing an ever increasing proportion of total national income. The second, and arguably more important, was that the modern welfare state was not a 'moral system', as the political left had been claiming for so long, but rather had evolved into a system which was encouraging individual self-interest and eroding social solidarity. For the first time, therefore, the conventional belief that there was a moral imperative driving the expansion of welfare was confronted head-on.

Far from promoting social cohesion, as people like Marshall had claimed, neo-liberals argued that the modern welfare system was creating social fragmentation. The true spirit of the modern welfare state was not altruism but self-interest, for the huge welfare budget was encouraging more and more people to get as much as they could for themselves out of the communal pot. Nor was the system particularly effective at helping the poor. Indeed, rather than solving social problems, the welfare state had created new ones, for it had fostered the emergence of a new 'underclass' which had grown dependent upon state handouts while the employed population laboured under increasingly onerous levels of taxation in order to support it.

Such arguments led neo-liberals to conclude that it was not only economically 'rational' for governments to cut their welfare budgets, but also that it was in some sense morally 'right' for them to do so. For too long, governments had been buying votes by expanding hand-outs to ever-increasing numbers of beneficiaries, indulging idleness by giving people money over long periods of time without demanding that they do anything to improve themselves or their condition, and exacerbating social divisions by taking money away from those who behaved 'responsibly' in order to support the increasing numbers of those who did not. The welfare state, in short, was not a moral system at all. Rather, it was a well-intentioned but ill-conceived system that, far from encouraging an altruistic concern for others, had actually ended up encouraging envy and stimulating selfishness.

How do you stop welfare free-riders?

Ever since increasing demands on parish relief prompted the British authorities to reform the Poor Law in 1834, governments in the Anglo countries have been struggling to find a way to separate those who really need and 'deserve' help from those who do not. The dilemma is simple: once government puts in place a system of social support to help those who cannot provide for themselves, it thereby immediately establishes an incentive for those able to work to abandon self-reliance and seek government aid instead. The problem is how to help the first group without encouraging the second.

This is a problem that has been addressed by modern 'game theorists' who refer to it as the 'free-rider' dilemma (see Olsen 1965; McLean 1987). Logically, the problem arises in any social group when the individual interests of its members come into conflict with their common interests as members of the group. The larger and more impersonal the group, the more individuals are likely to be tempted to pursue their individual interests at the expense of other members, and to ignore the collective interests that they share. Welfare state systems are a case in point.

Game theory recognises that, in the provision of public goods such as social security systems, the collective utility is maximised if everybody plays by the rules and cooperates. This means that it is in our common interests that we should all contribute what is required of us, and that nobody should claim from the system unless they really need to. Provided nobody exploits the system, contributions stay low and everybody is covered against future mishaps. However, once individuals begin to break ranks, or to 'defect' (the term used in game theory), then the system swiftly breaks down and everybody ends up losing. Fearful of missing out, group members scramble to claim their share of the collective resource before others can get hold of it, and very soon everybody is trying to take out more resources than they put in, leading to the collapse of the system (Hardin 1977).

Despite the fact that everybody loses from such behaviour, it is a fundamental axiom of game theory that 'rational utility maximisers' will tend to pursue their own individual interest at the expense of the common good (and thus, in the long-term, at their own expense too). This is because, for as long as others continue to play by the rules, any given individual stands to gain a lot more if they defect than if they cooperate, and once people start defecting, others lose out unless they do likewise. This means that collective welfare systems have an inherent tendency to generate self-interested behaviour which eventually undermines them.

This problem seems to have been particularly acute in the welfare systems of the Anglo countries, and they have developed their own distinctive strategies for trying to cope with it.

Despite the significant differences in their systems of welfare, the English-speaking countries (the United States, Australia, New Zealand, Canada and the United Kingdom) have been said to form a distinctive cluster – what Esping-Andersen (1990) calls a 'liberal welfare regime' – when compared with other advanced welfare states.[1] According to Esping-Andersen, these Anglo-Saxon liberal regimes share in common an emphasis on social assistance as a safety net, use of means testing to target payments specifically to those in need, enforcement of strict entitlement rules, and a concern to discourage malingering by setting benefit levels below minimum earnings. This suggests that these countries have traditionally sought to solve the free-rider problem mainly by means testing (in order to target help to the most needy), and by setting low levels of benefit, or attaching unattractive conditions to receipt of benefit (in order to deter people who are not in real need from claiming).

These systems contrast vividly with the conservative or corporatist regimes found in Catholic Europe (where welfare support is based on entitlement through social insurance administered by the state, and benefits are graduated according to the scale of contributions that have been made), and even more starkly with the social democratic regimes associated with Belgium, Holland and Scandinavia (where all citizens are included in a single, universal scheme which has traditionally offered high levels of benefit funded by high levels of personal taxation).

Esping-Andersen sees the key difference between these different types of systems as lying in the degree to which they make it possible for individuals to escape the requirement to perform paid labour in order to survive (what he calls 'commodification'). Comparing the age pension, sickness and unemployment benefit provisions across eighteen different countries, he showed that the Anglo-Saxon countries have the most 'commodified' welfare systems while the Scandinavian nations have the most 'decommodified' systems. In the Anglo countries, welfare is deliberately restricted so as to make it a less attractive option than working. In the social democracies of Scandinavia, by contrast, the welfare system comes much closer to a fully decommodified system where 'citizens can freely, and without potential loss of job, income or general welfare, opt out of work when they themselves consider it necessary' (Esping-Andersen 1990: 23).

All of this raises an obvious question. What is it about countries like Denmark and Sweden that has enabled them to operate these relatively decommodified welfare systems without (apparently) encountering the crippling problem of mass free-riding which would almost certainly arise if such a system were introduced in any of the Anglo countries?

Part of the answer may be that the Scandinavian countries do suffer from relatively high levels of free-riding, but they

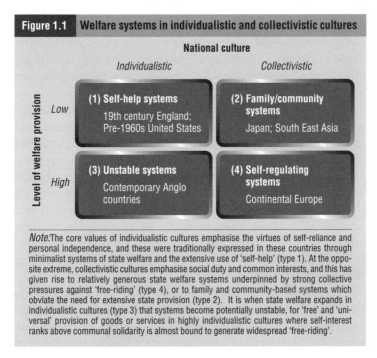

Figure 1.1 Welfare systems in individualistic and collectivistic cultures

National culture

	Individualistic	Collectivistic
Low	**(1) Self-help systems** 19th century England; Pre-1960s United States	**(2) Family/community systems** Japan; South East Asia
High	**(3) Unstable systems** Contemporary Anglo countries	**(4) Self-regulating systems** Continental Europe

Level of welfare provision

*Note:*The core values of individualistic cultures emphasise the virtues of self-reliance and personal independence, and these were traditionally expressed in these countries through minimalist systems of state welfare and the extensive use of 'self-help' (type 1). At the opposite extreme, collectivistic cultures emphasise social duty and common interests, and this has given rise to relatively generous state welfare systems underpinned by strong collective pressures against 'free-riding' (type 4), or to family and community-based systems which obviate the need for extensive state provision (type 2). It is when state welfare expands in individualistic cultures (type 3) that systems become potentially unstable, for 'free' and 'universal' provision of goods or services in highly individualistic cultures where self-interest ranks above communal solidarity is almost bound to generate widespread 'free-riding'.

choose not to make a fuss about it. Certainly these countries have higher levels of welfare receipt among their working age populations than does Australia, and this would seem to support this possibility. But even if this is part of the answer, it simply pushes our question back one stage, for we then need to explain why free-riding is not seen as a particular problem, especially if it is actually more widespread than in the liberal welfare regimes.

The more fundamental explanation for why these relatively decommodified systems do not collapse under the weight of free-riders probably lies in the fact that they have evolved much more collectivistic cultures than the Anglo countries have.[2] This means that they have less need to rely upon official controls and enforcement because individuals and communities are more inclined to regulate themselves and their members. If this is the case, then it follows that social democratic welfare regimes based on generous entitlements and high quality provision are probably only sustainable in countries where, for whatever reason, individuals are prone to recognise a strong commitment to the interests of the collectivity. Indeed, such regimes will only emerge in the first place in cultures like those of Sweden where individuals are already predisposed to monitor, police and regulate their own and their neighbours' inclinations to 'defect'.

Generous welfare regimes based on a high level of trust will, however, prove extremely unstable if introduced into individualistic cultures where self-regulation in the interests of the collectivity is less developed, and where group pressures to conformity are likely to be much weaker (see Figure 1.1). It is notable in this respect how difficult it has been for the authorities in Australia and Britain to encourage people to inform upon those they know to be abusing the welfare system – 'dobbing' and 'snooping' have often been regarded in these more individualistic and privatised cultures as reprehensible rather than an act of civic duty.

Compared with other parts of the world, the Anglo countries are peculiarly individualistic in their cultures. MacFarlane (1978) has traced the origins of Anglo individualism as far back as the twelfth century when he believes that

England was already a nation of 'rampant individualists', and it seems that this distinctive inheritance has survived to this day. For example, in his review of the cultures of contemporary capitalism, Albert (1993) draws a sharp distinction between the more collectivistic and cooperative institutions and practices of the 'Rhine model' countries and the much more individualistic and competitive character of the 'Neo-American' model of capitalism practiced in the Anglo countries. He shows how this distinction is reflected in a wide variety of institutional differences including their financial systems, their systems of industrial relations, and their welfare systems.

Perhaps the most convincing evidence that a cultural divide underpins the distinction between the Anglo countries, with their liberal welfare systems, and the continental Catholic and Scandinavian nations, with their corporatist and social democratic welfare systems, can be found in a huge attitudinal survey of fifty national cultures conducted by Hofstede (discussed in Smith and Bond 1993). He found that the western, developed countries tended to be much more individualistic than Asian nations and those with less developed economies, but within the western bloc he also reported that the Anglo countries were more strongly individualistic than the others. The United States ranked as the most individualistic culture in the world, with Australia second, Great Britain third, and Canada fourth. The Scandinavian and Germanic countries ranked much lower (although the Netherlands scored as high as Canada). Thus, the same clustering of Anglo countries reported by Esping-Andersen in his analysis of welfare systems, and by Albert in his analysis of different capitalist systems, is repeated by Hofstede in his analysis of national cultures.

It is this individualism that helps explain the peculiar character of the contemporary welfare reform debate in the Anglo countries. If it is true that collective systems of welfare entitlement are always likely to be unstable when located in strongly individualistic cultures, then it is no surprise that a renewed concern with monitoring and controlling access to welfare should have arisen in the Anglo nations over the last twenty years as a response to the loosening of control and expansion of eligibility that took place in the 1960s and 1970s. The concern, in essence, is that the system has been swamped by free-riders, and the determination to reform it is being driven by the desire to reintroduce the traditional distinction, which seems to have become blurred, between those who really need help and support and those who are exploiting the common good for their own selfish purposes.

This concern was captured by the Federal Minister for Family and Community Services, Senator Newman, in her speech launching the current welfare reform initiative: 'There are examples around Australia where job opportunities are available and our entrenched culture of welfare dependency has meant that certain members of our community are not only prepared, but feel entitled to exploit the social safety net instead . . . [W]here there are jobs available, even though they may fall short of the initial expectations of the job-seeker, it is neither fair nor moral to expect the hard working men and women of this country to underwrite what can only be described as a destructive and self-indulgent welfare mentality' (Newman 1999a: 5-6). In other words, the collective system is being exploited by free-riders, and reform is needed to protect the interests of those who are still playing by the rules.

The welfare systems in countries like Australia, Britain and the United States have become less discriminatory and more generous since the 1960s. What we are seeing now is an attempt to pull them back into a form which is more consistent with the strongly individualistic cultures of these countries. Today as so often in the past, there is a growing suspicion that the welfare system is supporting too many people who could and should be supporting themselves. It is for this reason that these countries have been leading the search for new ways of getting welfare claimants back into the workforce.

Does the welfare system encourage idleness?

In June 1998, over four and three-quarter million Australians were receiving income support payments (this and subsequent statistics are taken from the Department of Family and

Community Services 1999a and 1999b). This represents a five-fold increase since 1965 when there were fewer than a million.

Just under half of those in receipt of payments in 1998 were above retirement age, and nearly 400,000 more were receiving student assistance. This leaves over two and a quarter million people in other categories, most of whom were unemployed (35 per cent), on Disability Support Pension (24 per cent), or receiving Parenting Payment (27 per cent, of whom 16 per cent were lone parents). It is these three groups around which most of the discussion about welfare reform revolves.

All three of these groups have swollen in size since the mid-sixties. Those receiving the Disability Support Pension or its equivalent have increased more than five-fold in this period, with most of the increase coming in the last fifteen years, when numbers doubled. The number of single parents receiving payments has increased by a factor of twelve since 1965, from under thirty thousand to well over one-third of a million. Their numbers have also been rising steeply in recent years, from a quarter of a million ten years ago to nearly four hundred thousand today. Finally, those on unemployment allowances have increased from 13 thousand to 790 thousand since the mid-sixties, a factor of sixty, although most of this increase occurred in the late seventies and early eighties. Between 1985 and 1998, the number of people claiming unemployment allowances increased from just over half to just over three-quarters of a million.

Today, more than 18 per cent of the population of work-force age is receiving income support payments as compared with just 3 per cent in the early- and mid-sixties. Welfare spending has grown much faster over this period than population size, the economy or government revenues – GDP per head has doubled since 1960, the real value of taxes has tripled, but the real cost of welfare spending has gone up five-fold (Warby and Nahan 1998). It is not difficult to see why the government is worried about these trends.

It is sometimes suggested that these figures exaggerate the extent to which dependency on income support has 'really' grown or is 'really' a problem. Travers (1998) points out that some of the increase in the number of recipients of Parenting Payment reflects improved rates of take-up following government publicity campaigns, rather than an increase in the number of poor parents needing support. Similarly, Henman (1999) argues that as the nation has become wealthier so the government has quite rightly become more generous and has extended help to a broader range of people including those who are earning low incomes. The rise in the number of people working part-time has also increased the number of workers who receive a top-up on their wages through the income support system.

All this is true, but as Peter Dawkins demonstrates in chapter 11, it does little to change the overall conclusion that the number of people who rely solely or almost exclusively on income support payments has expanded substantially over the last twenty to thirty years (the periods of most rapid growth being the mid-1970s, the early 1980s, and the first half of the 1990s). As we have already noted, the result is that 18 per cent of the workforce age population is now receiving income support. Even if we now remove from this statistic all those (such as part-time and low-paid workers) for whom income support represents a top-up on wages (defined generously as those for whom welfare payments constitute less than 90 per cent of their total income), this proportion only drops four percentage points, to 14 per cent. In other words, one in seven Australians of workforce age today relies almost entirely on income support payments, and this represents a much higher level of dependency than in the 1960s and 1970s. The blow-out is no statistical artefact – it is real.

Alan Buckingham shows in chapter 4 that these trends are not unique to Australia. They were repeated in the other Anglo countries too, and in many cases they were sharper elsewhere (for example, the rise in numbers claiming disability payments, and the increased number of sole parents claiming welfare support, have both been more marked in the United Kingdom than in Australia in recent years). It was this marked upward trend in rates of dependency on welfare payments that stimulated the neo-liberal reappraisal of welfare which developed in the Anglo countries during the 1980s.

The critique rested on the argument that the welfare system has expanded to a point where it is supporting substantial numbers of people who would once have been expected to support themselves. The evidence for this lay in the statistical trends which we have been reviewing, for these are consistent with the view that increasing numbers of people may have deliberately been opting for government income support rather than for work or other forms of family self-reliance.

The most influential critic of welfare who began arguing for such an interpretation during the 1980s was Charles Murray. In his book, *Losing Ground*, first published in 1984 and re-issued ten years later, he maintained that the expansion of welfare in the United States in the 1960s had undermined the ethic of personal responsibility and had promoted idleness and dependency by changing the short-term costs and rewards attaching to different patterns of behaviour. His fundamental argument was that people respond rationally to incentives. When the state expands welfare provision, it makes it more profitable to become a claimant, and it makes it correspondingly less attractive to remain in a low-paid, boring job. Even though, in the long term, work may still offer a better prospect than welfare, many poor people respond more readily to short-term signals, and when welfare became more attractive from the 1960s onwards, they reacted as rational utility maximisers, just as game theory predicts that they would.

In the United States, where the main welfare benefit was Aid for Families with Dependent Children (AFDC) paid to single mothers, Murray argued that increased generosity had encouraged precisely the behaviour which was creating the problem which AFDC was intended to resolve. Put simply, AFDC made it easier for poor single women to have children without marrying and thus to put themselves into a situation of long-term welfare dependency. In order to demonstrate this claim, Murray showed how a couple with children stood to improve their income if they split up, leaving the woman to rely on AFDC payments, rather than staying together with the man working in a low-paid job. He further reinforced the point with evidence from a ten-year trial of a Negative Income Tax scheme which was introduced experimentally across several American states. According to Murray, the results showed that provision of a minimum welfare income floor had a devastating effect on the experimental groups as compared with the control groups. They reduced their working hours, they took longer to find a job, and their rates of marriage break-up spiralled.[3]

Applied to Australia, Murray's analysis would suggest that the six-fold increase in the proportion of the workforce age population in receipt of social security payments since 1960 in large part reflects an increase in the number of people who now choose (quite rationally) to claim benefit rather than work for a living. Rather than indicating an extraordinary six-fold increase in the number of people in need over the last 35 years (a period, incidentally, when the nation doubled its wealth), this would suggest that the expansion of the welfare system has simply created its own demand, and that Australia is now locked into a vicious circle in which provision of benefits and demand for state support chase each other ever upwards.

In chapter 12, Michael Raper strongly rejects this line of argument. He points out that the Australian welfare system, with its tight means testing and eligibility rules, has always encouraged people to work wherever possible, and that welfare payments are in any case set at such a low level that they are unlikely to offer any serious incentive to avoid work where it is available. In his view, the belief that welfare has generated a disincentive to work is 'pejorative and inaccurate.' Income support dependency has risen in Australia due to a combination of factors over which individuals themselves have had little or no control. In particular, despite the fact that the national wealth has doubled, there are now fewer jobs available for those with few skills, there is a higher incidence of disability, there has been an increase in early retirement, and more parents now have to raise their children without a partner to help them.

Raper is clearly right to remind us that economic circumstances and the structure of employment opportunities have changed since the 1960s. The Welfare Reform Group's *Interim Report* explicitly recognises, for example, that there has been an increasing polarisation between affluent and poor communities, and between households where two or more adults are working and households where nobody is working. The increase in the nation's wealth has, therefore, gone side-by-side with a sharpening of the income gap between the prosperous and the poor, and it is quite reasonable to suggest that levels of need have therefore risen even as the country as a whole has grown wealthier.

Nevertheless, some of Raper's arguments and assumptions can be challenged. It is difficult to accept that the huge rise in the number of disability pensioners reflects a real increase in rates of disability today as compared with ten or twenty years ago, especially when we remember that average health levels have improved in this time. Rather, as the Welfare Reform Group's *Interim Report* suggests, it is more likely that increasing numbers of non-employed individuals have successfully managed to have themselves re-classified as disabled, for not only is the payment higher than the unemployment benefit, but also there is no requirement on those in receipt of the Disability Support Pension to seek work or undertake training. If this is the case, then it would lend support to Murray's belief that people will respond 'rationally' to unintended incentives in the welfare system, adjusting their behaviour in order to maximise the financial benefits to themselves while minimising the demands that are made upon them.[4]

Nor should we accept without comment Raper's implicit assumption that increasing rates of single parenthood have nothing to do with the rational choices of the individuals concerned. In chapter 9, Lucy Sullivan argues that changes in the Australian welfare and tax systems over the last thirty years have fuelled the increase in the number of lone parents while eroding the traditional nuclear family. She reviews the impact of welfare changes in Australia since the introduction of the Supporting Mothers Benefit in 1973 and concludes that the federal government has brought in a series of changes that have eroded young men's incentive to work while making couples on relatively low incomes better off if they separate than if they stay together.

In many ways echoing Murray's argument that welfare payments have enabled single women to have children without a partner to support them while also encouraging couples to avoid making a long-term commitment to each other, Sullivan goes on to argue that Australian governments have ended up penalising self-sufficient families on low to moderate incomes in order to pay for the spiralling growth in the numbers of single-parent households dependent upon the state for most or all of their income. Thus, she identifies a vicious circle in which increased welfare spending led to higher taxes which dragged larger numbers of traditional families into poverty, thereby further increasing the demand for income support and necessitating another round of tax rises.

Sullivan's contention that the Australian tax and welfare systems have created perverse incentives that have influenced the way people behave is to some extent supported by evidence presented by Peter Dawkins in chapter 11, as well as in the Welfare Reference Group's *Interim Report* (see Appendix 4: 49-50). For example, Dawkins shows that the traditional family type, consisting of an employed husband and a non-employed wife raising two children, faces 'effective marginal tax rates' (that is, deductions from income due to tax levied and withdrawal of welfare payments) of between 61 and 104 per cent across a wide range of gross weekly earnings. While recognising that recent tax changes have helped restore incentives for some groups, Dawkins nevertheless leaves us in no doubt of the need for the welfare system also to address this problem, and he reviews a variety of reform options through which this might be achieved.

Sullivan's argument goes further than this, however. Not only does she claim that the welfare system has weakened the incentive to work, but she also maintains that it has undermined the traditional family by driving it into poverty with high taxation while supporting other, less viable, household types with generous welfare payments. Her argument here echoes Murray's position that single parenthood is for most people inherently unsustainable without outside financial support. Previous generations knew this, which is why the two principal routes to single parenthood (unmarried pregnancy, and divorce or separation) were by today's standards uncommon, and why unmarried mothers and divorcees often met with social disapproval. However, when the culture started to change and governments responded by increasing financial support for single parents, single parenthood became economically viable. This meant that more people were able to countenance a course of behaviour which would have been disastrous a generation earlier, and the more common it became, the less social disapproval it attracted.

This argument is much more contentious than the simpler proposition that the tax and benefit system has discouraged work, and in chapter 2 Mead takes issue with it. He claims that there is no evidence that the welfare system caused the weakening of the two-parent family in America, although he does accept that the recent American welfare reforms may result in a fall in the numbers of young unmarried mothers. Mead's view is that the causes of the increase in rates of single parenting over the last thirty or forty years lie much deeper than Murray's analysis of economic costs and incentives would suggest, and he emphasises the influence of cultural over economic factors in the explanation of such trends. Most economists today would probably agree with him, for there is actually little evidence that financial incentives have more than a marginal effect on marriage behaviour or fertility rates.

Mead's argument against Murray seems to cast doubt on Sullivan's belief that changes in the Australian welfare system have undermined the traditional family form while underpinning less sustainable alternatives. It is true that traditional families on modest incomes can face very high effective marginal tax rates, just as single-parent households have benefited from changes over the last thirty years, but there is little firm evidence to suggest that these financial signals have triggered major changes in social behaviour.

Having said this, we should not lose sight of the fact that lone parenthood would not have been a viable option for most people without the expansion of state benefits (in Australia about three-quarters of lone parents are on income support, and in Britain their dependency rate is even higher at around 90 per cent). Provision of benefits may not have *caused* the increase in the rate of single parenting, but it has almost certainly *enabled* it to continue growing.

This appears to be the view of the British Labour MP, Frank Field. He argues in chapter 3 that the main economic cause of the weakening of the traditional family in the United Kingdom was the collapse of manufacturing employment, for this made it more difficult for young men to earn a living sufficient to support a family. Nevertheless, Field goes on to recognise that the British tax and welfare system may have *reinforced* this trend by benefiting single parents at the expense of two-parent families, for at the same time as young males were becoming less eligible marriage partners, the state was putting in place the means for young women to raise their children without a husband.

Here, it is relevant to note evidence, discussed by Alan Buckingham in chapter 4, that recent American welfare reforms which have abolished unconditional aid to single mothers have begun to reverse the rising trend in pre-nuptial births in the United States. This would certainly seem to suggest that changing welfare incentives can influence individuals' behaviour with regard to marriage and fertility, although these measures have been fairly draconian, and it may well be that changes at the margin would have much less of an impact.

We should therefore be cautious before we endorse Michael Raper's rebuttal of the argument that the welfare system has encouraged higher levels of 'irresponsible' behaviour. Whether the expansion of welfare since the 1960s has undermined the traditional self-reliant family and promoted the growth of single parenthood remains arguable, but there are strong grounds for believing that it may well have weakened the incentive for claimants to find work. If this is the case, then the next question to be answered is whether those without a job would be likely to respond to stronger work incentives. Put another way, do the jobless really want to find work?

Does long-term reliance on welfare create a culture of dependency?

Murray's analysis in *Losing Ground* (1994) basically held that many welfare recipients are rational utility maximisers who have calculated that welfare dependency offers them a better deal than working. However, in *Beyond Entitlement* (1986) and *The New Politics of Poverty* (1992), another American welfare critic, Lawrence Mead, took issue with this. He argued that economic calculation is much less significant in influencing people's behaviour than the values and norms which they share as members of a given culture, or sub-culture. Mead's analysis subsequently became influential in helping shape the welfare reform agenda in Britain and Australia as well as in the United States, and he summarises his argument in chapter 2.

Mead rejects Murray's view that many welfare claimants deliberately avoid work. Rather, he suggests that many of them accept work as a goal, but have only a weak sense of personal efficacy. They would in principle like to get jobs and take more responsibility for their own lives, but they feel unable to do so. Even when jobs are relatively plentiful, they find it hard to find and keep them, for they lack the social skills and personal competence to organise their lives in the way that is necessary in order to function effectively in the employment market. They are willing to do 'the right thing', but are seemingly incapable of delivering on their promises. Such people are most unlikely to respond in a rational and calculative manner to changes in the trade-off between work and welfare. They are in Mead's words 'dutiful but defeated'.

Writing in the context of the United States, where many of those on the welfare rolls are black, Mead attaches no moral 'blame' to these individuals, and he accepts that in many cases, the 'culture of dependency' which they exhibit can be explained as the product of factors, such as racism, which go back many generations and which lie outside of their power to fix. He is also clear that their capacity to cope has often been blighted by poor parenting and disrupted family lives when they were young. None of this, however, changes the fact that long-term reliance on welfare makes these people's lives even worse. What they need, according to Mead, is not a fortnightly welfare cheque, but rather a combination of 'help and hassle' to break the cycle of dependency and push them into self-reliance.

Mead's argument is evaluated by Frank Field in chapter 3. Field thinks that Mead over-emphasises the significance of cultural factors and pays insufficient attention to structural labour market problems. Writing from a British context, he is certain that the main problem over the last quarter of a century is that, for certain categories of people, the jobs have simply disappeared.

Field's critique in some ways echoes the comments of William Julius Wilson in his debate with Mead back in 1987 (Mead and Wilson 1987). In that debate (and in his book, *The Truly Disadvantaged*), Wilson claimed that the main cause of long-term unemployment among American inner city blacks is that the manufacturing jobs have left town. In his reply to Wilson, Mead insisted that the problem is not so much the non-availability of jobs, but the scarcity of attractive jobs. In the United States, he claimed, there are plenty of jobs that the non-working poor could do, but they are generally in the service sector, pay the minimum wage, and offer few career prospects. Unless they are pushed, Mead believes that many long-term unemployed people will simply find reasons or excuses for avoiding such work, even though it may offer an initial stepping stone to something better down the line.

Mead's argument may stand up in the vibrant and low-unemployment economy of the United States, but can it equally be applied to Britain and Australia where unemployment rates are significantly higher?

In the case of Britain, Field thinks not. He suggests that in the British inner cities, it was the collapse of traditional male jobs in manufacturing which generated long-term welfare dependency. Mead (in chapter 2) responds to this in much the same way as he responded to Wilson back in the 1980s – he accepts that there are unemployment black spots in Britain, just as there are in America, but he still maintains that the evidence demonstrates that jobs can be found even in the most depressed areas, and even during recessions.

What is perhaps more interesting than the disagreement between Mead and Field is the convergence in their positions. Thus, while insisting that structural economic change caused the problem in the first place, Field agrees with Mead that one result of the prolonged joblessness that followed the collapse of manufacturing in Britain was that many claimants lost what he calls the 'habit of work'. He agrees with Mead that the resulting 'culture of dependency' has become a problem, and he concurs with Mead's strategy of 'help and hassle' as the way to break it. The principal difference between Field and Mead is therefore not in the identification of the problem, but is in their prescriptions for fixing it. According to Field, in areas of high unemployment, governments need to intervene on the demand side (to help create more jobs) as well as on the supply side (to push more people into the labour force), whereas Mead tends to put all his emphasis on the supply side alone.

Australian critics of Mead's position are much less conciliatory than Field is. Michael Raper (in chapter 12) and Fiona MacDonald and Don Siemon (in chapter 10) argue against Mead's belief that welfare has generated a dependency culture, and they assert that there are simply no jobs available in Australia for most of those on income support to do.

MacDonald and Siemon are of the view that the globalisation of the economy has destroyed many full-time blue-collar jobs in Australian manufacturing while creating in their place more casual work, more part-time work, and more 'underemployment', and they doubt Mead's claim that those without work can graduate to more secure and better-paid jobs if they first get a foothold on the ladder by accepting low-paid, short-term work. They further suggest that groups like single parents lack 'real opportunities', not only because there are few jobs available for them to do, but also because there are inadequate provisions of child care services and workplaces are often too inflexible to accommodate employees with family responsibilities.

Similarly, Raper claims in his chapter that the jobs are simply not there for people with low skills, and he sees no point in demanding that they look for work which is not available. Backing up this claim, he points out that there are currently six unemployed people for every notified vacancy in Australia.

According to Peter Dawkins, in chapter 11, these arguments are too simple because unemployed people can and do find jobs even when the unemployment rate is high. Even in a labour market where there were sixteen people chasing every vacancy, Dawkins demonstrates that a job-seeker with average levels of skill and competency would have a better than even chance of finding a job within six months.[5] This is important, for it not only supports Mead's claim that it is still possible to find work in times and places of high unemployment, but it also reminds us that there is a constant turnover in the composition of those claiming income support.

The debate about welfare dependency really centres on long-term claimants, because it is here that Mead's concern about welfare breeding a 'culture of dependency' is likely to have most purchase. Appendix 3 of the Welfare Reform Group's *Interim Report* shows that long-term dependency is surprisingly common in Australia. Taking all categories of workforce age claimants together, 70 per cent of those who were receiving income support in September 1995 were also receiving it nearly four years later, in June 1999.

Long-term dependency is more common in some categories of claimant than in others. The report shows that once people move onto the Disability Support Pension they are unlikely to move off it before retirement – four-fifths of those claiming this pension in March 1999 had been claiming continuously for at least two years. Single parents, too, tend to experience quite long periods in receipt of Parenting Payment – in March 1999, 58 per cent had been on the payment for a continuous two-year period, and 80 per cent had received it for more than two years in total (the equivalent figures for parents who were partnered were 36 per cent and 65 per cent respectively). Although lone parents do move off Parenting Payment as their circumstances change, research conducted by the Department of Family and Community Services (Bagnall 1999) found that 70 per cent of those moving off payments were back again within twelve months.

Turnover rates are considerably higher among unemployed people claiming the Newstart Allowance, only a quarter of whom had been unemployed for a continuous two-year period in March 1999, although more than half of them had been unemployed for more than two years in total. However, the statistics also show that about 7 per cent of people on Newstart in 1995 had moved to the Disability Support Pension by 1999, and this lends support to those who believe that the increase in disability pensioners is at least in part due to transfers from unemployment.

The fact that nearly three-quarters of working age welfare claimants in 1995 were also claiming four years later suggests that long-term reliance on income support in Australia is common. This could be explained by Mead's claim that prolonged reliance on welfare habituates people to dependency and sustains a dependency culture, for it does seem that there are some people who spend a long time on income support and who may have trouble getting off it. However, these statistics alone cannot demonstrate that such a culture of dependency actually exists, still less that it is to blame for the rising numbers of people who depend for their incomes on welfare payments over relatively long periods of time. To evaluate this claim, we need to turn to research on the values and behaviour of the welfare dependent population itself, and three chapters in this book (chapters 5, 6 and 7) begin to address this.

In chapter 5, Frances McCoull and Jocelyn Pech show that in the United States and the United Kingdom, as well as in Australia, children who grow up in welfare-dependent households are more likely to end up dependent on welfare themselves. Reviewing the international evidence, they find in all three countries that a young person's probability of unemployment and/or welfare dependency is roughly doubled if he or she comes from a family where the parent or parents were themselves on welfare. In Australia, where they investigate the income support records for over three-quarters of those people who turned sixteen in the first three months of 1996, McCoull and Pech find that high levels of dependency on both unemployment and family payments during late adolescence are significantly associated with both family background and a history of parental reliance on income support. Children of sole parents and children with parents on income support double their chances of becoming 'heavily welfare dependent' (defined as being on income support for more than half of the time since their sixteenth birthdays) before they reach the age of twenty.

This research may offer some support for Mead's argument that long-term joblessness is essentially a cultural problem, for it is consistent with the idea that welfare-dependent parents develop a distinctive set of values and attitudes which they then transmit to their children, thereby predisposing them to a life on welfare support as well. However, McCoull and Pech offer no explanations for the correlations that they present, and we should be wary of jumping to conclusions. The sorts of correlations that they report could, after all, be explained by geographical factors (parents on income support might live in localities with few job opportunities which means that their children would also experience more difficulty finding work), or by individual psychological ones (if joblessness is increasingly associated with low intelligence, as Murray and Herrnstein (1988) suggest, then jobless parents with low IQs will tend to produce more than their share of low-intelligence children who will in turn find it more difficult to find work).

The first step in determining whether the link between parents' welfare dependency and that of their children is a result of the transmission of a distinctive culture is to see whether such a culture actually exists among young people who are claiming income support. It is this question that Wendy Stone and I address in chapter 6 where we summarise some findings from a series of focus group interviews conducted with groups of 16-19 year-old males and females in Victoria.

This research documented a strong 'work ethic' among both school students and those in jobs or training, and it also found that some unemployed young people on the government's Job Placement, Employment and Training (JPET) schemes were determined to seize their opportunity and equip themselves for work. However, the research also clearly revealed the existence of what we defined as a 'dependency culture' among some unemployed teenagers who showed little serious inclination to find a job, little interest in training or pursuing qualifications that might improve their job prospects, and a high level of fatalism which was sometimes underpinned by a hopeless entanglement in a drugs culture. Drawing on Durkheim's terminology, we summarise what we found as a state of 'anomie' characterised by negativity, drift, and lack of structure or purpose. In Mead's terms, these young people were certainly 'defeated', even if they did not appear particularly 'dutiful'.

Where does this culture of dependency among some unemployed young people originate? Stone and I speculate on whether it is likely to have been passed on from their parents, but given the pattern of fractured family relationships that so many of them reported to us, we rather doubt it. Instead, we tentatively suggest that, while parental influence can certainly explain why so many young people are so strongly committed to a work ethic, it is probably a *lack* of family influence that explains why a minority have drifted into a dependency culture. If this is right, then the emergence of a dependency culture among young people may represent a 'default' position to which they tend to gravitate in the absence of positive socialisation and effective parenting during their formative years.

The young unemployed are only one of the groups where relatively high levels of income support dependency are concentrated. Another consists of indigenous Australians. As McCoull and Pech report, Aboriginal young people are three and a half times more likely than others of their age group to become heavily dependent on welfare during their late teens.

In chapter 7, Noel Pearson examines the causes of high levels of welfare dependency in Aboriginal communities, and he leaves us in no doubt that the problem today is cultural, a conclusion consistent with Mead's claims in America. Pearson argues that long-term reliance on state welfare has undermined the resilience and self-reliance of Aboriginal Australia. The modern welfare system has, he says, been a 'destructive influence' over traditional Aboriginal mores and values, for it has destroyed the norms of reciprocity which once under-pinned the Aboriginal custom of sharing, and it has fostered a 'victim mentality' among those who have come to rely upon its largesse. What Pearson calls 'passive welfare' – the transfer of money from the government with nothing expected or demanded in return – is turning his fellow Aborigines into 'wasteful, aimless people', and is leading inexorably to a 'disintegration of our communities and the annihilation of our culture'.

Just as Field (chapter 3) argues that it was economic dislocation that stripped British inner city working class men of their jobs, and which therefore led to their dependency on welfare in the first place, so too Pearson traces the cause of long-term joblessness among Aborigines in Australia to a change in the local economy. In this case, the incorporation of Aborigines as full Australian citizens in 1967 resulted in the enforcement of equal pay for white and black workers, but this in turn led to a huge loss of Aboriginal jobs in the pastoral industry and hence to a drift to the towns and an increase in reliance on income support.

Similarly, just as Mead (chapter 2) accepts that the plight of inner city blacks in America has roots in the history of slavery and racism, so too Pearson traces the ultimate cause of the plight of the Aborigines to their 'colonial dispossession' since the time of European settlement. By seizing the land, the colonisers disrupted forever the traditional subsistence economy and therefore destroyed the capacity of Aboriginal peoples to take care of their own material needs.

Like Field and like Mead, Pearson is therefore not looking to 'blame' the recipients of welfare for their current condition. Traditional Aboriginal culture was robust, resilient and self-reliant, and it has been factors beyond the control of Aboriginal communities – racism, dispossession, trauma – that have broken down this culture and led to the present problems. But also in common with Field and Mead, Pearson is clear that the welfare system has made matters worse. Despite a vast improvement in the material circumstances of Aboriginal communities over the last thirty years, Pearson finds that on a range of indicators the strength of Aboriginal society has been deteriorating, and is now far less functional than it was thirty or forty years ago. The explanation, according to Pearson, lies in the growing habituation of the people to passive welfare.

In Pearson's view, the basic problem is that the modern welfare system demands too little from those at whom it is targeted. Echoing Murray's argument in his book, *In Pursuit of Happiness and Good Government* (1988), Pearson believes that human beings take pride in themselves through their achievements, and they realise their capacities through the exercise of personal responsibility and initiative. When people are given money for no reason other than that they are deemed to need it, they not only hand over control of their lives to those who are handing out the cash, but they also lose any sense of the link between action and its consequences. They get a cheque whatever they do. Or as Pearson puts it, money loses any rationale in the way it is 'earned', and this means that it also loses any rationale in the way it is spent. This then results in welfare payments being squandered and in people losing the will and the capacity to take responsibility for themselves and their families.

According to Pearson, it was not social problems in the Aboriginal communities that led to welfare dependency, but welfare dependency that created the current torrent of social problems. In all likelihood, however, the causation has probably run both ways. This applies not simply to the Aboriginal communities but to Australian society as a whole.

Social problems – growing youth unemployment, a rise in marriage breakdowns and single parenthood, a collapse in demand for unskilled labour – do lie behind the rise in welfare spending since the early 1960s, but the state's response has itself also triggered new problems. The relationship is dialectical – or, to put it in everyday language, the welfare system has been chasing its own tail for the last thirty years. Changes in the family have led to increased demands for welfare support for lone parents, for example, but this increased funding has itself enabled a further rise in the rate of lone parenting. Problems of youth unemployment have triggered an increase in welfare spending on young people, but this has in turn led some young people to see the welfare system as a viable alternative to work or education and has therefore reinforced the rising trend of youth joblessness. The collapse in demand for unskilled labour in regional Australia hit many Aboriginal workers particularly hard, but their switch to long-term income support then eroded the will to work and has now made some of them virtually unemployable.

Recognising the complexity of these processes of mutually reinforcing causation, analysts like Lawrence Mead, Frank Field and Noel Pearson have begun to converge on a recognition that, while structural circumstances can create problems of long-term joblessness, habituation to welfare can in turn foster a culture among claimants that hinders their ability to take advantage of the opportunities that may still be available to them. For all the disagreements that separate them, therefore, these writers seem to agree that part of the reason for high rates of long-term welfare dependency in Australia is the cultural change wrought by the welfare system itself.

It is increasingly clear that the polarisation in Australia between the traditional left-wing view that welfare claimants are the victims of structural forces beyond their control, and the traditional right-wing view that they simply choose not to work, is unhelpful. One does not have to subscribe to theories about a new Third Way in politics to recognise that traditional boundaries between left and right are blurring, and that the debate on welfare reform has been moving beyond these old lines of battle.

This is probably what the Minister had in mind when she concluded her speech launching the current welfare reform initiative with a plea to the media to ensure that 'the debate that our community must have does not become a sterile exercise characterised by cheap political point scoring and sensational headlines' (Newman 1999a: 9). Whether her wish is granted remains to be seen. New lines of intellectual and political cleavage can be disorienting, and there will always be those who prefer the comfort of their well-worn ideological foxholes to the feeling of exposure and vulnerability which comes from moving onto a new and unfamiliar terrain of battle.

What should be done?

The newly emerging policy consensus, not only in Australia but in the other Anglo countries too, is that welfare should wherever possible be made conditional upon some input from recipients – what the Australian government calls 'mutual obligation'. Where the arguments begin, however, is over what kinds of obligations it is reasonable to demand of people. In particular, there are disagreements over whether participation should be voluntary or compulsory, and over whether it should always entail work or should be broadened to encompass training or even (as in the Welfare Reference Group's *Interim Report* recommendations) non-economic forms of 'social' participation.

Lawrence Mead's position, grounded in the American experience, is that only compulsory work requirements are effective. In chapter 2, he argues that voluntary participation schemes are ineffective, because people are too defeated or disorganised to take advantage of them, and that training schemes (offered as an alternative to work) are also ineffective, because people need to get used to the daily routine of working in order to break their habituation to welfare, and training simply puts this off to another day.

In his review of recent policy developments in Australia, Britain and the United States in chapter 4, Alan Buckingham supports Mead's position. Noting that welfare reform in Britain and Australia has been relatively timid as compared with developments in the United States, Buckingham suggests that the culture of dependency has been largely unaffected by recent changes in these two countries because they have shied away from enforcing work.

In Britain, for example, the Blair government's Welfare to Work initiative has imposed work or training requirements on young unemployed people, but participation by those on single parent and disability benefits has been left voluntary, and take-up rates have been disappointing.[6] Much emphasis has been placed on the new Working Families Tax Credit, which is designed to make employment financially more attractive than welfare, but a recent report estimates that this will entice only 27,000 more people into work (Blundell et al. 2000). The new tax credit may be effective as a way of boosting the take-home incomes of relatively low-paid workers, but it is a cumbersome way of getting more people into employment in the first place, costing over fifty thousand pounds for each new job filled. Buckingham concludes that the British New Deal program is proving very costly and largely ineffective. Even when people have successfully been placed in jobs, more than half of them have been back on the unemployment register within six months.

Australia has for much of the 1980s and 1990s been ahead of Britain in pursuing the new welfare reform agenda, but Buckingham believes that here too the reforms have yet to have much of an effect. He believes that one of the main reasons for this is that both countries still allow claimants to opt for education or training courses to fulfil their obligations, and he cites recent OECD evidence that training schemes for the unemployed rarely lead to subsequent employment. This argument receives some support from Peter Dawkins, in chapter 11, and from the Welfare Reference Group's *Interim Report*, both of which draw on evidence collected by Martin (2000) who finds that training programs can work for mature women returning to the labour force, but that they are largely ineffective for other groups. Indeed, the *Interim Report* notes in an appendix that across the OECD countries 'almost no training program worked for out-of-school youths' (Appendix 6: 97), yet it is precisely this group which in Australia is being herded into training in large numbers as a result of the Job Placement, Employment and Training (JPET) program.

Several of the contributors to this book remain unconvinced by these arguments in favour of compulsory work obligations. In chapter 12, Michael Raper insists, against Mead, that any activity requirements attaching to receipt of welfare should be voluntary, and that training is likely to prove more effective than work placements in helping people become self-reliant in the long term, since the collapse of low-skilled jobs means that there are few opportunities for people to participate effectively in the labour market unless they have some skills and qualifications. Similarly, in chapter 10, MacDonald and Siemon explicitly reject Mead's view that work offers the best route out of long-term poverty and welfare dependency. They point out that many of the jobs which are likely to be available to low-skilled welfare recipients are short-term and low paid, and they argue that single mothers in particular should not be expected to find paid employment when they still have dependent children. In their view, Work for the Dole does not increase the number of people in work; it simply makes life harder for those who are forced to go looking for jobs that do not exist.

The most incisive critique of Mead's position comes from Anna Yeatman, in chapter 8. She begins by pointing out that Mead has moved a long way from the principles of neo-liberalism which originally underpinned the New Right's critique of the welfare state. Where neo-liberals seek to minimise the role of government and to leave individuals as far as possible to determine for themselves how they should behave, Mead wants to use the government to enforce what he believes is the most appropriate form of behaviour – namely, a commitment to work. This, says Yeatman, is paternalism, not liberalism,[7] and she argues that Mead's position implicitly assumes that he knows what is best for people (that they should achieve self-respect through work), and that he has the right to force them to comply with this judgement.

This line of argument leads Yeatman into a familiar and very old debate within political philosophy and political sociology about whether we can define other people's 'best interests' even if they fail to recognise this for themselves. Her conclusion is that it can be legitimate to impose such paternalistic judgements upon others, but only under certain tightly specified conditions. In the particular example of work requirements being imposed through the welfare system, she claims that this is only legitimate if individuals themselves would like to find work, if employment is the best solution to the poverty in which they currently find themselves, and if (in the case of those with children) it can be shown that their children benefit as a result of them working.

Yeatman seems to doubt whether these requirements are met in recent and current moves to reform the welfare system in the Anglo countries. In the United States, where 'welfare mothers' have been forced out to work, she believes that most would actually prefer to combine limited employment with a continued child care role, and she doubts whether the children of these mothers are benefiting from being placed into full-time child care facilities in order to enable their mothers to fulfil their welfare obligations. She also argues that forced participation in today's labour market is likely to result in poverty-level wages (as well as in subordination to the 'patrimonial authority' of employers) and that compulsory work in return for welfare therefore fails to meet the requirement that it should offer an effective route into self-reliance.

Yeatman's arguments raise a host of philosophical and theoretical issues, not the least of which is how she can deem it 'illegitimate' for the donor in a social relationship (in this case the taxpayer, mediated by the government) to impose certain requirements on a 'recipient' before handing over money. Her discourse rests on the assumption, examined earlier in this chapter, that receipt of welfare is somehow an unequivocal moral right, for only by starting off from such an axiom can she conclude that the paternalistic imposition of conditions by a donor may be an 'unjustifiable' restraint on their generosity.

Leaving aside such arguments, however, it is possible to evaluate the positions taken by Mead and Buckingham on the one hand, and by Raper, Yeatman, and MacDonald and Siemon on the other, by considering the recent American experience. As noted above, the American welfare reforms, ushered in by the *Personal Responsibility and Work Obligations Reconciliation Act* of 1996, have gone much further than any of the welfare reforms introduced or even proposed in either Australia or Britain. The new legislation replaced the old Aid for Families with Dependent Children (AFDC) payments with a system called Temporary Assistance to Needy Families (TANF) which limited any individual's right to welfare to a lifetime total of just five years (although this does not include food stamps or Medicaid). The new system also imposed compulsory work requirements on lone-parent claimants once their youngest child reaches a specified age (this varies from just 12 weeks in

Wisconsin, to 12 months in other states). State agencies administering this new policy generally help welfare claimants search for work, and they make various forms of help available to enable them to find child care while they are working. Claimants who cannot find work are given a work placement, for which they receive basic welfare payments until such time as they find a job for themselves.

By current Australian and British standards, this new policy regime (which is broadly consistent with Mead's principles of 'help and hassle') looks draconian. But the question is whether it has been effective in reducing welfare dependency and improving the wellbeing of those American families who were previously receiving AFDC payments.

Judged against the American government's primary goal of reversing the thirty-year rise in the size of the welfare rolls, the reform has proved a resounding success. Between 1994 and 1998, at a time when the number of claimants in both Britain and Australia was still rising, the Americans managed to reduce their nationwide AFDC/TANF caseload by 42 per cent (Kalisch 2000). In Wisconsin, where change began earlier and has gone further than in most other states, the rolls fell to just 7,700 cases by 1999, a dramatic drop of 90 per cent in just four years (DeParle 1999).

Critics like Henman (1999) have suggested that these huge reductions in levels of welfare dependency were probably due more to the expansion of the American economy through the 1990s than to the impact of legislative changes, but research reported by Kalisch (2000) indicates that only 20 per cent of the overall reduction can be explained by improved labour market conditions. Besides, as Mead points out in chapter 2, in earlier periods of expansion in the American economy the welfare rolls have not shrunk. The reduction in welfare caseloads since the mid-1990s is unprecedented, and there is little serious doubt that it was caused primarily by the move to a new welfare system.

Where there is more room for debate is over the impact of these changes on the wellbeing of those who have left the system. Here, research has shown that around two-thirds of former claimants succeeded in finding jobs, but a quarter did not find paid work and did not have a partner in paid work either (Loprest 1999).[8] Most of those who left the system have managed to stay off welfare, although 30 per cent did find themselves back on benefits within two years of leaving.

Loprest reports that most former welfare recipients are in relatively low-paid jobs, and this would seem to bear out Yeatman's argument that, in moving people from welfare to work, the American reforms did not necessarily improve their material wellbeing by any appreciable amount. Interestingly, however, Loprest and Brauner (1999) also found that between a half (in Washington) and three-quarters (in South Carolina) of those who had left welfare reported that their lives are 'better now' than they were before, and this would seem to fulfil Yeatman's requirement that any imposition of work conditions is only justifiable if it results in an improvement in the quality of people's lives. Most former welfare recipients seem, therefore, to have benefited from this reform, and most (60 per cent) said that they were confident that they would not be going back on welfare in the future.

In addition to gauging the impact on the former welfare recipients themselves, Yeatman also requires us to consider the impact on their children. This is even more difficult to determine, and as Mead himself recognises, there is a legitimate argument to be had about whether it is better for the children of lone parents to have a parent at home looking after them all day, or whether it is preferable that they should grow up with the role model of an adult earning a living.

Mead believes that children in two-parent families are better off if one parent works and the other stays at home, but that children living with only one parent do better if that parent goes out to work. Such evidence as there is on this tends to support his contention that children of lone parents often do better if that parent goes out to work, but the explanation appears more complex than Mead allows (see Barnett 1992; Caughy et al. 1994). Given the economic and cultural poverty often associated with their home backgrounds, children of lone parents can benefit from time spent outside the home in high quality institutional day care where they receive more mental stimulation and contact with peers. This would suggest that any move to enforce work obligations on lone parents would have to ensure that good quality child care provisions were in place if the children are to benefit. It is noticeable in this respect that the American reforms have gone hand-in-hand with higher rates of spending on things like child care and personal counselling than were ever incurred under the old arrangements. Wisconsin, for example, now spends 40 per cent more per welfare family than it did before (Australian Broadcasting Corporation 2000).

Overall, then, the story of the American reforms seems, on balance, a rather positive one. This should not be taken to imply that Australia and Britain should now follow America in toughening up the welfare reform process. The United States context is very different from that in both Britain and Australia, and what works in one place may not work in another.

In chapter 3, for example, Frank Field notes that, even if it were deemed desirable, it is simply not politically feasible at this time in Britain to enforce employment requirements on single parents with young children in return for benefits, and in chapter 9, Lucy Sullivan suggests that such reforms would not attract much support in Australia either. This is borne out by a recent survey by Eardley (1999) who found strong (80 per cent) public support in Australia for compulsory work in return for dole for younger claimants, but who reports that only 40 per cent supported extending this principle to the over-fifties, that only 20 per cent felt it should apply to those claiming Disability Benefit, and that only 18 per cent believed it was reasonable to demand that sole parents should find full-time work once their child/ren started primary school (although more than half thought that they should find part-time work). As I noted at the start of this chapter, there is still a strong sense in Australia and Britain that the welfare state is a moral system, and unless or until such public sentiments change, it would probably be electoral suicide for any party or government to propose radical reforms on anything approaching the American scale.

Nor are political considerations the only grounds for caution. Perhaps the Achilles heel of the new American system, which is only now becoming visible, is the five-year lifetime limit to welfare entitlement. We saw earlier that nearly one-third of those who left the American welfare rolls have subsequently returned, and taken together with those who never left at all, this makes for a substantial number of people who are now beginning to exhaust their entitlement. In Wisconsin, the first small tranche of 48 people came to the end of their five years in October 1999, and in every case they were granted an extension (DeParle 1999). In New York and California, where one-third of the nation's welfare recipients live, state governments have announced that payments will be reduced but not eliminated once the five years elapse. It seems that, having pared down the numbers on welfare, those who are left represent a hard core who are unlikely to get jobs no matter what threats are made, and when it comes to the crunch, even the hard-nosed reformers of Wisconsin seem unwilling to cut off people who have been working for their welfare cheques simply because they have failed to find jobs of their own.[9]

It is also important to remain cautious about the likely costs of reform. As the Wisconsin state government found, welfare reform may reduce the number of claimants, but it does not necessarily reduce the government's bill overall, for extra money has to be found to provide expanded child care places and to pay for the more intensive one-to-one counselling for those seeking work.

The danger for Australia is that reform here might incur the same sorts of costs as the new American system without achieving its benefits. It is noticeable that the Welfare Reform Group's *Interim Report* anticipates a move to an 'individualised' system of casework, comparable with that now found in the United States, and it also accepts the need to help lone parents with child care if they are to be enabled to return to work. Both of these proposals would be extremely expensive to realise, and the proposed merging of pensions and benefits into a new, single Participation Support Payment would represent a further, substantial increase in expenditure given the government's stated commitment to maintaining the current value of pension payments in any reform. Perhaps recognising the strain that its proposals are likely to put on government spending, the authors of the report anticipate phasing in their recommended changes over a ten-year period.

If the proposed reforms are likely to lead to a major hike in per capita welfare spending, then it is crucial that, as in America, they also reduce the overall number of claimants. However, judging by the proposals outlined in the *Interim Report*, it is likely that any reduction in the numbers of people claiming income support would be modest. For example, no limit on lifetime eligibility for welfare is envisaged in the report so there will be no mechanism to cut off those income support claimants (70 per cent of the total) who were on the rolls in Australia in both 1995 and 1999. Nor does the report anticipate moving to a 'workfare' system under which all able-bodied claimants of workforce age would be required to undertake some form of employment in return for their benefits. Indeed, not only does the report endorse the continuing use of training schemes as an alternative to work for some claimants (despite the fact that evidence demonstrates that such schemes do little to get people back into jobs), it also envisages allowing claimants who have caring responsibilities to engage in 'social participation' in return for their benefits, a form of activity which, however useful it might be, is unlikely in itself to reduce their long-term reliance on welfare payments.

Perhaps these early proposals from the Welfare Reform Reference Group represent the realistic limit on how far the welfare system can be changed under present conditions in this country. As Peter Dawkins notes in chapter 11, the proposals offer no quick fix, but rather they nudge the welfare system down a different path which may take many years to complete. Whatever changes lie in the future will probably need public opinion behind them if they are to survive, and they will need at least the tacit support of service providers and the voluntary sector if they are to be successfully put into practice.

Such considerations suggest that we are unlikely in the short to medium term to see policy makers in Australia seriously considering the sorts options which have recently been adopted by their American counterparts. This in turn suggests that the current level of welfare dependency in Australia, encompassing one in seven of all adults of workforce age, is unlikely to change very dramatically in the foreseeable future.

Notes

1. It is important to recognise that, despite their commonalities as 'liberal' systems, there are also significant differences between the welfare systems of the different Anglo countries, and Esping-Andersen's attempt to treat them all as a common category has been challenged (for example, Castles and Mitchell 1991). Britain clearly has much bigger socialised health and housing systems than either Australia or the United States, for example. Social security systems also differ quite sharply. For most of the twentieth century, the British system has incorporated elements of 'continental-style' social insurance, while Australia has relied entirely on means-tested income support payments funded out of general taxation, and until recently tried to ensure that wages are set high enough to cover the needs of families with an employed male 'head of household' without further help from the state. In the United States, 'welfare' developed much later than in the other two countries and has traditionally been limited to child support payments for lone mothers, together with specific provisions (such as food stamps) aimed at families with very low incomes. As Deacon (2000) notes, social insurance schemes covering sickness, unemployment and old age do exist in the United States but are not seen as part of the 'welfare system' by American commentators.

2. It is notable in this respect that the Anglo countries differ from most continental European nations on a number of things that might indicate a relatively strong commitment to the collectivity. The Anglo countries, for example, have all so far resisted the introduction of compulsory national Identity Cards, and none of them have compulsory peacetime national service, yet such policies are common and are widely accepted throughout continental Europe. See Saunders (1996) for a more extended discussion.

3. This evidence is particularly pertinent for current debates in Australia given that the Welfare Reform Reference Group writes quite favourably in its Interim Report about the possible introduction of some variant of a basic income or Negative Income Tax. However, it has also to be recognised that different Negative Income Tax experiments in the United States often produced different results, so the evidence may not be as conclusive as Murray believes (see, for example, Danziger et al. 1981, and DSS 1981).

4. About half of those claiming the disability payment today have either 'musculo-skeletal' or 'psychological/psychiatric' disorders (Newman 1999b), and while not denying that things like bad backs and

depression can certainly inhibit the capacity to work, it is precisely in these 'grey' areas that medical discretion in diagnosis is probably at its broadest.

5. Equally, of course, it has to be remembered that any attempt to push more people of workforce age into the labour market will increase the unemployment to vacancy ratio (that is, the numbers of people chasing each job) thereby lengthening the average time it would take for a job-seeker to find work. If, implausibly, *all* those of workforce age in Australia today were now to be redefined as job-seekers, this would raise the current ratio of vacancies to jobless by 500 per cent, there would be 80 people chasing each vacancy, and the average job-seeker would take two and a half years to find employment. I am indebted to Peter Whiteford for bringing these calculations to my attention.

6. The Welfare Reference Group's *Interim Report* notes that only one in four lone parents turned up for the preliminary interview. The British government has now made such interviews compulsory for all new social security claimants

7. This is a charge, incidentally, with which Mead himself agrees, for in chapter 2, he explicitly recognises that his proposals amount to a new 'paternalism' in which government is used to enforce behavioural standards which in earlier times would have been imposed through socialisation within strong family units.

8. Loprest reports that, of those with no earnings at all, half are still receiving some form of social security or child support, while half – 12 per cent of all those who have left the welfare rolls – have no visible source of income at all.

9. It remains to be seen whether this softening of the five-year rule encourages more free-riders back into the system. Clearly the American reforms still have not fully resolved the recurring problem of how to offer help without encouraging idleness.

Chapter 2

Welfare reform and the family: lessons from America

Lawrence Mead

In America, the decline of the family connotes several ways in which parents have become less committed to their children, and to each other. Half of marriages now dissolve in divorce and about a third of children are born to unmarried mothers. Fathers are far less present in the lives of their children than they once were. In many families, both parents work, so children get less attention than they once did. Some commentators trace the rise in social problems among youth to the changes. Other than high work levels, all these trends are most pronounced among the poor.

Welfare and the family

Is welfare to blame? Some conservatives, notably Charles Murray, argue that welfare and other social benefits have tempted the poor into dysfunction. They could get support from government if they had babies out of wedlock and refused to work, but not if they got married and supported themselves. If parents neglected their children, they knew government would take over (Murray 1994).

However, the hard evidence for this position is weak. Access to welfare, or the level of benefits, appears to have only a small influence on whether women marry or have children out of wedlock. The decline of the family appears to have deeper roots – in greater cultural permissiveness and perhaps in greater affluence. Today, a single mother often can support herself and her children without a husband, if not through welfare then through employment or help from friends and family.

And government has found no clear way to promote less unwed pregnancy or stronger families. Liberals[1] suggest that to provide better family leave, child care, or other social benefits would somehow strengthen the family – but all these things would make it even easier for women to raise children on their own, or for parents to neglect their own responsibilities to children. Conservatives say the answer is to take away existing benefits, so that parents will have only themselves to rely on. But in an affluent society with many sources of income, merely reducing government support would change little.

To directly strengthen the family may be beyond the reach of government. Change will hinge mostly on more diffuse changes in the culture to make it less permissive – to promote marriage and stigmatise parenthood outside marriage, as society used to do. Such changes appear already to be occurring in the United States, as I note below. The climate on family matters has recently turned more conservative, and divorce and unwed pregnancy are falling.

Public policy can do much more to overcome the other leading problem of poor adults – a failure to work consistently. If there is any way for government to strengthen the family in America, it will probably emerge from current efforts to enforce work among welfare recipients, and also to improve the payment of child support. Below, I lay out the logic behind American work requirements in welfare and then suggest some connections to the family problem.

The work problem and opportunity

In the main, sustained poverty among the working-aged and their children in the United States is due to lack of employment, especially work that is steady and full-time. Around three-quarters of American adults, including single mothers, work at some time during a year, and around half work full-year and full-time. Indeed, the population is more fully employed than ever before in our history. But among the poor as the government defines them, only 41 per cent of adults report any earnings at all in a year, and only 13 per cent of them work full-year and full-time (US Department of Commerce 1999). Among single parents on welfare, fewer than 10 per cent report working at a given moment, although the real level – if unreported work is counted – is perhaps one third. There are working poor – people with large families or limited earnings who remain needy despite working. But the number of non-working poor is much larger.

Academics tend to trace non-work and thus poverty back to a set of social barriers that prevent poor adults working – above all, a lack of accessible jobs and child care, but also low wages, racial discrimination, and the disincentives against work set up by welfare itself. But the evidence that such barriers actually prevent work is weak, just like the evidence that welfare creates unwed pregnancy. That is especially true for the long-term poor – those who remain needy for more than two years at a stretch. It does not appear that social unfairness often defeats all employment for the poor; more often, it depresses the quality of job they can get. Social barriers, that is, cause inequality among workers, but seldom poverty among the non-workers (Mead 1992).

Frank Field, in chapter 3 in this volume and in other writings, argues that, at least in Britain, non-work is often due to a sheer lack of jobs. In Britain, the welfare rolls include more men than they do in America, and the recessions of the 1980s and 1990s had a devastating effect on employment, especially for unskilled men. That is why many men in blighted localities like Birkenhead now subsist on the dole, abandoning hope for work or marriage.

I concede that a loss of jobs plays some role in causing poverty and dependency in very depressed areas. But American research does not support the idea that this is true of the labor market generally. Studies that set out to prove an absence of jobs typically fail to do so (for example, Newman 1999). Nor is this true only during good economic conditions such as we have currently. Even in depressed cities, and even during recessions, legal jobs at *some* wage are commonly available to most jobless who seek them at a given time. The cause of poverty is far more that the jobs pay poorly and –

above all – that the low-skilled typically do not stick with them.

American policy experience confirms this. We find that programs that merely give non-workers better chances to work on a voluntary basis do little to overcome poverty. This includes training for better jobs, work incentives that allow welfare recipients to keep more of their benefits if they work, or even government jobs. Such measures do little to raise work levels. That is because they do not cause many more jobless poor to take jobs than were working before. So in America, most experts have abandoned such proposals, even on the left.

We have to recognise that today's long-term poverty is seldom the result of steady workers being shut out of all employment or paid starvation wages. Poverty of this structural type was much more prevalent before 1960, when the economy was a lot less generous and systematic bias against racial minorities still existed. Indeed, work levels among the poor ran much higher prior to 1960, before recent equal opportunity reforms and economic expansion, than they do today. Then, the poor were typically needy *despite* work. Today, they are usually needy for *lack* of it.

Liberals want to offer new chances to poor people by inventing new social programs. Like some American liberals, Frank Field advocates job creation by government. Conversely, conservatives recommend greater reliance on the private sector. Both sides assume that some change in social structure can liberate the needy to get ahead. They both make what I call the 'competence assumption' – that poor adults are able to advance their own self-interest, if not society's. The problem is only to give them chances and incentives that will align their self-seeking with the wider social good. That premise is deeply rooted in the social justice and equal opportunity policies of the past. It was valid as long as most of the poor worked consistently, at least in some job.

It is no longer valid when many poor adults become dysfunctional – that is, when they cannot achieve even their own self-interest, let alone society's. It is difficult to call failure to work when one is poor anything but dysfunctional. The same goes for failure to get through school, drug addiction, or bearing children that one cannot support. Researchers strain to locate some impediment that would explain these behaviours, for then those who engage in them might not be deemed irrational and dysfunctional. Without stronger evidence that such impediments exist, additional benefits and incentives to promote work become pointless.

In America, as elsewhere in the West, the historic issue between left and right was the proper size of government. How much should it tax and spend, and how far should it intervene in private society to equalise opportunities and rewards among ordinary people? The left says only bigger government can achieve openness and justice, while the right sees government as the obstacle and wants to cut it back. But America has learned that merely to change the scale of government does not itself overcome poverty. Large expansions of government aid in the 1960s and 1970s lowered poverty mainly among the elderly and disabled, who are not expected to work. But among the working-aged, work levels fell. More limited cuts in aid during the 1980s and early 1990s left working-aged poverty virtually unchanged, because work levels did not rise. That is why America has lately taken more direct steps to move the poor into jobs.

A culture of poverty

To explain serious poverty, we must refer back to what sociologists of the 1960s called the 'culture of poverty'. The culture of poverty involves a mindset that I call 'dutiful but defeated'. Studies show that most poor adults have orthodox social values. They want to work, maintain their families, and so on. But they feel unable to do so in practice. They perceive myriad obstacles outside themselves that make them unable to work. These include all the things spoken of by liberal scholars – lack of jobs and child care, lack of training, lack of health care or other support services. But when we inquire how pressing these constraints are, we typically find that they do not actually prevent all employment. Other low-income people somehow overcome them and succeed in working regularly. New programs to ease the barriers on a voluntary basis do not cause more poor to work steadily.

Much more, the problem is a lack of mastery within an individual's personal life – an inability to get organised for work and then to sustain that commitment over time, overcoming problems as they arise. Poor adults typically can find jobs, but they lose them because they fail to show up for work regularly, due to health or family problems. Or they lose positions because of conflict with supervisors or co-workers. If the problems really were external, then we would find that poor adults seldom held jobs at all, or that benefits to overcome barriers, such as child care, would have more effect on work levels than they have done.

To say this is not to point blame at a personal level. The culture of defeat that surrounds the poor is as much a collective cause of poverty as any external barrier. They are not individually responsible for it. But at the same time, the immediate roots of non-work usually are not impersonal, so no further social reform, however egalitarian, can overcome them. Even a socialist society would find it had to *require* the poor to work, because merely treating them fairly does not produce change. This is what even the British Labour Party has discovered, as its New Deal shows.

Inability to function may indeed connect to the opportunity structure, but chiefly well back in time. In America, the root of most of today's serious poverty probably goes back to the historic denials of opportunity for blacks and other minority groups, who today make up a majority of the long-term poor. For blacks, the trouble goes back to the decades of unequal opportunity that followed the defeat of slavery in the Civil War. Jim Crow – the Southern racial caste system – and the exclusion of black workers from the Northern factories took its toll. The majority of blacks kept faith, prepared themselves, and when civil rights came, were ready to advance into the working and middle classes. But many others lost faith in America and themselves. The disillusionment of poor blacks and, later, Hispanics, caused the family and work levels to crumble in poor areas just when the doors of better opportunity opened.

Comparable stories could be told about other countries. The scars of class as well as race figure heavily in the making of dependency throughout the West. Frank Field speaks of a 'hysteresis' whereby prolonged non-work causes people to lose even the capacity to work. But to say this, again, confers no solution. Blighted memories prevent further opportunities in the present from solving the social problem. Today's seriously poor typically do not believe that they will ever have a chance to make it, even if society now wishes them to. Their despair has become immune to social change. Welfare reform must address dysfunction as a behaviour, not because it has no social causes, but because the roots are lost in history where they cannot be reached.

The family and functioning

The family is often the connection between past injustice and present poverty. The opportunity structure appears to have little influence on personal behaviour in the present. Social arrangements affect how people are rewarded if they function, but not whether they function. Rather, the ability to cope stems largely from one's family and upbringing.

Most children acquire a sense of possibility not because society is fair to them but because adults near to them are. By identifying with parents and teachers, they internalise values. By meeting parental expectations, they also derive a sense of mastery that makes them approach life hopefully, without defeating themselves. The wider world has no comparable influence. If parents are effective, children will be well formed even if the surrounding society is unfair. Among blacks, exemplary figures such as Martin Luther King or Colin Powell were the products of a segregated society but also of strong families that upheld demanding standards for them. Those families empowered them to go forward and break down barriers in the surrounding society.

Today, conversely, increasing rates of family breakdown have undercut functioning even though society has become much more fair. It is chiefly through dysfunctional parents that the malign influence of past injustice reaches forward to blight our own time. Today's poor adults often neglect or abuse their children because they were mistreated by their parents, as they were by their parents, and so on. Those earlier parents failed, in part, because they were ground down by a hostile or indifferent society. Today society may be more enlightened. It provides chances to get educated and get ahead, and to try again if one fails, that were unknown a century ago. But it cannot – without abolishing the family – interrupt the transmission of a heritage of defeat.

Once children leave the family to go to school, there is remarkably little government can do to change them or to enhance their capacities. By the time they become known to the authorities as problems – for crime or truancy – they may be too impaired ever to take full advantage of the chances actually available to them. Their feeling of hopelessness really arises in the first instance from weak or abusive parenting, even if they project it onto the environment. Thus, by itself, no improvement in the wider setting can make them hopeful, because none can undo those early experiences.

The solution lies in rebuilding the family, not society. Government has no easy way to do that, but the best single thing it can do is to restore order in poverty areas. It must restrain the behaviour of people who cope poorly, who otherwise would injure themselves and their children, in hopes that the children will function better. It must restore the influence of more constructive authority figures, both parents and others. This means enforcing the law, but also raising educational standards in the schools, and above all enforcing work in welfare.

It is chiefly by working that parents convey a belief to their children that there is opportunity outside the front door. If welfare parents do not work, no program to help their children is likely to achieve much. To a child, to have functioning parents is worth twenty-five Head Start programs. Only if parents work and fulfil other civilities, such as obeying the law, can they have the self-respect needed to command the respect of their children.

Work enforcement

American government is enforcing values on all these fronts with rising success, but the most dramatic breakthrough has come in requiring work within welfare. In America, welfare reform mostly means work enforcement. The focus is on the program now known as Temporary Assistance to Needy Families (TANF), which largely supports single-parent families. (Programs for the unemployed and disabled have as yet received less reform attention, in part because they are less generous than in other western countries.) Traditionally, very few welfare mothers worked, compared with a large majority of mothers not on welfare, including single mothers.

Thirty years of research and experience have shown that many more welfare mothers will go to work, or leave welfare if they are required to enter work programs as a condition of aid. Just participating in mandatory work activities strongly promotes employment, and the effect is greater if the programs emphasise working in available jobs rather than education or training for better jobs. While education and training can help people get better jobs later, it is best in the short run if the non-workers simply accumulate a work history in jobs they can already get. Since the 1980s, the best programs of this type have shown that employment and earnings on welfare can be raised substantially, despite the social and economic barriers that supposedly prevent work. Mandatory programs outperform voluntary ones chiefly because they cause more recipients to go to work, as against merely raising the earnings of those already working (Mead 1997c: chapter 2).

Serious work enforcement in American welfare goes back about twelve years. Under the most recent national welfare law, the Personal Responsibility and Work Opportunity Reconciliation Act of 1996, which created TANF, states received more discretion to decide who should be covered by welfare, but they were also required to put even more welfare adults to work than before. Half of the adult recipients are supposed to be working by the year 2002. The gathering force of work demands, plus a thriving economy and many jobs, have driven the TANF rolls down by over half in the last five years – the sharpest fall in the history of program.

Mandatory work programs are a lot less punitive than they seem on the surface. Their philosophy is not to hold the poor personally culpable for their failures. Rather, it is to hold them at least partially responsible for their futures. The notion is that government will make special efforts to support work, through child care and other services. But in return, welfare adults must make serious efforts to work. Through shared effort, society and the individual can together overcome dependency and poverty (Mead 1986). Most recipients respond to that appeal. Most go to work or otherwise avoid welfare. Remarkably few are thrown off the rolls for refusal to cooperate.

Some researchers think low unemployment gets most of the credit, but we should remember that a good economy never before produced a welfare decline anything like this. During the booming 1960s, welfare also boomed, and when the nation last had low unemployment, in the late 1980s, the welfare rolls *increased* by 30 per cent. What has made the difference today is the growing reality that going on welfare means having to work. Today, there are many jobs available, as there have been before – but recipients are being driven to take them as never before. That has caused a great many simply to leave welfare or never seek it, and to go to work instead.

Evidence on the effects of the decline is not all in, but what we know to date is strongly positive. About two-thirds of recipients who have left the rolls are employed, according to state surveys. While some are not, they typically have secured support from friends and family or from other social programs, and active hardship (homelessness, children driven into foster care) is rare. Federal surveys of the population show that work levels among poor adults, including single mothers, are soaring while poverty is falling, albeit more slowly. The proportion of poor female heads of family who worked rose from 43 to 57 per cent between 1993 and 1998, with most of that coming just in the last two years. In the same period, the poverty rate fell from 15 to 13 per cent (US Department of Commerce 1994-99, 1999).

States differ in how firmly they are enforcing work. Among states with large, urban welfare caseloads, Wisconsin has most firmly demanded work as a condition of aid. The state has driven its welfare rolls down by around 90 per cent since 1987. Yet, according to a recent survey, Wisconsin in 1997 had the highest work level among single mothers and low-income parents and the lowest child poverty rate of thirteen states studied (Urban Institute 1999). The state also ranks high on other social and health indicators that affect children, and most of these conditions are improving in the state (Annie E. Casey Foundation 1999). Nothing but welfare reform could explain such trends. More must be done to raise the incomes of former recipients, many of whom remain below poverty despite working. But from what we know now, work enforcement looks like America's greatest success against poverty since the problem became a national issue almost forty years ago.

Admittedly, this success depends critically on a strong political consensus. In America, the public will to have welfare adults work for their benefits is nothing short of ferocious, and that demand has finally governed our policy. All groups share in that demand, including minorities and the poor themselves. I realise that the will to enforce work is a good deal weaker in Australia, Britain, and other western countries. That is partly because in these societies work by mothers is still less commonplace than it is in the United States, and also because the cultures are less suspicious of dependency. On the other hand, these other countries typically have more working-aged men living on benefit, and the politics probably do support demanding that they work. Australia's Working Nation and Work for the Dole policies have this objective. They actually pre-dated the much noted British New Deal, as Buckingham notes in chapter 4 of this volume.

The family connection

My sense is that the decline of the family is, in fact, a stronger concern in Australia than rising dependency. The concern is not so much that more people are living on benefit and not working as that more children are growing up without two parents, and that fewer couples are having children at all. The focus is not on the welfare state so much as on the decay of private society.

Can welfare reform do anything about that? Very little, one might argue. Requiring single mothers to work for aid infringes the original purpose of family welfare, which was to free them from employment so that they could devote themselves to raising children. Even if one accepts that this is impolitic today, requiring work might hurt children. But if strengthening the family has not been the main goal of work requirements, that process still has some favourable family effects. Along with other programs built on enforcement, work tests could become the germ of a more constructive family policy, at least for the poor. '

Work requirements focus on adults. But we have research that suggests that for a single mother to work probably is good for children too, on average, contrary to the original presumptions of welfare. If a mother works, her children tend to do better in school, controlling for other factors. The reasons probably are that a working mother gives a good example, and her own morale improves, making her a better parent. It is two-parent, not single-parent, families where the child may gain if the mother does not work (Mead 1996). Research on the effects on children of the recent welfare changes is still in process, but welfare mothers do say that for them to work is popular, not unpopular, with their children. In one welfare reform experiment in Milwaukee, Wisconsin, families that agreed to work 30 hours a week in return for wage subsidies and other special benefits saw their children do markedly better in school, particularly boys (Bos et al. 1999: chapter 7).

The current welfare reform aims much more at raising work levels than at reducing unwed pregnancy among the poor. One reason for that is the weak evidence that welfare is responsible for that problem. Another is that interventions in the family are a lot more controversial among the public than enforcing work. Nevertheless, unwed pregnancy is currently falling in America, and welfare reform is probably one of the reasons. The connection is not that states are cutting off aid to single mothers – they are not – but is rather the clear message of personal responsibility that suffuses the welfare reform movement. Poor women are being told that, if they get pregnant, they will have to do more to help themselves, and this causes more of them to avoid pregnancy until marriage. Demands to work impose a much needed structure on the lives of poor adults (particularly youth) outside the family, and that brings more order to their personal lives as well.

Some experimental programs have appeared that try to enforce good behaviour in ways beyond employment. One type is services for teenage mothers that require that they stay in school or attend parenting classes as a condition of aid. It is easier to raise work or school levels than to reduce further pregnancies, but the programs that have the most effect on births are also the most directive, and this supports the enforcement model (Besharov and Gardiner 1996). Other programs that combine benefits with requirements – what I call paternalism – have appeared in criminal justice, drug addiction, education, and homeless policy. Most show promise (Mead 1997c).

The work emphasis in welfare supports the family because lack of earnings is itself a major reason why families break up among the poor, or fail to form. Mothers who work are less likely to have to go on welfare than those who do not, and they are more likely to meet and marry men who are working, rather than the men who hang around neighbourhoods without working. The potential effects on male work effort are even more important. Failure to provide earnings is the main reason why poor fathers abandon their families – or are kicked out by their spouses. The best single thing social policy could do for the family would be to raise work levels among low-income fathers.

Work requirements in TANF might appear to have little application to fathers, because the program supports mainly single mothers. They are subject to the work requirements, not the departed fathers, who usually do not draw welfare. Actually, traditional welfare did support some two-parent families, and since TANF some states have changed the rules to make it easier for such families to qualify. Those fathers, as well as teenagers not in school, are already subject to work tests. More important, the fact that the mother now has to work causes her to put more pressure on the father to work himself, or at least pay child support. In Wisconsin, as the welfare rolls have risen, the number of mothers claiming and receiving child support has risen. To a degree, the support of single-parent families is shifting its base from welfare to child support, a development that, if well-managed, could support stronger relationships among the parents.

Furthermore, strengthening child support enforcement is a goal of the American reform second only to raising work levels on welfare. Efforts to make more absent fathers pay to support their families go back twenty-five years. As a condition of federal welfare funding, states have been made to set up special agencies to find the fathers, establish paternity, and then collect support payments. Few low-income fathers pay regularly, in part because they have work problems of their own. That has led to work enforcement efforts for them that parallel the ones in welfare. While few absent fathers can be made to work in return for aid, they can be made to do so on pain of going to jail for non-payment of support. Again, experiments that combine requirements with new support services show promise. There is also experimentation with 'fragile families' programs that attempt to build ties among unwed parents so that the father never quits the family at all. The goal is, not just child support enforcement, but marriage. Very likely, these programs aimed at child support and family-building will be the next frontier for social policy in America (Mead 1997c: chapter 4).

All of this, admittedly, addresses the family problem only among the poor. Among the middle class, the problem probably has somewhat different causes. There, parents are probably working too much for the good of their marriages and children, rather than too little. The antidote is more likely to come from general shifts in the culture, rather than changes in social policy. Currently, there are movements in the society to reaffirm the norm that marriages last and that parents, including fathers, devote serious attention to their children. The incidence of divorce and unwed pregnancy is at least falling, although not yet to the levels of the 1950s. Some conservatives even speak of a restoration of traditional society (Murray 1995). These positive trends, however, are related to the social policy developments like Siamese twins.

The same public will to enforce agreed values is also – albeit more hesitantly – driving the movement to rebuild private society.

This much is clear: enforcing work and other civilities will accomplish more than changing the financial incentives that surround the family. There is much interest in Australia currently in altering the tax as well as benefits systems in ways that will promote the stability of the family and the care of children. The American experience, however, is that such incentives have next to no influence on actual family behaviour, just as they have little influence on work levels among the poor. The slim effects of such schemes cannot justify the immense analytic effort devoting to designing them.

Since the Australian social security system covers up to a quarter of the adult population, many of the recipients will have a work history. And since the system is strongly means-tested, the financial disincentives to going to work and raising one's income can be substantial. In these circumstances, disincentives may have more to do with low work levels than they do in America. However, the cost of reducing these deterrents is also high. To reduce the 'tax' on rewards from going to work, one must either cut benefits for the most needy or extend eligibility for aid higher up the income scale. One appeal of work requirements is that they raise work effort without a need to reduce targeting. One can continue to focus aid on the neediest while using administrative oversight to be sure that recipients take looking for work seriously.

The illusion is to imagine that basic social behaviour ever had much to do with economic payoffs. Mostly, people work or stay married because they think it is right, and not because it is in their self-interest in any narrow sense, although it usually is. To get them to work or stay married, there is no substitute for a clear message that society expects it. In the family arena, if not in the financial markets, social authority absolutely trumps economic incentives. The attraction of incentives for governments is not that they work, but that they avoid antagonising voters. They promote a behaviour we want but leave it as a choice. Government does not have to say clearly that the behaviour is right, and the alternative wrong. But experience teaches that if we want to restore social order we will have to say that. There is no substitute for setting standards for individual behaviour and enforcing them, either through law or the more diffuse sanctions of public opinion.

Enforcement and justice

Poverty would be easy to solve if only resources, and not governance, were required. Both left and right naturally search for some way to 'invest' that would overcome the social problem without addressing conduct. For liberals, that means spending more on poor families through welfare or intensive service programs. For conservatives, it might mean special education programs to build up skills, job placement programs, or job creation in the private sector. But the effect of even the best such efforts is limited and long-term. It would be better to invest in high-quality social administration because bureaucracy – unpopular though it is – increasingly must manage the lives of the seriously poor.

What paternalist programs do is mimic the combination of 'help and hassle' for budding citizens that effective families provide. This combination does more to help people function better than either help without requirements or plain severity could do alone. Government must manage lives for only limited purposes – to promote work and the other competences required of citizens. But in so doing, on current evidence, it can also indirectly foster stronger families. As parents are forced to face their responsibilities by the society, they will be more likely to commit themselves more fully to one another. Public expectations must apply the pressure to uphold marriage that the forces of scarcity once did.

Traditionally, social policy sought to promote, not functioning, but social justice. The idea was that society owed some recompense to the needy, whose failure to prosper reflected the pressure of social and economic structures beyond their control. That view was especially strong outside the United States, where the welfare state often had roots in the socialist movement. But it presumed that the beneficiaries were already citizens in full standing. And that in turn presumed, tacitly, that they were workers, or lived in a family that had a work history. The very image of welfare as a 'safety net' presumes that individuals are trying seriously to upraise themselves. When they no longer do this, as is true for most of today's seriously poor, then the focus on justice cannot be maintained. The competences assumed by citizenship must first be reaffirmed, above all work. Only then can questions of justice and redistribution get back on the political agenda (Mead 1992).

That shift is already occurring in America. Exactly because more welfare recipients are working, society is more disposed to be generous to them. State and federal governments are raising work incentives and other benefits tied to jobs in order to 'make work pay'. Because the working poor earn more, they also qualify for more help from government, not less, as liberal critics of welfare reform feared. Helping struggling 'working families' (the 'battlers' in Australian parlance) is just as popular as aiding the non-working poor was unpopular.

Indeed, the political climate in Washington has shifted left in areas beyond welfare. The anti-government Republicans who passed the last welfare reform in 1996 are in fast retreat. The current political campaign focuses on the new things government might do, in such areas as education and health. One reason for that is that the booming economy has helped balance the federal budget, but another is that it is harder to argue today than it was a decade ago that the potential beneficiaries of new social benefits would be 'undeserving'.

A deeper moral is that welfare, and the welfare state, cannot only be about rights and claims. Those who claim rights must also have obligations. Those who would be free must first be bound. Parents who would bequeath freedom to their children must first live orderly lives. The chief problem for today's seriously poor is no longer social injustice but the disorders of private life. For these Americans, the way forward is no longer liberation but obligation. In the short run, welfare reform American-style can look negative, even punitive. But the payoff is a stronger and, above all, a more integrated society. This is the road that the rest of the western world must also travel.

A return to stronger families will not lead to an age of reaction, as many fear. We should remember that all the major reformist movements of the past – the labor movements, civil rights, feminism – broke out in societies that were far more cohesive at a private level than they are today. Strong families generated strong citizens who got through school and worked. That gave them, if they were disadvantaged, the fortitude and the social standing to assert new rights.

In contrast, welfare is the narcotic that has drawn the teeth of any successor movements. Today's poor may be disadvantaged, but they are also dependent, and the combination is fatal. How likely is it that Aborigines in Australia, or Native Americans in the United States, can reverse past injustices when they have become virtual wards of the state? They must first return to full citizenship. That requires that they reclaim from welfare the responsibilities that they have abandoned to it. They must recover strong families where adults function as workers and parents. They must prepare their children, by example, for vigorous lives.

Note

1. In this chapter, the term 'liberal' is used in the North American sense of 'social democratic' or 'progressive'.

Chapter 3

Welfare dependency and economic opportunity: a response to Lawrence Mead

Frank Field

According to Charles Murray (1994), the ready availability of welfare corrupts the populace and accounts for the inevitable surge in the numbers on benefit. While taking issue with Murray, Lawrence Mead nevertheless believes that some families have now become so dysfunctional that they are not only unwilling but also unable to work without being compelled to do so (see chapter 2 in this volume). He doesn't explain why such a state of affairs exists.

Mead makes his contribution to the debate in his customarily attractive manner. He distances himself from those conservatives like Murray who view the decline in family norms as a consequence of the temptations presented by social security. He writes: 'To directly strengthen the family may be beyond the reach of government' (p. 45). But then he quickly cheers himself up (and no doubt his readers) by adding shortly afterwards: 'If there is any way for government to strengthen the family in America, it will probably emerge from current efforts to enforce work among welfare recipients'. Reforms based on enticing the poor to work have had little success. Hence America 'has lately taken more direct steps to move the poor into jobs' (p. 48).

Elsewhere (Field and Owen 1994) I have given an overall view of how the debate over the relation between work and welfare has moved cyclically during the present century. I would not deny that the existence of welfare can impact on behaviour, and therefore the character of claimants (Field 1995, 1996), and like Mead, I too wish to argue for the development of a more pro-active welfare whereby such payments are made much more conditional on seeking jobs. But we must remember that the composition of the welfare rolls in Britain is radically different from that in America. The British rolls are not dominated by single-parent claimants to the degree they are in the States.

It has been the collapse of manufacturing employment which has transformed the composition of Britain's welfare rolls. This collapse changed welfare from being primarily concerned with retired claimants to a system dealing with people of working age. It has been the contraction of the job market for semi-skilled and unskilled males which has had the greatest impact, both directly and indirectly, on the composition of those on welfare and the length of time spent on welfare, and thereby on the functioning of families.

Unemployment and the welfare rolls

In the early post-war period in Britain, the welfare rolls[1] were composed largely of claimants who were retired. This dominance of aged pensioners was such that their numbers rarely fell below 70 per cent of claimants. This position held right up to 1970, and even then aged pensioners remained in a clear majority until 1980. The fall in the proportion of aged pensioners was not brought about by fewer pensioners claiming; in fact the opposite has occurred, with numbers of aged pensioners on welfare rising almost threefold. Rather, it was the impact of two major recessions in Britain which revolutionised the composition of the welfare rolls.

The first of the two major post-war recessions, starting in 1980, saw the number of unemployed people on welfare rise from less than 20 per cent of the total to over 40 per cent in the space of three years. By 1983, for the first time ever during the post-war period, there were more unemployed benefit claimants than there were aged pensioner claimants. That position was further reinforced by the recession that began in the early 1990s.

The severity of these recessions is seen in the data on the numbers in work in Great Britain. The size of the labour force rose in most years in post-war Britain. When earlier post-war recessions occurred, the fall in employment rarely amounted to more than half a million, or 1 in 50 of the total number of jobs. Moreover, a complete recovery was recorded within the space of two or three years. The recessions of the early 1980s and 1990s were of a quite different order. In the three years after 1980, 1.5 million jobs were lost. Almost 2 million jobs were lost in the recession beginning in 1990 and the total number of jobs had still not recovered to its 1990 level eight years later.

Loss of male jobs

These two recessions have had a lasting impact on the employment levels of male workers. While the total number of jobs in the economy has risen overall by a little over 2 million since 1979, the number of male jobs has fallen over the same period by half a million. While the number of women in work has risen by 2.5 million, this growth in the female labour force has not been uniform throughout the country. In some inner city areas the number of women workers has fallen, although by far less than the dramatic collapse in the number of males in work in the same areas. The loss of male jobs has been particularly noticeable in the trades offering semi-skilled and unskilled workers job opportunities.

The constituency of Birkenhead which I represent in Parliament illustrates how growing national prosperity accompanied by a buoyant national labour market conceals considerable job deficits in some local labour markets. That Birkenhead is typical of inner-city areas in Britain can be seen from a recent study by the Joseph Rowntree Foundation (Turok and Edge 1999). In 1979 there were 20,900 men working full-time in Birkenhead, as well as 2400 men in part-time employment. By 1997 the number of men in full-time work had dropped to 12,500 and the number of male part-time workers had also fallen, to 2100.

In case anyone sees these data as supporting the Murray thesis – welfare availability tempting people onto benefit – it should be noted that these years were marked by the closure of much of the heavy manufacturing base in Birkenhead, including the shipyard and the steel mill. The number of women in full-time work in the constituency stood at 7700 in June 1978 rising to 11,300 three years later. By September 1997 the number of women in full-time work had fallen to 8,800. Similarly the number in part-time work in the constituency, which had stood at 12,300 in 1978, had fallen to 9,100 twenty years later.

I therefore disagree with what one commentator (Deacon 1997) has billed as Mead's 'most striking argument', namely, that the availability of jobs is not the key issue in explaining the rise in the welfare rolls. Mead believes that the jobs are there, but that the long-term workless poor, while 'dutiful', are 'defeated' and are therefore incapable of getting or retaining them. Pro-active welfare is relevant, for even in those areas of the country registering a major jobs deficit, some jobs still become available. But pro-active welfare by itself is not adequate in those areas where the job cull has been massive. Here workers have every reason to feel defeated.

Impact on behaviour

In the years following the 1980 recession, economists began talking of 'hysteresis'. By this they meant that the recession had been so severe, and had so enfeebled some local economies, that the market could not engender its own recovery. But the severity of the recession not only affected how the local economy worked. It also had a similarly devastating impact on the behaviour of many people. It was the recession which pushed people onto the welfare rolls, and thereby changed the behaviour of some claimants. It was not that behavioural changes resulted in welfare claims, but that being thrown onto welfare led to behavioural changes.

How was behaviour affected? Hysteresis on individuals and families resulted in the breakdown for many of the habit of work. It is as simple as that. In areas like Birkenhead, the norm whereby young males smartly moved from school into work was destroyed. Worklessness became the norm in some tightly defined areas. The hopelessness of being part of a huge stagnant pool of unemployed labour can defeat all but the most determined of individuals. And this hopelessness was not assuaged by drugs.

The marital status of males was damaged by this change. How can you start to plan a life together when all that is brought financially to the contract is a meagre welfare cheque? So marriage became an endangered species in the poorest areas, and a new norm was quickly established in its place. In one of the poorest parishes in Birkenhead, a yearly total of 170 or so funerals was matched by as few as three marriages.

It was not only young workers who were affected, although as a group they bore the brunt of the jobs collapse. Older redundant male workers faced similar difficulties in finding a job in a far tighter labour market. But successive Conservative governments, wishing to see the unemployment count fall as elections approached, were active in persuading employment staff to transfer claimants to Incapacity Benefit, or at least to register them as sick.

The collapse in the job market also impacted on the numbers of young single parents. Why marry a fellow – supposing an offer is there – when a benefit claim as a single parent results in more money proportionately than by marrying, particularly if the boyfriend also claims his welfare cheque, together with housing benefit, and sub-lets his flat while living with his girlfriend? More money to be sure, but hardly a more stable environment for children to grow up in.

Here is just one example of benefit rules affecting behaviour once people are on the rolls. But it was not simply the collapse of suitable jobs for men with few skills which led to fewer men being able fulfil their financial responsibilities as fathers. The self-same changes to the local labour market operated against women as well. Over a 20-year period, the number of full time and part-time jobs for women workers in Birkenhead fell by 2500 and 2200 respectively. Fewer full-time job opportunities now exist for young women before marriage, and there are also fewer part-time job opportunities for mothers to combine with family responsibilities should a marriage have taken place. And news on this front travels fast along the grapevine from older sisters and friends finding difficulty in supplementing their family income with part-time work. Faced with greater difficulty in getting a full time job, and with far fewer young men able to accept the financial responsibility of fatherhood, some young women opt rationally for lone parenthood, usually (but not invariably) soon after they have left school.[2]

The case for pro-active welfare

To recognise that the main cause of the transformation in the nature of the welfare system lies in the economy, is not to argue for retention of the status quo. A welfare system designed to look after aged pensioners is clearly unsuitable once that operation is geared to a very large majority of claimants of working age – hence the move in Great Britain to make welfare pro-active.

New Deal, introduced in Britain in 1998, is the most far-reaching of the welfare changes introduced so far by the Blair Government. All unemployed claimants without family responsibilities who are below the age of 25 and who have been unemployed for ten months have to accept one of a range of full-time options, including subsidised work, or lose benefit. This scheme is being extended to other claimants without family responsibilities.

The case for national pro-active welfare schemes is twofold. The first is that, as has been already noted, the delivery of welfare was originally geared almost exclusively towards aged pensioners, and these are no longer the majority of claimants. No-one seeking to set up a system of welfare in Britain today would design the one that was put in place in the early post-war years which were characterised by full employment. With a tighter job market, and fewer jobs for life, an active employment service helping claimants into work is required.

But second, such a service was also necessary to counter the feelings among groups of claimants that looking for work is hopeless, or is not an attractive enough proposition. That was a view which took root after the first major recession, and was reinforced by the second. While pro-active welfare is most relevant in areas registering high employment, it also has a role in areas still characterised by high unemployment. If I can cite the example of Birkenhead again, the Wirral Employment Service, whose jurisdiction covers Birkenhead and the surrounding region, helped 15,105 people into work in 1995–96, a time when the local labour market was still fragile following severe recession.

By concerning itself with the skill levels and attitudes of claimants, pro-active welfare can play a part in improving the quality of labour on offer; and the availability of such labour may itself help stimulate job creation by employers who might not otherwise consider such a development. But while it is crucial to develop still further this 'help and hassle' strategy which underpins pro-active welfare, this approach alone will not see significant reductions in unemployment in those areas suffering a major job deficit. In areas of persistently high unemployment, New Deal Mark 2 will need to consider much more direct means of influencing the demand for labour, as well as keeping a continual interest on the supply side issues.

Single parents

New Deal in Britain extends to single parents on benefit. The New Deal for Lone Parents targets single parents who have been on Income Support for more than eight weeks, and whose youngest child is in full-time schooling, with a package of job search, training and after-school care to help them into work. But the crucial difference between this part of the New Deal and those applying to all other able bodied workers, is that the scheme is voluntary. Lone parents are invited to the employment office for an interview, but until recently there was no sanction on those who refuse this invitation, let alone anything more demanding.

This part of the New Deal was implemented nationally at the end of October 1998. By the end of June 1999, 72,190 lone parents had attended an interview; of these, 6,450 had left the scheme and found jobs. The impact of the scheme has therefore been very limited – the number of single parents on benefit in Britain has begun to fall, but this fall was only recorded after the number of jobs in the economy began to increase (the movement out of the current recession was first apparent in Scotland, and it is significant that the number of single parents claiming benefit began to fall first in this area).

The New Deal scheme for single parents is based on self-selection, and while some single parents have been helped into work, the likelihood is that many of these would have made that transition anyway. Nevertheless, the scheme is important in changing the ethos of welfare from one of passive receipt to one of greater reciprocity of duties. It expresses the idea that it is the duty of the state to provide benefit, and the duty of the claimant to be an active working citizen as soon as that becomes a possibility.

An assumption behind the view of many of those advocating more conditional welfare for single mothers in Britain, as well as those blazing the trail in America, is that single mothers working leads to better functioning families. That may be so for single mothers with older children. In Britain single mothers have a right to draw benefit until their youngest child has reached age sixteen. At some stage this rule will be reviewed. While policies helping those single mothers with younger children move into work when they wish to do so command considerable but not universal support in Britain, an approach which made the drawing of benefit conditional on seeking work, either after two years on benefit, or once children began school, would not win the support of the House of Commons, and would likely be strongly opposed by a majority of voters.

Given this electoral bulwark against change, it is a pity the Government has not experimented more with ways of encouraging single parents back to work. It has so far cost £5,611 (A$14,000 approximately) for each single parent moving back into work on the New Deal. Wouldn't it have been a worthwhile pilot to offer in one or two local areas, say, £2000 (A$5,000) to those single parents able to get back to work for at least a year? Here again is a difference with Mead. Some incentives are important in stimulating good behaviour. The Government's obsession with whether the poor's marginal tax rate is 70 per cent instead of 90 per cent is relevant on grounds of fairness, but not in making an effective contribution in moving people back to work.

It is through a policy of trying to raise skills of pupils in schools, of continuing that process for people once successfully placed in work, or seeking work, together with the development of pro-active welfare policies to support people seeking work, that Government policy may help engender conditions conducive to stable families in areas of greatest poverty. But the hysteresis effect on people's behaviour following two major post-war recessions, and the changing views of what constitutes normal behaviour, is most clearly seen in inner city areas where a cumulative process of disintegration appears to be at work. This should caution against claiming too much for what Government policy may achieve. Destruction is far, far easier than reconstruction. Stable families require an economy producing family wages and a surrounding culture which recognises and encourages the concept.

Conclusion

That Britain, like America, is reforming much of its welfare so that payments are conditional on actively seeking work, should not disguise the significant differences between the two countries. Welfare in America is primarily concerned with payments for single mothers. This is not the case in Britain, where unemployed males and disabled workers are also major welfare beneficiaries. But these differences should not detract from a common concern about the number of children being raised in fluid single-parent families (that is, families where there is a series of boyfriends resulting in a number of children by different fathers).

Lawrence Mead sees the shoe-horning of welfare claimants into work as possibly providing the most effective way of strengthening American families. I have argued that it has been the collapse of unskilled jobs, concentrated as these losses have been in inner city areas, which has intensified the impact on society of changing views about marriage. The perceived near irrelevance of marriage for many poorer people has been reinforced by tax and welfare systems giving privileges to single-parent status. Getting claimants in inner city areas back to work is highly desirable on its own grounds, and will only be achieved by operating on both the demand as well as the supply sides of labour.

But, as Lawrence Mead himself observes, 'To directly strengthen the family may be beyond the reach of government', at least for governments understandably concerned only with the short term, and where the wish to find that ever elusive panacea is as strong as ever.

Notes

1. I use 'welfare' as a shorthand to refer to the basic means-tested income for those out of work. In Britain, this payment is currently known as 'Income Support'.

2. This trend has been reinforced by tax and benefit changes which give a privileged position to the single parent over the married couple. In this way, the welfare system sends out strong messages about behaviour, and the populace, being rational, picks up the vibes quickly.

Chapter 4

Welfare reform in Britain, Australia and the United States

Alan Buckingham

Over the last couple of years in Britain, welfare policy has been subjected to one of the most radical rethinks since the publication of the Beveridge Report in 1942. The reforms that have emerged from current thinking are based on the British Labour Government's espousal of a new set of ideas about social issues. Influenced by a number of respected thinkers (including Frank Field and Lawrence Mead), New Labour has adopted a philosophy emphasising the reciprocal obligations of citizenship, and has argued for a new 'contract' between the state and the individual: 'The new contract is essentially about duty. Duties on the part of government are matched by duties of the individual' (DSS 1998: 8).

The Blair government claims that past welfare policies encouraged passivity and dependency by paying benefits without placing sufficient demands on the recipients to find work. New Labour hopes that by requiring recipients to enter into a contract, it will encourage much more active participation in job search, and in education and training schemes. As people are helped into work they will also move off welfare and into self-sufficiency. By emphasising the mutual obligations of the citizen and the state it is hoped that a more inclusive and cohesive society can be created where everyone unites in the interests of the community.

This new way of thinking is said to represent a Third Way which rejects 'old' Labour's rights-based welfare philosophy, as well as the individualistic and market-led welfare policies of the Conservative Party. New Labour rejects the dependency and passivity that old Labour policies allowed, and it rejects the minimalist role of government towards joblessness and dependency that the Conservative governments of the 1980s adopted. Instead, both individuals and the state are expected to take an active role in securing escape from joblessness and dependency – and the primary way of achieving this escape is through steady employment.

British commentators have made much play of the innovativeness of New Labour's thinking. What many do not realise is that the policies that have emerged are very similar to the reforms that have been taking place in Australia in recent years. In fact, the major policy reform that the British government has introduced to deal with the problem of joblessness and welfare dependency – the New Deal – is heavily derivative of the past Australian Labor government's Working Nation reform and the more recent Coalition government's Work for the Dole program. In turn, these reforms can be traced back to the American Workfare reforms.

The basic principle underlying all of these policies is the notion of 'reciprocal obligations'. Under this philosophy a deal is struck between the state and the individual whereby the state pays benefits and is pro-active in helping individuals back into work, in return for which individuals must meet their obligations of participating in the various schemes and searching for work.

Welfare dependency and the family

Changes in welfare policies or in approaches to joblessness are likely to have direct consequences for the family. The obvious example of this relates to lone parents, most of whom depend to a greater or lesser extent on welfare support. In Britain, Australia and the United States, the numbers of lone parents claiming welfare support have risen sharply over the last thirty years, and in all three countries it is reasonable to suppose that lone parenthood could not have expanded to the extent that it has unless government had provided cash support.

Welfare dependency among lone parents has been rising in both Britain and Australia, but the trend is much stronger in

Britain. As Figure 4.1 shows, Britain has a very high rate of lone parenthood (a third higher than in Australia), a high rate of never-married mothers (more than double Australia's rate), and a high rate of joblessness. In absolute terms the numbers in Britain are even more striking. Latest estimates show that 1.6 million families are headed by a lone parent, affecting 2.8 million children (Haskey 1998), while the social security bill for the 1.3 million dependent on welfare amounts to about £10 billion (about A$25 billion) (DSS 1999). Furthermore, spells on benefit for lone mothers are rarely brief. A recent study found that 43 per cent had been in receipt of the basic welfare benefit (Income Support) continuously for more than six years (Finch et al. 1999).

In the United States, there has been a long running debate over the deleterious effects of welfare and the role it is claimed to have had in creating a lone parent underclass caught in a culture of benefit dependency (Gilder 1980;

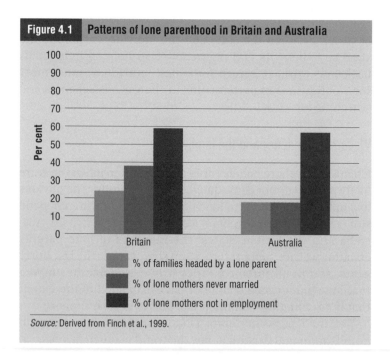

Figure 4.1 Patterns of lone parenthood in Britain and Australia

Legend:
- % of families headed by a lone parent
- % of lone mothers never married
- % of lone mothers not in employment

Source: Derived from Finch et al., 1999.

Murray 1994; Ellwood and Bane 1994). Clearly influenced by this debate, the recent Clinton welfare reforms in the United States have sought to change the conditions under which benefits are paid. In 1996 this process began when the major benefit for lone mothers, Aid to Dependent Families with Children (AFDC), was replaced with Temporary Assistance for Needy Families (TANF). As the name of the benefit implies, TANF is designed to be temporary; it limits families to two years on welfare in any one spell, and to a total of five years welfare. The clear message is that benefits are finite and cannot be seen as a long-term income source equivalent to work or the father's earnings. Another message the reform conveys is that welfare is not a right. In return for TANF, recipients need to meet rigorous job-search and training obligations. The immediate aim of TANF is to get lone mothers into work and off of benefits as soon as possible, and the welfare agencies are extremely pro-active in organising this. Lying behind this aim is the desire to reduce the number of out-of-wedlock births.

The belief seems to be that, by placing obligations on lone mothers to find work and get off benefits, there will be positive secondary consequences in achieving greater parental responsibility and strengthening family stability. One way this may work is by deterring many women from having births out of wedlock in the first place. Prospective lone mothers now know that they cannot expect to be provided for by the state; they must either find work or find a husband willing to support them and their child. Another way it may work is by increasing the incentives of those who are lone mothers to marry, for it is only by finding a new and committed partner that they can now choose to stay at home and care for their child rather than go out to work full-time.

The evidence from the United States is that these reforms are having their desired effect. In the state of Wisconsin, where rigorous welfare to work policies have been in existence for some time, there has been an 18 per cent fall in the number of ex-nuptial births to black Americans between 1990 and 1996, and between 1993 and 1998 there has been a 40 per cent drop in the number on welfare (Murray 1999).

Male joblessness and implications for the family

Joblessness and welfare dependency amongst men also has implications for the family. The American sociologist William Julius Wilson (1987) has argued that men without jobs do not make attractive marriage partners because they do not command an income sufficient to sustain a family. For Wilson, the lack of 'marriageable' men is an important reason why there is such a high rate of ex-nuptial births and lone parents in poor neighbourhoods in the United States. He argues that single women who cannot find stably employed partners to father their child may choose lone parenthood and benefit dependency instead.

A consequence of this is that large numbers of jobless males remain unmarried, without a role to play in supporting a family. Yet the duties attaching to marriage and supporting a family may be crucial in 'locking' men into responsible behaviour: 'Young males are essentially barbarians for whom marriage – meaning not just the wedding vows, but the act of taking responsibility for the wife and children – is an indispensable civilising force' (Murray 1996: 41). Men who do not have the responsibility for supporting a family do not have to stay in work, do not have to keep up to date with the payment of bills, and generally do not have to think about anyone else than themselves.

The idea that there is an association between male joblessness and failure to marry is supported by empirical evidence. I have conducted research on the underclass in Britain using a large longitudinal survey called the National Child Development Study (Buckingham 1999). This survey[1] followed a cohort from birth until thirty-three years old, and it shows that only just over half of those males who suffer from chronic worklessness and welfare dependency had married by their early thirties (this compares with over four-fifths of all other men in the cohort). In fact these men have difficulty finding partners altogether. Over two-fifths of chronically jobless men who had never married had also not had a steady relationship in the last ten years.

For writers like Murray (2000), this sort of evidence points to the emergence of a male underclass who have no stake in work, no stake in the family, and therefore no stake in society. Support for this comes from some startling statistics about British society that he has highlighted. Despite the fact that Britain is enjoying the lowest rate of unemployment for twenty years at just 4 per cent, worklessness among young men has been increasing rapidly. By 1999, 31 per cent of men aged 18–24 were jobless compared with 21 per cent a decade earlier (when unemployment stood at over 7 per cent).[2] The rise in young jobless men has been paralleled by an increase in the rate of men failing to marry the women whom they have made pregnant. In Britain in 1999, 38 per cent of all births were outside of wedlock, a rate three times higher than twenty years earlier. Finally, the indicator that the number of anti-social, lawless young men is growing is that Britain has experienced a doubling in the rate of violent crime in the last thirteen years (Office of National Statistics 1998, 2000). The rate is now higher than that in the United States.

The British Labour Government seems not to acknowledge an association between male joblessness, low rates of marriage and anti-social behaviour, but it does recognise that many of the jobless feel a lack of inclusion in society. Its response to this problem, embodied in the concept of 'stakeholding' (Kelly at al. 1997), is to give individuals the skills, education and job opportunities necessary to provide them with a 'stake' in society, thereby overcoming their 'social exclusion'. This philosophy is reflected in the New Deal, where high quality training and education form the centrepiece of a program aimed at getting the jobless back into work.

Comparing Britain and Australia with the United States

In Britain, Australia and the United States, recent welfare reforms are based on the assumption that they should operate so as to reduce the number of benefit-dependent jobless men and women. 'Passive' welfare policies, where benefits are paid without corresponding expectations about job seeking, have been replaced by 'active' polices, where the obligations of benefit recipients to seek work are matched by the efforts of the welfare agencies to help find work.

In the United States the Clinton reforms are highly active in requiring lone mothers collecting welfare to meet tough obligations to find work and move off welfare. For unemployed men, there is no federal unemployment benefit at all. In Australia and in Britain the welfare policies are not as hard on the jobless, and the duty of the welfare agencies to offer help for job seekers is stressed rather more. The Australian Work for the Dole reform is based on the principle of mutual obligation – that in return for welfare, unemployed people have the obligation to seek work actively and strive to improve their competitiveness in the labour market. Similarly, in Britain the New Deal reform seeks to establish a new contract between citizen and state, with rights matched by responsibilities (DSS 1998).

Under Work for the Dole and the New Deal, young people who have been unemployed for longer than six months are automatically placed on the schemes and they are required to supplement their job searching with training, education, community work or subsidised employment. Claiming welfare without job seeking and/or job training is not tolerated, and benefit sanctions are applied to those who do not comply.

Despite these common themes, however, there are two crucial differences between the three countries. One lies in what is deemed to be stopping the jobless from working. Whereas the American reforms are based on the assumption that the major factor in joblessness is lack of personal motivation to find or take work, the British reforms still assume that joblessness results mainly from the external barriers that individuals face. The thinking in Australia seems to fall somewhere between these two positions.

The other major difference is the overall aim of the reforms. The Clinton reforms aim to cut the numbers on welfare, which in turn, it is hoped, will reduce the number of ex-nuptial births and deter lone parenthood. In contrast, the British New Deal and Australian Work for the Dole reforms do not seek to push lone parents into work and off welfare. In both countries, the sorts of obligations that have been imposed on other claimant groups (such as the young unemployed) have not so far been extended to cover sole parents, and both governments have been careful not to appear to be attacking this group.

These two differences have a fundamental impact on the way that the policies have been implemented, as well as the likelihood of their success. Let us consider each in turn.

Low work motivation versus barriers to employment

According to the British Labour Government's 1998 welfare reform green paper, worklessness occurs because, 'People face a series of barriers to paid work' (DSS 1998: 1). For the unemployed the major barrier is presumed to be the mismatch between the skills and education they have, and the level of skills and education expected by potential employers.

Reflecting this assumption, the government has essentially copied the reforms of the Keating Australian Labor Government by making training, education and job placements the centrepiece of the New Deal for the unemployed. The emphasis is not on getting the jobless into work as soon as possible, as is true of the Clinton reforms, but is on educating and training unemployed people in order to prepare them for work. Whereas the American reforms assume that it is work motivation that is lacking, the British reforms assume that the jobless would willingly take work if only the barriers to employment were not there.

The same assumption applies for lone mothers as for the unemployed: lone mothers on benefit would like to work but barriers stop them from finding a suitable job. In fact, the barriers they face are thought to be even greater than those that face the unemployed. Not only are there skill barriers but there are financial and child care barriers as well. The financial barrier is that lone mothers are not working because they will be no better off in work than remaining on benefits. The child care barrier is that lone mothers cannot work because there is a lack of child care facilities and they lack the money to pay child care costs.

In order to lessen the financial barrier to employment, the British government has introduced the Working Families Tax

Credit (WFTC). This in-work benefit reduces the taper in benefit withdrawal for those who find work so that work always pays better than benefit dependency. In fact the incentive to work is very strong, with WFTC offering a guaranteed minimum income of £200 (A$500) per week for a full-time worker. In order to lessen the child care barrier the government has introduced the Childcare Tax Credit which provides financial help to cover up to 70 per cent of child care costs for low- and middle-income families.

The problem with these sorts of policies, however, is that there is little evidence that 'barriers to work' really are the major cause of continuing joblessness. It is difficult to see how lack of skills could be the problem, for example, when labour force participation rates have dropped sharply across all social classes in America and Britain (Jencks 1990; Nickell and Bell 1995). Regardless of level of skill and education levels, men are less likely to be participating in the labour force.

Joblessness and dependency seems to be more closely related to personal choice than lack of opportunity. As Layard et al. (1994: 16) have argued, in Britain, 'Even when unemployment is high, there are not queues for all vacancies . . . if people are unemployed, it is generally because they have decided against these jobs'. Undoubtedly, people with fewer skills and lower education have unequal opportunities in finding the best work, but they are not excluded from work altogether, as the British government's current policies seem to assume.

Even where lack of skills is the problem, moreover, the British government is far too optimistic about the likely success of training and work experience programs in getting people into work. As a recent OECD report found, in respect of those who had not been in regular employment for a long time, 'the effectiveness of generalised training or work experience programs with these groups has been found to be low' (OECD 1998a: 126). Evidence from the United States suggests that the success of such schemes is more closely related to the obligations they impose on finding work: 'The major determinant of whether clients enter jobs . . . is simply whether the program expects them to; the labor market and the skills of the clients are secondary' (Mead, in Mead and Wilson 1987: 13).

Data recently released by the British Department for Education and Employment (DEE) on the those entering New Deal schemes between July and September 1998 seem to bear out the claim that the training and educational elements of the program are of marginal importance in getting the jobless into work. The New Deal for unemployed people is not a cheap fix for joblessness. It costs in excess of £3000 (A$7,500) to get each person into a subsidised or unsubsidised job – even more in the case of single parents (see Field page 69 of this volume). Yet the core performance measures on which the government has chosen to judge the success of the scheme raise serious doubts about its success. Despite the British government's emphasis on vocational qualifications in the New Deal, its own statistics show that fewer than 5 per cent of those who complete the New Deal gain any recognised qualifications.

In fact, the major barriers the British government claims are responsible for joblessness – lack of work experience, skills and education – do not appear to be closely related to likelihood of finding work once on the New Deal program. The heart of the scheme is the 'options' stage, where participants must chose between a subsidised job, education or training, voluntary work, or work for the community's environment. The aim is to help the jobless gain skills and work experience. However, less than one in seven of those who entered this stage of the scheme managed to secure a job and leave the New Deal program. More effective has been the initial stage of the New Deal, known as the 'gateway', where advisers try to get participants into work as soon as possible. Advisers arrange job interviews on the participants' behalf and participants are taught basic work readiness skills, such as how to apply for a job. By the end of this stage, one-third of participants find work.

In belated recognition that lack of work motivation and lack of work readiness may be major causes of continued joblessness, the British government has recently announced

Table 4.1	Work commitment comparing working-class and underclass British males			
	Strongly agree or agree (%)	Uncertain (%)	Strongly disagree or disagree (%)	N
If I didn't like a job I'd pack it in even if there was no job to go to				
Semi/unskilled working-class	16	14	70	850
Underclass	39	21	41	264
p < .0001				
Having almost any job is better than being unemployed				
Semi/unskilled working-class	58	14	29	851
Underclass	47	9	44	262
p < .0001				
Once you've got a job it's important to hang on to it even if you don't really like it				
Semi/unskilled working-class	54	16	31	847
Underclass	47	14	40	263
p < .05				

Notes: Percentages may not sum to 100 due to rounding. All p. values refer to separate chi-square tests.
Source: Buckingham 2000.

plans to intensify the 'gateway' by including a two-week course that tries to make the unemployed more work-ready by teaching them how to talk to fellow employees, suggesting appropriate dress for work, and teaching them the importance of turning up to work on time.

Unfortunately, however, the problem of worklessness runs much deeper than just trying to get the unemployed into work. The DEE data show that of those on the New Deal who do find work, three-fifths return to unemployment within six months. One reason for these returns could be that those on temporary contracts fail to find further employment when their contracts terminate. An alternative explanation is that many lack long-term commitment to stay in paid work.

Many British sociologists are reluctant to accept the latter explanation. They believe that the chronically jobless are no different from employed members of the 'working class' as regards their commitment to work; they are simply the unfortunate members of the working class who have fallen into unemployment (Morris and Irwin 1992; Gallie 1994). Evidence from the National Child Development Study suggests they are wrong (Buckingham 1999; see also Saunders and Stone, chapter 6 of this volume, for Australian evidence on this issue). Table 4.1 shows that underclass males who have displayed a history of weak work attachment have a significantly lower commitment to work than men employed in semi- and unskilled manual occupations (that is, men who are unambiguously 'working class'). They are, on average, more willing to turn down jobs, or to leave jobs, which they consider unacceptable or not of the right quality. Instead of queuing up for any available work, as the British government assumes, there are significant numbers of chronically jobless males who remain quite choosy about the sort of work they will accept.

This evidence is supported by how they behave when in work. The longitudinal evidence indicates that chronically jobless men who find work frequently find it difficult to sustain employment. Although these men had been employed in as many jobs over the last ten years of the survey as other men, their job tenure was much shorter than the average. The longest job these men had been able to sustain since leaving school was, on average, less than three-fifths as long as the rest of the male cohort (64 months as compared with 118 months). Many of these jobs ended because of redundancy or the termination of a temporary contract, but many also ended through choice or dismissal. In fact since leaving school, chronically jobless men had been dismissed three times more often than other male cohort members.

Taken together, the evidence from the early performance of the British New Deal reform and from the British cohort study indicates that men who have a record of joblessness and welfare dependency appear to have some difficulty finding work and a lot of difficulty staying in work. It is not that lack of skills or education act as barriers excluding the chronically jobless from work, but that they lack the motivation and personal control to find work and then stay in work.

The Australian government appears to be ahead of the British government in recognising that low motivation is a genuine problem in getting the chronically jobless into work. The Working Nation scheme initiated by the Australian Labor

Government during the early 1990s, like the British New Deal reform, was premised on the need to help the jobless overcome barriers. However, just as with the New Deal, the results could best be described as mixed. Training and educating the unemployed did not open up a new vista of opportunities for employment as was hoped, for only 22 per cent of Job Compact participants were in unsubsidised employment three months after leaving their placements (Finn 1999: 61). Instead, the evidence suggested that a large amount of 'churning' was going on where the unemployed would go through the system only to find themselves back collecting benefits again at the end. Furthermore, many of the employers in the scheme who offered temporary job placements were negative about the work attitudes of the unemployed (DEET 1996: 91).

In response to this experience, the Coalition government's Work for the Dole reforms adopted a tougher set of policies that shifted the emphasis away from the need for help in overcoming barriers to the need for the unemployed to find work at the earliest opportunity. This reflects the idea behind policy reforms in the United States, that education and training is less important than getting the jobless to be motivated about finding work. Accordingly, spending on training programs has been reduced and obligations of job search have been increased.

Work of some kind is a condition of benefit payment, and for those who fail to meet this obligation, the penalties are much harder than in the British New Deal. Non-compliance with the various job search requirements can result in the non-payment of benefits for up to twenty-six weeks. And in order to check that the jobless are complying with their obligations to find work, case managers carefully scrutinise the job search diaries compiled by every client. Work for the Dole does not allow the jobless to free-ride by collecting benefits without also making strenuous efforts to find work. According to a recent OECD report on western welfare systems, the Australian Work for the Dole reform amounts to 'a "zero tolerance" approach to long-term unemployment' (OECD 1998: 81).

Welfare reform and lone parent welfare dependency

Just as the assumptions about the barriers stopping jobless males from working have proved suspect, so too have the assumptions that financial barriers stop lone parents from working. The British Labour Government set up the in-work benefit, WFTC, in order to overcome the financial disincentives of paid work by 'making work pay'. However, in the United States evidence on such in-work benefits casts doubt on their effectiveness. Ellwood and Summers (1986: 96) found take-up to be low because, 'welfare mothers do not seem to be very sensitive to work incentives'. Neither is there much evidence that lack of child care stops lone mothers from working. According to a study of 850 lone parents in Britain, 'child care was not the major barrier for the majority of lone parents' (Ford 1997: 63). Rather, as Hakim (1995) has argued, many women simply want to stay at home and bring up their children themselves. Moreover, if women do want to work, arranging child care seems to be much less of a barrier than commentators often suppose. For example, the country in Europe with the highest full-time rate of female employment – Portugal – is also the country with non-existent child care services (Hakim 1995: 438).

An evaluation of the New Deal pilot scheme funded by the Department of Social Security found that financial and child care barriers are of much less importance than self-imposed barriers. As Finch et al. (1999: 53) note: 'Many did not want to work "yet", deciding instead to focus on their role as a parent.' Contrary to New Labour's assumption that lone mothers are queuing up to work, the researchers found that as many as 78 per cent of them did not even take up the offer of an interview with a New Deal adviser.

Now that the New Deal has moved beyond the pilot stage the results look even less convincing. The figures for January 1999 show that since the program was set up, 163,383 letters had been sent to lone parents inviting them for an interview, but only 6,262 (3.8 per cent) had got jobs. Furthermore, one-fifth of lone parents who did get jobs left them after six months (*The Independent*, 14 March 1999).

In Britain, participation in the New Deal is voluntary for lone parents; they are simply sent a letter asking them to attend an initial interview with an adviser. Although the overall goal is to promote movement from Income Support to paid work, there is no compulsion placed on lone mothers to seek work or even take up suggestions regarding courses that could help improve skills or education. Indeed, it is only recently that the government has begun to oblige lone mothers to attend the initial interview.

In reality the New Deal for lone parents is a one-way deal: offers of help in training, education and job search are provided without any expectation on the part of lone parents that they participate. Reflecting this, the advice on the government's Web page to lone mothers states: 'It's entirely up to you to choose whether to join the New Deal (http://www. newdeal.gov.uk/english/engtxt.asp)'. A major reason for this arrangement is that the Labour government thinks lone parents should have a choice about whether they wish to work or not. British New Deal advisers simply 'provide a "tailored" package of help and advice on jobs, benefits, training and child care' (Finch et al. 1999: 13). This contrasts sharply with the situation in the United States where the TANF advisers' primary role is to get lone mothers into paid work and off benefits as soon as possible.

The British government's assumption that lone mothers are ready and willing to take work may partly reflect some early evidence that was positive about the rate at which lone parents exit from welfare. Brown (1990) argued that only 27 per cent of single mothers and 37 per cent of divorced mothers were on benefit for longer than five years. A major reason for these relatively short durations is that lone mothers tend to marry quickly. Using evidence from a study by Ermisch (1986), Brown claimed that the median duration of lone parenthood for never married women is just thirty-five months.

However, because the estimates of welfare durations were derived from the calculation of single spells of welfare claiming, they heavily underestimated the true degree of welfare dependency amongst lone parents (because lone parents frequently have more than one spell on benefit).

When all spells of welfare claiming are added together, American evidence shows that over 80 per of lone mothers who claimed the old pre-Clinton reform benefit (AFDC), spent more than five years collecting it.

Similarly, my analysis using the British National Child Development Study shows that at age thirty-three, a quarter of lone parents had spent over half of their economically active careers jobless and collecting benefit. For these women marriage had not offered a swift escape route from benefit dependency because marriage did not come quickly. In fact, of those who did marry after the birth of the child, it took an average of ten years to find a husband.

This evidence highlights just how ingrained welfare dependency is for some lone parents, suggesting the existence in Britain of an underclass of women who spend very long periods of their lives collecting benefits. Given this, it comes as little surprise that the British government's policy of opening up employment choices and opportunities through the New Deal has been met with such apathy by lone parents. It seems that when given the choice many would rather do what they know best and stay at home with their child, than seek paid work.

American experience suggests that what works is an approach which directs and compels lone parents to work, and does not allow long-term dependency. The recent American welfare reforms, which have withdrawn the right to infinite welfare, have effectively undermined the long-term economic viability of lone parenthood. This is not something which New Labour in Britain is willing to countenance. Although its stated aim is to 'rebuild the welfare state around work' (DSS 1998: 23), the Blair government is unwilling to enforce work obligations and place limits on welfare claiming because it does not want to be seen to be attacking lone parents.

New Labour is therefore caught in a dilemma. It wants to reduce joblessness and dependency, but it is not prepared to withdraw support for a form of family life that for most people inevitably leads to joblessness and dependency. Because lone-parent families are rarely economically viable, the only remaining way to get lone mothers back to work is by subsidising them when in employment. This has in turn entailed the replacement of one in-work benefit – Family Credit – with a far more costly one – Working Families Tax Credit. But there is serious concern that these sorts of in work benefits do not pull people out of welfare dependence because claimants become stuck in low paid work attached to the financial support of the in-work benefit (Marsh 1997: 126). Put another way, the price of getting lone parents back into work is continued benefit dependency.

Conclusion

Australia, Britain and the United States have all now established 'active' welfare policies, but they work in different ways, reflecting differing assumptions about why the jobless are not in work.

There is a degree of convergence between these governments over youth joblessness, with a growing recognition that some of the major obstacles to finding work are self-imposed. However, neither the Australian nor the British governments are likely to follow the American policy of offering no welfare to young unemployed people, even though both governments are increasing the obligations attached to benefit receipt.

The Australian experience of the Working Nation reforms indicated that poor motivation was at least as important as lack of skills or education in explaining continued joblessness among young people. Work for the Dole tries to deal with this by placing much more emphasis on the participants' obligations to seek work. In Britain, the mixed success of the New Deal is also leading the government towards greater emphasis on obligations and sanctions, although it is still some way behind the Australian Coalition's reforms. Estimates indicate that in the first year of the New Deal, fewer than one in four hundred participants had been subjected to benefit sanctions for non-compliance (*The Independent*, 28 May 1998), but under proposals announced in 2000, penalties for non-compliance will be tougher and more frequently invoked. As the Chancellor explained: 'We have kept our side of the bargain by providing the opportunities. It is now for young people to look at the one million vacancies and the opportunities that exist and show they have a responsibility to take them up.' (*The Times*, 17 September 1999).

In respect of lone parents the picture is rather different, with no clear consensus between governments. Clearly, governments cannot have it all ways. Either governments must adopt the American approach, which enforces work obligations and places limits on welfare entitlements at the cost of making lone parenthood a non-viable lifestyle choice, or they will have to support free choice in family arrangements at the cost of long-term dependency among those who choose lone parenthood.

In Australia, the Reference Group on Welfare Reform (2000) has explicitly addressed the issue of extending the 'mutual obligation' principle to include some lone parents, and a pilot Parenting Payment Intervention scheme has obliged lone parents who have been collecting welfare for more than five years, together with those who have recently left work to go on benefit, to attend an interview to discuss ways of getting back into work. It also seems likely that eligibility for Parenting Payment will at some point be changed to exclude parents of older children.

None of this is anywhere near as demanding as the mutual obligation conditions now being required of those who register as unemployed, but the same philosophy of getting people off welfare and into self sufficiency is apparent, and there is a clear commitment to promoting a culture of self-reliance and personal responsibility among lone parents as well as other groups of claimants. The Australian government now explicitly recognises the link between welfare, independence and the family, for as Prime Minister John Howard has suggested (Bagnall 1999: 47): 'The stable functioning family still represents the best social welfare system that any community has devised and certainly the least expensive.'

Notes

1. The cohort consists of men and women born in one week in 1958. There have been five waves, the last in 1991 when there were 11,407 respondents. The chronically jobless and welfare dependent amounted

to 5 per cent of the cohort. Buckingham (1999) explains how this group is defined.

2. The increase in joblessness among young men cannot be accounted for by the rise in the proportion of men aged 18–24 in full-time education. In fact, the proportion of men in this age group participating in full-time education increased by just 3 per cent between 1989 and 1999 (GSS 1989; DEE 1999). In so far as more people are attending full-time education, it is the growing participation rate of young women and mature people of both sexes that accounts for the bulk of the increase.

Chapter 5

Trans-generational income support dependence in Australia: early evidence

Frances McCoull and Jocelyn Pech

The term 'trans-generational welfare dependence' refers to a cycle of sustained income support dependence across two or more generations within families. Until recently very little has been known about the extent of this phenomenon. Interest in the topic has commonly been generated by the occasional media story which 'confirms' the existence of a problem by identifying one or two families with multiple family members across generations receiving income support. Anecdotal evidence and conjecture have therefore typically defined the parameters of debate.

Views on the issue are divergent. Some people argue that such cases are the exception rather than the rule and consider it unfair to blame the victims of poor labour markets, economic restructuring or family breakdown for their circumstances. Others believe firmly in a culture of welfare dependence, arguing that parents either transmit undesirable attitudes about education, employment and income support to their children, or at least fail to transmit positive attitudes. Peter Travers (1998: 117) summarised this view of welfare dependence as incorporating 'the notion of a cycle whereby dependence, poverty, and generally feckless behaviour are perpetuated from one generation to the next'.

Wherever the truth lies, there are important issues for policy makers and governments to address. We know that some families in Australia appear particularly prone to joblessness and consequently tend to rely heavily on income support. But we do not know how many of these families there are, whether the problem is increasing, or what differentiates families who are long-term poor and income support dependent from those who are not, including families with low incomes from work. And if we can establish that the children of income support recipients are more likely to experience unemployment, lone parenthood or other difficulties as adults, we still do not know what factors might reduce or (inadvertently) increase these risks.

In the Department of Family and Community Services we have started a long-term research project to attempt to answer some of these questions. Our intention is simple – to help inform, design and deliver policies and programs which improve the life chances of children from disadvantaged families.

In this chapter we provide an overview of some of the existing literature on this issue and outline early findings from our research. At this stage we have limited our focus to the financial (rather than psychological) aspects of dependence; that is, the extent of reliance on the income support system for individual or family income.

Trends in the labour market and poverty

Australia has traditionally been considered an egalitarian society. We pride ourselves on our capacity to provide relatively equal opportunities for all citizens and would like to believe that the life chances of children are not affected unduly by the education, employment and income support experiences of their parents.

Only a quarter of a century ago (1973–74) Australia was a world leader in social mobility (Erikson and Goldthorpe 1992, cited in Travers and Richardson 1993). However, subsequent economic and social developments have threatened our sense of egalitarianism and may have eroded the extent of social mobility in this country.

Since the mid-1970s the labour market has been characterised by persistently high rates of unemployment, especially long-term unemployment. An increasing number of jobs have become part-time and/or casual, and market incomes have become more unequal. Rates of lone parenthood have risen dramatically over this period and there has been an increasing polarisation among two-parent families between those with two incomes and those with none.

Partly as a consequence of these trends, there has been a large increase over the past two decades in the numbers and proportions of Australian children living in low income families that are without paid work and/or reliant upon income support.

First, the number and proportion of Australian families with children under the age of fifteen who had no parent in paid work increased from about 180,000 (14.5 per cent) in 1986 to around 390,000 (17 per cent) in 1999 (ABS 1997a). Just under three-quarters of the parents in these families were not in the labour force. Among the quarter who were unemployed, perhaps 40 per cent had been unemployed for more than one year.

Second, the proportion of Australian children living in families receiving income support (those in which at least one parent received a social security pension, benefit or allowance) doubled across the twenty-year period between 1978 and 1997, from 11.5 per cent to 23 per cent. In 1998 almost 1.2 million children lived in such families, about 60 per cent of them with only one parent.

Even so, we know little about how many children experience long periods of poverty or how their life chances are affected by that poverty. As Esping-Andersen said at an OECD conference in November 1996: 'It is undeniable that bad jobs, low pay, unemployment, and poverty afflict more and more people. Yet if people's experience of marginality and want is only temporary, life chances will not be seriously impaired . . . We face a crisis of polarisation only if the losers of today are losers for life, and if they pass their underprivilege on to the next generation.'

Review of the literature

What existing information sheds light on these issues? Australian evidence is still limited because we have very little in the way of longitudinal data. For this reason the following literature review draws heavily on overseas evidence, in particular from the United States. In that country two major longitudinal surveys – the Panel Study of Income Dynamics, begun in 1968, and the National Longitudinal Survey of Youth, begun in 1979, have spawned a large research literature. While we do not suggest these findings can simply be generalised to the Australian situation, they and findings from British research based on the National Child Development Study may be indicative.

American research

In a recent survey of the United States literature, Corcoran and Chaudry (1997) reported that while many persistently poor children (about half of African-Americans and three-quarters of whites) do not experience poverty in early adult life, growing up poor did increase the probability of long-term poverty in adulthood by three times (from 8 to 26 per cent) for poor blacks and eight times (from one to 10 per cent) for poor whites.

Looking at data from four longitudinal surveys on the longer-term effects on children of growing up in a non-intact family, Gottschalk et al. (1994: 102-106) found that young people from non-intact families were significantly more likely than young people from intact families to experience a number of adverse life events. They were more than twice as likely to drop out of high school early, two to four times as likely to have a child outside marriage before the age of twenty (girls), and one and a half times as likely to be workless in early adulthood (boys). Despite this, only a minority of children from both intact and non-intact families experienced such high risk life events. These effects were consistent across racial groups and socio-economic classes.

Corcoran and Chaudry also found that about half of the difference between the groups was attributable to differences in family income and the remainder to other factors, such as parental behaviours and residential mobility.

Studies of welfare receipt across generations have also found some evidence of a transmission. However, most research is restricted to analysis of mother and daughter receipt, because the bulk of welfare in the United States has generally been directed to this area.

A number of researchers (for example, Rainwater 1987; McLanahan 1988) have found that daughters of welfare recipients were more than twice as likely as the daughters of non-recipients to receive welfare themselves. These studies have attracted some criticism for failing to control adequately for the correlation between welfare receipt and low income. Nevertheless, they find support in research by Gottschalk (1992: 268) which concluded that the 'mother's participation is significantly correlated with both early births and daughter's participation in AFDC [Aid to Dependent Families with Children], even after controlling for family background and income, as well as a host of other observed characteristics'.

Even so, most daughters of welfare recipients do not go on to become welfare recipients themselves. Duncan (1984: 91) found that 'most adult children from welfare families were not receiving welfare income themselves, and most of the adults who were receiving welfare income did not come from welfare households'.

United Kingdom research

British research tends to provide support for many of these findings. Johnson and Reed (1996) found that young men, who at the age of sixteen had unemployed fathers, were twice as likely as the average to have experienced significant unemployment by the age of thirty-three. These researchers found no evidence that women whose parents were unpartnered, unemployed or low income were more likely to be lone parents at age thirty-three, although they did not discount the possibility that this may have been the case at younger ages.

John Hobcraft (1998: 86) found 'general evidence of the transmission of social exclusion and disadvantage across the generations and the life course', although he was cautious about drawing inferences about causality. He examined the relationships between three important variables – childhood poverty, contact with police by age sixteen, and family disruption (defined as having been born out of wedlock or the parents' relationship having ended) and eleven indicators of social exclusion. The latter included demographic, psychological, educational, economic and social welfare outcomes.

Hobcraft found strong associations between his three variables and one control variable (childhood scores on educational tests) and most of the indicators of social exclusion. Childhood poverty and contact with police were most strongly associated with lack of qualifications in adulthood. Family disruption, on the other hand, was most strongly associated for women with a range of demographic outcomes (including early parenthood and extra-marital births) and, for men, with homelessness. While adult receipt of income support was significantly associated with a wide variety of childhood disadvantages, the relationship was generally not as strong as for other outcomes (Hobcraft 1998).

According to Kathleen Kiernan (1997), people whose parents divorced during their childhood had lower educational attainment and higher rates of unemployment by age thirty-three. They were also more likely to have partnered early, cohabited rather than marrying, become parents at a young age, and had higher rates of partnership dissolution. Controlling for a number of background factors that pre-dated the divorce, such as financial hardship, school achievement and behavioural problems, explained much of the difference in economic outcomes but somewhat less of the difference in family formation behaviour.

Australian research

While Australian evidence on these issues is sketchy and incomplete, it tends to suggest similar patterns of trans-generational correlation. For example, young people from low socio-economic backgrounds are significantly less likely than other young people both to finish secondary school and to take up post-secondary education (Chapman 1992; RHEFP 1998). However, this disadvantage does not appear to extend to rates of completion of post-secondary qualifications. Among those who proceed to further education, students from low socio-economic backgrounds have similar success and retention rates to other students (RHEFP 1998: 92).

Australian Bureau of Statistics data show that young people whose parents are not in work have lower labour force participation rates and higher unemployment rates than young people with at least one parent in work. The 1992 Survey of Families (ABS 1994) found that young people without a parent in paid work were one and a half to two times more likely to be unemployed than young people with at least one parent in work.

More recently, the Australian Bureau of Statistics Survey of Employment and Unemployment Patterns found that young people with one or both parents in work were significantly more likely to have found stable employment over a one-year period than young people whose parents were not in work. In these data, father's employment appears to be have been more influential on young people's employment outcomes than mother's (ABS 1998a: 106).

Summary

Overall, evidence from overseas, and to a lesser extent Australia, suggests that family poverty, lone parenthood, parental unemployment and welfare receipt are associated to a greater or lesser extent with less favourable outcomes for some children.

Research design

In order to understand the Australian situation better we have started building a longitudinal data set which provides a composite picture of family receipt of income support. In the following sections we outline early findings from this research. We report on the characteristics of parents from different family income types, the number of young people who enter the income support system in their own right at an early age, and the extent to which the receipt of income support by young people is associated with their parents' receipt of income support.

On the basis of our literature review we have formulated two early hypotheses to guide our research. The first hypothesis is that young people whose parents receive income support will be more likely to experience during their teenage years a number of life events that lead to them also receiving income support. These include leaving school early, becoming unemployed, becoming homeless and/or having children before the age of twenty-one. The second hypothesis is that the probability of these outcomes will increase as the degree of parental disadvantage and income support dependence increases.

The research data set contains selected information from family payment and income support records of just under 53,000 young people and their 92,000 parents. It comprises all young people who were recorded on the Department of Family and Community Services family allowance database in December 1995 and who turned sixteen between January and March 1996. It captures slightly more than four-fifths of all young people in Australia who turned sixteen during that time, excluding only young people from the most well-off families.[1]

A complex data-matching process was used to assemble thirteen data 'snapshots', taken at quarterly intervals from January 1996 until January 1999. These snapshots provide a comprehensive social security history of both the young people and their parents over the three-year period.

For this analysis, we categorised the families in the data set into three family types, depending on their social security status at 1 January 1996. In doing so, we were using social security status as a proxy for degree of disadvantage, rather than as a variable in its own right. Because of the highly targeted nature of the Australian social security system there is a high correlation between many indicators of disadvantage and income support receipt. Each family type contains both one and two-parent families.

Middle-high income families were either non-recipient families (who had previously received family allowance for the young person but were no longer doing so) or families whose only current social security entitlement was family allowance at the minimum rate.[2] Most families who were not currently in receipt of family payment would have lost family allowance entitlement because their income or assets increased beyond the upper limits for that payment.

Low income working families either received family allowance at more than the minimum rate[3] (but no adult pension or benefit) or, in the case of some two-parent families, one adult received a social security pension or benefit (most commonly Parenting Allowance) while the other was in low-paid work. *Income support recipient families* were the lowest income families in the data set. In these families, both parents, or the lone parent, received a social security pension or benefit.

Table 5.1 summarises the numbers of families and the likely range of taxable income for families of each family type, based on a one-child family. These income figures should be regarded as indicative only, as there are a number of reasons why a particular family may have had a higher or lower income at that point in time.[4]

This categorisation represents a hierarchy of disadvantage and income support dependence, from the not disadvantaged and not dependent (middle–high income families) to the most disadvantaged and most dependent (income support recipient families). Middle–high income families are classified as not dependent since even in the case of those who received some family allowance, this was primarily for horizontal, not vertical, equity reasons and this support formed a low proportion of the family's income. They account for almost 60 per cent of the families in the data set.

Low income working families had a degree of income support dependence which ranged from low to moderate. They

Table 5.1	Numbers of families in data set and approximate ranges of taxable income for a one-child family, by family type			
Family type	Families		Taxable income* range ($pa)		Income support dependence (rating)
	No	%	From	To	
Middle-high income	31528	59.8	27768	na	Not dependent
Low income working	9227	17.5	19847	27767	Low to moderate
Income support recipient	11987	22.7	8734 (s) 14674 (c)	20816 (s) 25124 (c)	Moderate to total
Total	**52742**	**100.0**			

Note: * Income excluding family payments and any other non-taxable entitlements (for example, guardian allowance or rent assistance). For income support recipient families, figures marked (s) are for lone-parent families and those marked (c) are for couple families.
Source: Longitudinal data set, Department of Family and Community Services, 2000.

were considered to have insufficient personal income to meet all the needs of their children. The level of income supplementation from income support varied considerably in this group, generally depending on the level of earnings of the working member. Almost three-quarters of these families received no income tested support for the parent(s).

A little less than a quarter (23 per cent) of families were defined as income support recipient families. While these families had varying degrees of dependence in terms of the proportion of family income supplied by social security

Table 5.2	Characteristics of primary parent by family type, January 1996			
Characteristic	Family Income			
	Middle-high	Low	Income support	Total
Male (%)	2.6	3.7	6.3	3.6
Lone parent (%)	14.1	20.0	59.2	25.4
Australian-born (%)	88.7	77.8	69.9	82.5
Overseas born: English-speaking (%)*	3.8	6.2	7.8	5.1
Overseas born: non-English-speaking (%)	7.5	16.0	22.3	12.4
Indigenous Australian+ (%)	0.5	2.4	3.7	1.5
Mean age (yrs)	42.5	41.2	42.1	42.2
Aged under 40 (%)	26.6	41.0	38.5	31.8
Aged 50 and over (%)	7.0	6.6	12.1	8.1
Mean no of children#	2.7	3.3	3.2	2.9
More than 4 children (%)	5.1	16.6	15.8	9.5
Mean age of youngest child (yrs)	12.4	10.5	11.1	11.8
Youngest child under 6 (%)	5.7	16.3	15.1	9.7
Mean age at first birth: mothers only (yrs)	24.2	23.3	23.9	24.0
First birth before age 21 (%)	19.8	30.5	33.7	24.8
Ever received income support (parent or partner) (%)	6.6	38.9	100.0	33.5
Public housing tenant (%)	1.2	7.4	20.2	6.6
N families	31528	9227	11987	52742

Notes: * Canada, Ireland, New Zealand, United Kingdom, United States. + Individuals whose social security records contain an indigenous identifier. Not all indigenous Australians receiving social security payments identify as indigenous. # Number of children listed on family allowance record.
Source: Longitudinal data set, Department of Family and Community Services, 2000.

transfers, the majority of families in this group were almost wholly dependent on income support. A minority of families in this group would have been less dependent overall than some of the low income working families in the second group.

Three income groups compared

First, we look at families of origin. Table 5.2 summarises the incidence of various family and parental characteristics within each family type. A consistent finding is the relatively clear divide between middle to high income families and the other two family types on many of these indicators. On most characteristics low income working families far more closely resemble income support recipient families than middle–high income families.

The incidence of many characteristics was considerably higher in low income working families and income support recipient families than in middle–high income families. Comparing parents from the highest and lowest family income types, the latter were: more than twice as likely to have been born overseas; four times as likely to be lone parents; seven times as likely to identify as indigenous; and sixteen times as likely to live in public housing.

Low income working and income support recipient families were considerably more likely than middle–high income families to be larger and/or younger. They were about three times as likely both to have five or more children and to have a youngest child under the age of six. Mothers in these families were more than one and a half times as likely to have had a child before the age of twenty-one.

Table 5.3, which shows the distribution of some of these characteristics across the three family types, reveals a consistent finding. Each characteristic was considerably over-represented in income support recipient families and under-represented in middle–high income families, relative to the proportion of families in each category. This was particularly the case for public housing tenants and those who had ever received income support (where over two-thirds were in income support recipient families), and for parents who identified as indigenous and those who were classified as single parents (where over half were in income support recipient families). In the case of public housing tenants, this reflects the increased targeting of public housing to those receiving income support.

Next we examine the situations of the young people in our research cohort. The framework again includes the family type variable as above, but as a family background variable that reflects their parents' family type at January 1996.

Table 5.4 summarises the characteristics of the young people as at January 1996. It shows that young people born overseas were under-represented in middle–high income families and over-represented in the other two family types. The proportion identifying as indigenous increased with the degree of parental disadvantage, from 0.5 per cent of middle–high income families to 4 per cent of income support

Table 5.3	Distribution of certain family characteristics by family type, January 1996				
Characteristic	Group				
	Middle-high income %	Low income working %	Income support recipient %	Total %	Total N
All families	59.8	17.5	22.7	100.0	52742
Indigenous Australian	17.5	27.5	54.9	100.0	810
Lone parent	33.2	13.8	53.0	100.0	13383
Overseas born: non-English-speaking	36.2	22.7	41.1	100.0	6511
Overseas born: English-speaking	44.3	21.0	34.7	100.0	2703
Male primary parent	42.8	17.8	39.4	100.0	1922
More than 4 children	31.8	30.6	37.7	100.0	5015
Youngest child under 6	35.1	29.4	35.5	100.0	5094
First birth before age 21	47.9	21.4	30.7	100.0	13037
Ever received income support	11.7	20.3	67.9	100.0	17648
Public housing tenant	10.9	19.5	69.6	100.0	3485

Source: Longitudinal data set, Department of Family and Community Services, 2000.

recipient families. Low income working families contained the highest proportion of first-born children (including only children) and the lowest proportion of last-born children, while the reverse was the case for middle–high income families. Consistent with their larger average family size, the two lower income family types contained higher than average proportions of middle-born children.

Table 5.4	Demographic and other characteristics of young people by family origin type, January 1996			
Characteristic	Incidence within family origin type			
	Middle-high income %	Low income working %	Income support recipient %	Total %
Gender				
Male	51.8	52.2	51.4	51.8
Female	48.2	47.8	48.6	48.2
Country of birth				
Australia	95.9	90.2	89.7	93.5
Australia: Indigenous	0.5	2.5	4.0	1.6
Overseas: English-speaking	1.7	2.8	2.1	2.0
Overseas: Non-English-speaking	2.4	7.1	8.2	4.5
Birth order				
Oldest or only	42.3	48.1	45.2	44.0
Middle	22.3	33.3	30.5	26.1
Youngest	35.3	18.6	24.3	29.9
Had responsibility for child(ren) *	0.01	0.03	0.11	0.04
Income support receipt				
None	99.80	99.75	99.29	99.68
Unemployment	0.13	0.13	0.40	0.18
Other+	0.08	0.12	0.31	0.14
Homeless#	0.05	0.05	0.14	0.07
Total — Per cent	59.7	17.6	22.7	00.0
Number	31798	9345	12098	153241

Notes: * Young people who were receiving family payment in respect of one or more children, who may or may not have been their own. + Includes parenting payment, sickness allowance, special benefit and carer payment. # Young people receiving the 'homeless' rate of income support because of no parental home, physical, sexual or psychological abuse or severe family breakdown.
Source: Longitudinal data set, Department of Family and Community Services, 2000.

Only tiny minorities of young people had responsibility for children or had been assessed as homeless just before their sixteenth birthdays. Fewer than half a per cent received income support in their own right, and just over half of these did so because of unemployment.

Life trajectories of the young people 1996–99

The number of young people who were recorded as receiving family allowance for dependent children rose from less than half a per cent in January 1996 to 2 per cent (or just over 4 per cent of all young women) in January 1999. The majority of these women had care of only one child, although one in eight had care of two or more children. Throughout the period, young people from income support recipient families were between three and four times as likely as those from middle-high income families to have responsibility for children.

A proportion of young people receiving family allowance would not have been caring for their own children. To analyse fertility among the young women, we have assumed that any

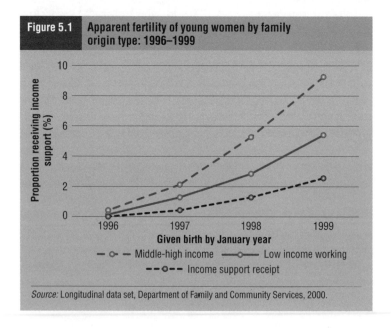

Figure 5.1 Apparent fertility of young women by family origin type: 1996–1999

Proportion receiving income support (%)

Given birth by January year

— ○ — Middle-high income   —○— Low income working
– – ○ – – Income support receipt

Source: Longitudinal data set, Department of Family and Community Services, 2000.

child listed on a young woman's family allowance record who was born when she was at least thirteen is her biological child. On this assumption, as Figure 5.1 shows, about 4.5 per cent of the young women in the birth cohort had become mothers by January 1999.

Young women from income support recipient families were about four times as likely as young women from middle–high income families to have had a child. The median age at first birth for all groups was around eighteen. Just under two-thirds of mothers were single, with mothers from middle–high income families slightly more likely to be partnered than mothers from the other two groups.

Table 5.5 summarises the young people's experience of the income support system from 1996 to 1998. Young people receiving student allowances are included in the 'no income

Table 5.5	Income support history of young people by family origin group, 1996–1998			
Characteristic	Receipt within each family origin group			
	Middle-high income %	Low income working %	Income support recipient %	Total %
1996				
None	94.5	88.3	76.8	89.4
Unemployment	4.6	10.1	20.9	9.2
Parenting	0.2	0.4	0.7	0.3
Disability/sickness	0.9	1.2	2.0	1.2
1997				
None	93.0	81.6	67.3	85.2
Unemployment	5.6	15.9	28.7	12.7
Parenting	0.5	1.1	2.1	1.0
Disability/sickness	1.1	1.8	2.8	1.5
1998				
None	84.6	71.5	57.4	76.1
Unemployment	13.6	25.4	37.5	21.1
Parenting	0.9	2.1	3.7	1.8
Disability/sickness	1.2	1.8	2.8	1.7

Source: Longitudinal data set, Department of Family and Community Services, 2000.

support' category largely because while student payments provide income support, receipt of these payments is unlikely to result in long-term income support dependence and associated labour market disadvantage. Indeed, receipt of student payments by young people from low income groups can be regarded as a positive outcome, since it indicates continued participation in education or training.

A small number of young people were receiving income support before their sixteenth birthday (1996). Around one in ten of the young people received income support at some time during the calendar year in which they turned sixteen and this had increased to one in four by the end of the year in which they turned eighteen. Unemployment payments were the most common, accounting for over three-quarters of income support receipt.

Figure 5.2 shows, for each family type, the growth in numbers receiving income support in each quarter. The Figure shows clear divisions between the three family types. Young people from income support recipient families were generally

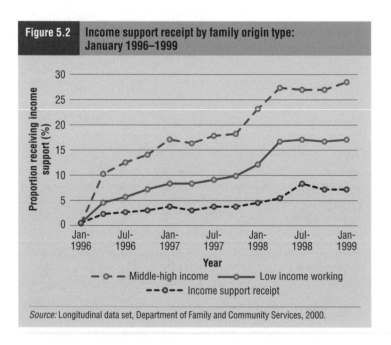

Figure 5.2 Income support receipt by family origin type: January 1996–1999

Source: Longitudinal data set, Department of Family and Community Services, 2000.

four to five times as likely as young people from middle–high income families to be receiving income support.

Each category of income support payments shows a similar pattern. If we take unemployment payments, for example, more than 20 per cent of young people from income support recipient families received an unemployment payment during 1996, compared with less than 5 per cent of young people from middle–high income families. Young people from low income working families were more than twice as likely to have received an unemployment payment as those from middle income families, but only about half as likely as young people from income support recipient families to have done so.

Over time the gaps between groups widened. During their eighteenth year (1998), almost 38 per cent of young people from income support recipient families received unemployment payments at some time, compared with fewer than 14 per cent from middle–high income families. Between 1996 and 1998, the gap between these two groups had increased by 50 per cent, from 16 percentage points to 24 percentage points.

Much the same pattern is repeated in respect of Parenting Payment. While receipt of parenting payment is relatively uncommon among parents in the general population, around 84 per cent of the young people who were responsible for dependent children in January 1999 received parenting payment. Young people from income support recipient families were three to four times as likely as those from middle–high income families to receive parenting payment. The annual rate of increase in the proportion receiving parenting payments was similar for young people from all family types, with numbers increasing by two to three times between 1996 and 1997, and doubling in the year after that. Nevertheless, parenting responsibilities accounted for relatively little income support receipt among young people aged sixteen to eighteen years. For all three groups, more than ten times as many received unemployment payments at some time during the period.

Relatively few young people received payments associated with disability or sickness. Most who did were receiving the disability support pension and the year-to-year variations suggest that about three-quarters of these accessed the

| Table 5.6 | Degree of cumulative income support dependence among young people by various personal and family background characteristics, January 1996–1999 |

Family origin type	Cumulative income support dependence					Total	
	Nil	Low	Mod	High	Max	%	N
Gender							
Male	71.1	16.4	6.1	5.1	1.3	100.0	27550
Female	71.5	15.1	6.4	5.5	1.5	100.0	25663
Dependent children (Jan 1999)							
None	72.9	15.8	5.8	4.4	1.2	100.0	52054
One	3.7	16.3	27.8	42.9	9.3	100.0	1031
Two or more	1.3	6.4	12.8	57.1	22.4	100.0	156
Country of birth/ethnicity							
Overseas: non-English-speaking	74.2	16.5	5.4	3.4	0.5	100.0	2412
Overseas: English-speaking	56.0	25.5	10.7	6.8	1.9	100.0	1058
Indigenous Australian	21.3	27.5	20.8	25.7	4.7	100.0	869
Other Australian	72.4	15.7	5.9	5.0	1.4	100.0	48902
Last pension/benefit received							
Unemployment	0.0	61.2	22.2	14.9	1.7	100.0	13323
Parenting	0.0	13.2	26.5	48.1	12.1	100.0	991
Disability support	0.0	5.0	10.8	38.9	45.3	100.0	855
Other	0.0	74.8	15.5	9.7	0.0	100.0	103
Family origin group							
Middle-high income	81.6	12.1	3.6	2.2	0.7	100.0	31798
Low income working	65.6	19.2	7.5	6.4	1.3	100.0	9345
Income support recipient	48.6	22.8	12.9	12.5	3.2	100.0	12098
Family origin group							
Lone parent	56.6	20.2	10.5	10.2	2.6	100.0	13520
Couple	76.3	14.3	4.8	3.6	1.0	100.0	39721
Country of birth (primary parent)							
Overseas: non-English-speaking	76.4	15.0	4.9	3.0	1.7	100.0	6567
Overseas: English-speaking	59.9	20.3	9.9	8.1	1.8	100.0	2739
Indigenous Australian	40.2	19.9	17.0	19.5	3.4	100.0	816
Other Australian	71.9	15.5	6.0	5.2	1.4	100.0	43119
Public housing tenant							
Yes	39.6	24.1	15.9	15.8	4.6	100.0	3523
No	73.6	15.2	5.6	4.5	1.2	100.0	49718
Total Per cent	71.3	15.8	6.2	5.3	1.4	100.0	
Number	37969	8404	3323	2810	735		53241

Source: Longitudinal data set, Department of Family and Community Services, 2000.

payment as they turned sixteen, probably as a result of congenital or otherwise long-standing disabilities.

Cumulative income support dependence

To examine the degree of cumulative income support dependence over the three-year period 1996 to 1999, we constructed five categories of dependence, derived from the number of quarterly snapshots in which a young person was recorded as receiving income support. Table 5.6 presents a summary of the relationships between these and various characteristics of the young people and their family income type.

The five categories are: nil – no receipt of income support over the three-year period; low – received income support in one to three-quarters; moderate – received income support in four to six quarters; high – received income support in seven to eleven quarters; and maximum – received income support in either twelve or thirteen quarters, and therefore likely to have received payment since before, on or shortly after, their sixteenth birthday.

Around seven out of ten of the young people in our data set did not receive income support between their sixteenth and nineteenth birthdays, and about one in fifteen experienced a high degree of income support dependence during that time.

Having the care of a child was highly correlated with receipt of income support. The higher levels of cumulative dependence experienced by young people with more than one child is probably simply a function of when they first had a child to care for.

Despite the fact that parents from non-English-speaking countries were significantly over-represented in the income support recipient group, young people from these families were the least likely to have been highly dependent on income support by the age of nineteen. Non-indigenous Australian-born young people came next, followed by young people from overseas English-speaking countries and indigenous Australians.

Information on the last payment received confirms that most youth unemployment is short term. More than 60 per cent of young people who last received unemployment payment had been receiving income support at three or fewer data collection points, while only around one in six had experienced high income support dependence. By contrast, 84 per cent of young people whose last payment was Disability Support Pension and 60 per cent whose last payment was Parenting Payment had received income support in more than half the quarters surveyed.

Compared with the average probability of about one in fifteen (6.7 per cent), the following four family background factors substantially increased the likelihood of a young person experiencing high levels of income support dependence between the ages of sixteen and eighteen: (1) coming from an income support recipient family (more than twice as likely); (2) living with only one parent at age fifteen (almost twice as likely); (3) having a primary parent who was identified as indigenous (three and a half times as likely); and (4) living in public housing at age fifteen (three times as likely).

Because there is a high degree of inter-correlation between these factors it is not possible at this stage to know which may be dominant or, indeed, whether other factors not captured in these data may have greater explanatory power.

There were only a few small subgroups of young people who were more likely than not to have experienced high levels of income support dependence by their nineteenth birthday. These included young people on disability support pension or parenting payment, and young people with the care of dependent children. Among young people identified as indigenous, almost half experienced no or low levels of income support dependence and for all other at risk groups there was a clear majority in the two lowest dependence categories.

Conclusion

It would be fair to say that early evidence is mixed. The findings provide some support for the hypotheses outlined earlier. Young people from income support recipient families were more likely than the average to leave school early, to experience unemployment, to have children before the age of nineteen, and/or to receive income support themselves. And again, the probabilities of these outcomes appear to increase with the degree of parental disadvantage and income support dependence.

Nevertheless, most young people from income support recipient families did not spend long periods on income support themselves during their late teens. But while only a small minority could be categorised as having been highly dependent on income support themselves, they were considerably more likely to have been so than other young people.

We have not yet addressed the issue of what causes some young people to enter the income support system at a relatively early age. We need to undertake considerable further analysis to draw any inferences about causal relationships.

We also need to develop a more sophisticated definition of income support dependence. In addition, we intend to survey a sample of the young people from our original cohort to collect information on variables that overseas research suggests might be important in identifying causative factors – for example, parents' educational attainment and employment histories, and the early school experiences of the young people themselves. We hope that with these improvements, our data set will yield more robust findings on the dimensions of trans-generational income support dependence in this country.

Notes

1. Families who were not eligible in 1996 for the minimum rate of family allowance had 1994-95 taxable incomes of over $61,000 and/or assets, excluding the family home, that were worth $559,250 or more.

2. At that time, minimum rate family allowance was $22.70 a fortnight ($590.20 a year) per child for the first three children in a family, with the rate rising to $28.90 a fortnight ($751.40 a year) for the fourth and subsequent children.

3. Maximum family allowance rates were $93.10 a fortnight ($2420.60 a year) for each child aged 0-12 and $121.10 a fortnight ($3148.60 a year) for each child aged thirteen to fifteen.

4. Calendar year entitlement to family payment is usually based on family taxable income for the previous financial year, unless it has varied by more than 10 per cent. In most cases, therefore, the family's recorded taxable income was for 1994-95. Income limits may have been higher where there were two or more children.

Chapter 6

Australian youth and the dependency culture[1]

Peter Saunders and Wendy Stone

Reliance on income support tends to run in families. As McCoull and Pech demonstrate in chapter 5 in this volume, Australian children who grow up in households where adults have long spells out of work and drawing on welfare payments are themselves much more likely to end up claiming income support when they reach adulthood. The question is why?

A cultural transmission of dependency?

One argument which has commonly been advanced is that welfare dependency is associated with a particular set of values, norms and beliefs – a distinctive culture – which is passed from generation to generation. Children tend to repeat the pattern of their parents because this culture of dependency is passed on to them through the process of childhood socialisation, and it then influences their own behaviour, just as it did that of their parents.

The modern origin of this kind of explanation lies in Oscar Lewis's work among the urban poor in Latin America in the 1950s. Lewis (1961) suggested that there was a distinctive 'culture of poverty' which arose as a way of coping with deprivation but which unintentionally helped to perpetuate it. He found that each generation of 'slum children' learns a set of beliefs and practices which helps them survive in the ghetto but which also makes it very difficult for them to escape it. Lewis believed that such a culture was largely confined to the Third World, but during the 1960s and 1970s some research in the United States suggested that it might exist there too (see, for example, Miller 1962). In Britain, however, a major review of research on poverty in that country concluded that there was little evidence to support the existence of such a culture there (see Brown and Madge 1982).

The idea of a 'culture of poverty' fell out of fashion in western social science from the 1970s onwards. Most sociologists at that time preferred to locate the causes of long-term poverty and unemployment in the social and economic 'structure' of contemporary capitalism rather than in the beliefs, norms and values of the poor themselves. More recently, however, the idea that poverty breeds a distinctive culture which exacerbates the plight of the poor has resurfaced in the concept of 'social exclusion'.

The language of social exclusion is, on the face of it, very different from that of the culture of poverty. Exclusion is, by definition, something that happens to people, not something that they bring upon themselves, and in this sense the concept has fully assimilated the structuralist critiques of the 1970s by locating the final responsibility for the plight of the poor outside of the individuals themselves. This is clearly demonstrated in continental European definitions of social exclusion which tend to focus strongly on structural factors (for example, Paugam 1995; Room 1995). In Britain, however, discussions of social exclusion have become increasingly reminiscent of the earlier concept of a culture of poverty, for they tend to emphasise the way material and cultural disadvantages reinforce each other to create a downward spiral from which individuals find it hard to extricate themselves.

For example, the Social Exclusion Unit in the United Kingdom maintains that youth unemployment, lack of education, deviant behaviour, and anti-education and anti-career attitudes all tend to reinforce each other. In a report on the 9 per cent of British young people who go through long periods where they are not in work, education or training, the Unit finds that they are much more likely than their peers to have appeared in court, to have taken illegal drugs, to become teenage parents, to reject the value of education and training, and to drop out of courses or jobs when opportunities are offered (Social Exclusion Unit 1999).

This approach to social exclusion clearly does not rely simply on a structural explanation of long-term deprivation. Included within it is a recognition that many of those who suffer exclusion express the sorts of individual values and behaviours which inhibit their ability to improve their situation, and which are much the same as the values and behaviours identified thirty or forty years ago in the culture of poverty literature. Both concepts recognise that individuals' lives may be shaped to a significant degree by factors beyond their control, but both also understand that deprivation can in turn be exacerbated and perpetuated as a result of a distinctive set of values and norms which effectively inhibit people from making the best of such opportunities as do come their way. This is not 'blaming the victim'. Rather, it is recognising that action is both 'structured' and 'structuring' – that the way people behave and think both reflects the social conditions in which they grow up and live out their lives, and unintentionally reproduces and develops that social context (Giddens 1984).

Three hypotheses

In this chapter, we consider whether there is any evidence for the existence of a dependency culture among young unemployed people in Australia. There are three possibilities, each of which has been forcibly advocated in recent writing on this topic (for a review, see Buckingham 1999).

Hypothesis I: Dependency culture as myth

The first hypothesis is that no such culture exists. As we have seen, this was the conclusion reached by a British review of the evidence twenty years ago, and it has long been the position taken by Marxist scholars who believe that the welfare-dependent poor are culturally and behaviourally no different from the working class as a whole. Seen in this way, those who are long-term welfare dependent are simply that section of the working class which has seen its employment opportunities disappear as a result of globalisation and capital restructuring. These people would work if they could, but there are no longer any jobs for them to do, and the argument that they have a distinctive culture is dismissed as an ideological myth designed to deflect attention from the real 'structural' cause of their distressed condition.

This hypothesis has been advanced by many left-wing British sociologists including Gallie (1994), Marshall, Roberts and Burgoyne (1996), and Dean and Taylor-Gooby (1992). Disconfirmation of the hypothesis would require evidence that people who rely on income support for extended periods do have different values, beliefs, expectations and behaviours than people from similar social and economic backgrounds who are in regular employment, and that these values and beliefs weaken the attachment to work, deny personal responsibility and agency, and ultimately legitimate withdrawal from the labour force.

Hypothesis II: Dependency culture as cause

The second hypothesis is the reverse of the first. Associated mainly with the political right, particularly in North America (for example, Murray 1994; Mead 1992), it holds that there is a distinct culture among many of those who are long-term welfare dependent, and that this is a major cause of their initial and continuing welfare dependency. As we saw in chapter 1, there are different versions of this thesis – Mead, for example, is quite strongly critical of Murray's arguments and is much less inclined than Murray is to emphasise the role of welfare benefits in encouraging idleness – but what they all share in common is the view that welfare dependency is primarily a problem rooted in the values of a distinct stratum of people – the 'underclass' – who ultimately lack a strong will to work.

The disconfirmation of Hypothesis II would require evidence that those who rely on income support for extended periods are no different in terms of their values, norms, beliefs and behaviours than other people from comparable backgrounds who do not rely on state welfare payments.

Hypothesis III: Dependency culture as outcome

The third hypothesis is slightly more complex than the other two. It shares with Hypothesis II the claim that people who have been dependent on welfare for long periods often exhibit distinctive values and norms, and that these tend to inhibit them from grasping any opportunities for self-reliance that may come along. On the other hand, it shares with Hypothesis I the claim that the initial causes of joblessness will often lie in the collapse of local labour markets rather than in any self-perpetuating culture of dependency. These two hypotheses are combined by arguing that a distinctive culture is the effect, rather than the cause, of long-term reliance on income support, but that there is a vicious cycle from lack of job opportunities to a fatalistic culture, and from fatalism to a continuing failure to find or hold down a job.

This third perspective was, broadly, the view developed by Oscar Lewis (1961) in his pioneering work on the culture of poverty, for he believed that this culture disappears once a realistic chance of changing things arises. We have seen that this perspective is also implicit or explicit in much of the British writing on social exclusion. It is also the line taken in the United States by Wilson (1987) in his critique of Mead's theory, in Britain by Frank Field (see chapter 3), and in Australia by Third Way politicians like Mark Latham (1998). It is also broadly consistent with Noel Pearson's arguments in chapter 7 of this book about the effect of state welfare on traditional Aboriginal culture.

Any attempt to disconfirm Hypothesis III will inevitably be more complex than is the case for the other two hypotheses. Clearly, if it were found that those who are long-term recipients of income support do not show any signs of sharing a distinctive culture of reliance, then (as with Hypothesis II) this would be sufficient grounds for rejection. If, however, there is evidence that such people do share a culture in common, then it would also be necessary to establish whether such a culture exists relatively independently of the structure of labour market opportunities. Only in this way can Hypotheses II and III be evaluated against each other.

Defining dependency culture

Before we can evaluate these three hypotheses against any evidence, we have first to be clear what a dependency culture would look like if we encountered one. Given that the term is now in widespread usage, it is perhaps surprising that it has rarely been explicitly defined (Henman 2000). Clearly at its heart lies the idea that some people are prepared to continue to live for the indefinite future reliant on welfare payments; but to constitute a distinctive 'culture', it must involve more than just this.

There can be no authoritative definition – concepts like dependency culture are ideal types, and inevitably their construction reflects the purposes of those who develop them. However, by drawing on the 'culture of poverty' literature, on research on the 'underclass', on writing about 'social exclusion', as well as on the literature explicitly addressing issues of 'welfare dependency', we have identified a set of definitional elements on which there is now considerable convergence, and we could probably achieve a reasonably wide consensus with a conceptual definition of dependency culture which embraces most or all of the following elements.[2]

Definitional elements of *employment and unemployment:*

- long and/or repeated spells of financial reliance on welfare payments, coupled with a belief that this is normal and acceptable as a life strategy;

- weak work attachment, indicated by a history of long spells of joblessness, poor timekeeping and attendance records when in work, and a typically short duration of jobs due to quitting or dismissal;

- weak work commitment, expressed in low levels of work motivation, absence of any 'moral commitment' to the principle of working for a living, and an unwillingness to accept jobs which are deemed unattractive or inappropriate.

Definitional elements of *education:*

- low attachment to education, revealed in patterns of early school leaving and truancy;

- low value placed on schooling and a lack of interest in training or opportunities for self-improvement.

Definitional elements of *family life:*

- weak family bonds, revealed in a pattern of disrupted relations with parents, siblings or children, and low levels of commitment to partners and/or serial partnering;
- an increased likelihood of early parenting.

Definitional elements of *lifestyles and aspirations:*

- a high likelihood of involvement in socially deviant and/or criminal behaviour, including self-destructive activities such as drug taking and alcohol abuse;
- low levels of participation in social organisations and civic activities of any type, low levels of integration into local neighbourhood or work-based networks, and little recognition of civic or social responsibilities;
- low self-esteem, a lack of belief in personal efficacy coupled with a willingness to let others take responsibility for solving one's problems, a high level of fatalism, no future-orientation, a victim identity and a sense of helplessness.

The list is not exhaustive. Other elements could doubtless be added, just as some of those on the list could be deleted or amended. Nor should we expect to find a sharp and clear boundary between people who 'fit' this ideal type and people who do not. The point of ideal types like this is that they give us the means to assess the *degree* to which behaviour or attitudes correspond to some pure yardstick. We may well find that many young people come close to one or two aspects of this ideal type, and it is unlikely that we will find any young people who fit every element exactly. We should not therefore expect to draw a sharp dividing line between those 'with', and those 'without', a dependency culture. Dependency culture is a matter of degree; it is not an absolute.

Research design

In the remainder of this chapter, we outline some of the findings from an exploratory study of the values, beliefs and attitudes of a small number of young people aged 16–18 years.

The research, which was undertaken for and funded by the Commonwealth Department of Family and Community Services in 1999 (see endnote 1), set out to determine whether there is any evidence for the existence of a dependency culture among people in this age group.[3] This question was addressed by means of sixteen focus groups carried out in Victoria and including young people from a wide variety of backgrounds and situations. Focus groups ran for between one and one-and-a-half hours, during which time participants discussed their views about work and unemployment, education and training, and family life, as well as exploring broader issues to do with current and anticipated future lifestyles.

Groups were recruited in both urban areas (populations in excess of 80 thousand) and rural areas (populations of 10 to 20 thousand), and in areas of high to medium and low socio-economic status, defined according to the Australian Bureau of Statistics Index of Relative Socio-economic Disadvantage, and by the proportion of the population in receipt of income support. Five groups were recruited by following the social networks of young people who had previously been interviewed by telephone (see endnote 3), the remainder by contacting community workers, secondary schools or TAFEs, and various agencies involved in providing services under the government's Job Placement, Employment and Training (JPET) scheme.

The sixteen groups involved a total of one hundred and fifteen individuals, all but one of whom agreed to complete a short questionnaire regarding their family background and personal characteristics. Analysis of these questionnaire returns confirms that the groups straddled a wide variety of young people. Approximately half of the participants were in full-time education, while roughly three in ten were unemployed and two in ten were in work or apprenticeship/training schemes. In one-third of cases, neither parent was reported as having completed Year 12 education, but in around 30 per cent of cases, at least one parent had gone beyond Year 12. Three in ten of these young people no longer lived in their parents' homes, and one-third of them reported that their parents were not living together. There were more males (62 per cent) than females in our focus groups, mainly because men heavily out-numbered women in focus groups conducted with school leavers (70 per cent compared with 30 per cent).[4]

The study was not designed to be representative, and it would be illegitimate to generalise from these findings to make any claims about the wider population of young people in Australia. The key purpose of the research was to discover whether elements of a dependency culture could be detected among any groups of young people, and a focus group methodology was appropriate for this. However, it is important to emphasise that the research cannot be used to gauge how extensive such a culture might be, should we encounter it.

Young people in full-time education

The focus groups conducted with young people who were still in full-time education revealed little evidence for the existence of a set of values and attitudes corresponding to the elements of a dependency culture as defined in our ideal type. Rather, the overall impression was of people with a clear commitment to the importance of education, a strong work ethic, and a belief that their destiny was in their own hands.

The commitment to education was sometimes instrumental – staying at school was seen more as a means to an end than as a value in itself. For some, staying on at school had more to do with inertia than with any positive decision – they could think of nothing better to do. And for some, it was the influence of parental encouragement that had been crucial.

(Female): My mum told me that I should work really hard because I have the opportunity to do something that they didn't do. So it's worth it I guess.

(Male): If it was up to me I would have quit school ages ago. I made like a deal with my parents. If I pass Year 12, my car's in the driveway. So that's the only thing keeping me at school – car of my choice.

Clearly, many of those who stay on at school are pragmatists, and we encountered various moans and complaints about school being boring or teachers being unreasonable. But these students did expect to succeed, and they were confident that they would be going on to further education or would find good jobs after Year 12, even though this would not necessarily be easy. There was a widespread commitment to the meritocratic ideal that hard work, motivation and ability will bring their own rewards, and they believed that their futures were in their own hands – it was a question of working hard. They were optimistic, ambitious and motivated.

> *(Female): If you don't aim higher in the first place then you're not going to get higher. If you aim high you're more likely to get it than not.*

> *(Female): I think if you like something in life you can have it if you really want to. You have a dream – then I think you can do it. You just have to want to do it.*

> *(Male): I believe if you put your heart and soul into something and you don't let anything stop you, in the end it's only going to be you who lets it die.*

This strong commitment to an ethic of personal responsibility was reflected in their views about unemployment. With relatively few exceptions (mainly among those in higher socio-economic status areas), these students believed that it was possible for people to find work if they tried hard enough, that many (although not all) unemployed people were deliberately choosing to remain on benefit rather than seriously search for work, and that it was unfair on those who did work that their taxes were being used to support those who refused to work.

These beliefs were sometimes grounded in first-hand accounts of family members or friends who were 'bludging' off the system and who were generally held in low regard.

> *(Male 1): They're just bums.*

> *(Female): Doing nothing.*

> *(Male 2): Sitting around.*

> *(Male 3): They're making no real efforts of doing anything.*

> *(Male 1): Losing jobs, that's the other thing they are good at!*

(Female): They go on the dole and sit on their bums – get paid sitting on their bum watching TV and they usually prefer to do that . . . My brother, his girlfriend, my ex-boyfriend, his friend, the whole family – they're not at school and they're getting paid for doing nothing. They are all on the dole.

People who were perceived to be 'genuinely' unemployed and seeking work were exempted from criticism, but those who just 'sat around' not looking for work were condemned as unfairly taking advantage of those who were working. This was particularly irksome for those (half of the participants) who had part-time or holiday jobs paying relatively low (junior) wages, for they resented having to support their peers who were not working.

(Female): What really annoys me is when I'm working I got $170 per week and I was working full-time, like 50 hours per week – no breaks, nothing. And they get the same amount of money as me, doing nothing.

Given these beliefs, it is not surprising that support for the principle of Work for the Dole was widespread among these school students.

(Male): At least they're going to be working for it and they are going to go – 'Hang on a minute, I'm working now for $200 where I can get a job and work for $400'. It might motivate them in getting a job.

(Male): At least you have to do something for the money. I wouldn't sit home and get the dole.

Anybody looking for evidence of a dependency culture among Australian youth will not easily find it among those still at school.

Young people in work or training

It is almost true by definition that young people who have successfully moved from school into employment or training are also unlikely to express values associated with a dependency culture, and so it proved. These participants shared many of the views and beliefs of their contemporaries who were still at school, although their experience of school had sometimes been rather different.

Some reported that they had left school because they had lost interest and motivation, or because they had been struggling to keep up with the work. Others claimed to have left school for positive reasons – they wanted to follow a particular vocational course of training, or they responded to an opportunity to work in an area that attracted them, or they preferred to study at TAFE and take vocational courses as part of their VCE studies. For some, the main consideration had been the money.

(Female): We're making more money, it's your shout at the pub.

However, leaving school did not represent a rejection of the broader goal of getting qualified. Like those who remained at school, those who had left for employment or for further training were generally well aware of the importance of qualifications if they were to succeed in life.

(Male): Like at the moment I'm doing electronics and not doing too bad at it, but when I finish this course I want to stay at the same school I am now, the same TAFE, and see if I can do my VCE there because I'm not finished with it. If I can, it will be better because I'll have my Electronics Certificate I and II, and I'll have my VCE Certificate, and it's easier to find a job.

Compared with the school students, employed young people seemed to express a sharper awareness of the labour market constraints which could make it difficult to find employment. They accepted the meritocratic ideal that hard work and ability brings success, but this was leavened with the idea that it was also important to know the right people and to be in the right place at the right time.

(Male): You've got to know what you want, but at the same time be in the place where you can get what you want. Yeah, it depends on where you are, and what you're doing – and whoever's around you, too.

(Female): I believe I worked really hard to get where I am. I mean I've been through a lot of shit to get to where I wanted to go.

(Male): Well, one thing that can help you out as well is who you know.

Like the school students, those who were working or training generally felt angry and resentful about people accepting the dole with no apparent intention of finding employment. It offended their sense of 'fairness' and made them feel they were being exploited:

(Female 1): A friend of ours is on the dole and she has no ambition and no intention of getting a job.

(Female 2): For her it's like one big holiday. It's okay for her to go out every day. She gets all this money, and like we work, and she still has more money than me. It's not fair.

(Female 1): It's not right. I wouldn't feel like taking other people's money for doing nothing – like just sitting around watching TV or whatever.

Not surprisingly, there was also strong support for the Work for the Dole policy in all of the groups involving employees or trainees.

Generally speaking, these young people were confident that they would be able to fend for themselves and make a success of their lives. As with the school students, so with the employees and trainees, there was little sign of what we have defined as a dependency culture.

The young unemployed

The young unemployed were not an homogenous category. Some were very committed to finding work and some had voluntarily signed up for training courses. Their values and aspirations had much in common with those of school students or young people in jobs or training.

(Male): You're better to be doing something, and earning it, than sitting on your arse.

(Male): I'll do any work. I worked as a baker apprentice, that was pretty shit. I worked that hard I made myself tired and I just wanted to sleep . . . I will work for $5.00 a day for a week just to give me a chance.

For these people, the work ethic seemed to be strong. They saw their problem as lack of opportunity rather than lack of motivation – either there were no jobs for them to do, or employers were demanding work experience that they could not offer.

Lawrence Mead argues in chapter 2 of this book that the chronically unemployed may *say* that they want to work, but some never seem quite to get around to it, and there is always some reason to be found which is said to be stopping them. This may also have been true of these young people, but some certainly seemed determined to make the most of the opportunities represented by the Work for the Dole program. They were positive about the JPET courses on which they were enrolled, and they recognised the chance of using them to get qualified.

(Male): My social worker said, 'There's a course. They'll teach you some experience and that, and you'll get a job out of it.' . . . I was unemployed, and I finished school, and I left home, 'n yeah, I just came here. And I've got an apprenticeship lined up already.

(Female): Well, I do enjoy doing the course. I don't want to be a dole bludger so I guess the only way I'm going to do it is to get my VCE [on JPET course].

This sort of commitment to work and training was by no means universal, however, and we also encountered clear evidence for the existence of elements of a dependency culture among some of the other young unemployed people with whom we spoke. Given the limitations of our methodology, we can make no estimate about the pervasiveness of this culture; all that we can claim is that it does exist to some degree among some young unemployed people.

Some, for example, spoke quite openly of their preference not to work, particularly in what they described as 'shit jobs'.

Such jobs as they had experienced had been poorly paid, boring and irksome, and relations with employers had been too hierarchical and authoritative. Their jobs had not lasted for very long, and sometimes training courses had not been completed.

> (Male 1): Oh, I get sick of the people I'm working for . . . Most of my jobs were in hospitality and I hated it. I hate the industry. I can't stand serving people.

> (Male 2): I had one guy, I'd be half way through the middle of something, and he'd just be sitting there looking at something, and he'd go, 'Get me that paintbrush there, mate'. And I'd go, 'Right, let's start again'. Just really annoyed me, you know – used to get my goat.

> (Male): I dropped out of the glazing course which I started because I did not like it . . . I almost finished the course before the glazing one, but I dropped out of that to do the glazing course. Now I dropped out of that one.

Some took a calculative line on work, saying that they would only work if the money on offer was better than they could get from the dole (sentiments consistent with Murray's argument that welfare benefits can act as a disincentive to work). Some claimed that it made more financial sense to stay on the dole than to find a regular job.

> (Male 1): You get paid – especially being young – you get paid more on the dole than you do working.

> (Male 2): Yeah, on the dole it's cash in hand.

> (Male 1): And like, your work turns out to be the same as the dole. It basically does, you know. So you're better off sitting on your arse because, like, instead of getting $4.65 an hour for slaving your arse off. Because that's what you're earning at, you know – the age of 18 and under – $4.80 an hour.

Pushed onto courses as a condition of receiving Youth Allowance, these young people did the minimum necessary to safeguard their benefit entitlements.

(Female 1): I have to come here otherwise I don't get paid.

(Female 2): If I don't turn up then I get my Austudy cut off.

(Female): You have to do two – well, four hours. You have to do two days of study a week or otherwise you don't get paid.

Some thought that working for their dole was exploitative or demeaning.

(Female): They shouldn't make you be like garbos or dig holes in the cemetery and stuff. What's that gonna do if you want to be a doctor or something?. . . I think they are ripping off the people for the work that they are doing. I mean that's the cheaper way for them to get things done.

Reflecting on their school days, these young unemployed people had little or nothing good to say. School had been boring, teachers had been unhelpful, the work had been inappropriate, the environment had been too hierarchical. Some reported incidents in which teachers had humiliated them, others complained of being moved up grades before they were ready. Three-quarters of them had left school before completing Year 12, and reports of clashes with teachers and repeated cycles of offending and punishment at school were common.

(Male): I didn't have a very good time at school. I spent most of my time out of school because I was suspended all the time. I did not like school and school did not like me.

This antagonism towards school was then reflected in an indifference about the value of formal qualifications, and the streetwise cliché that the best school is 'the school of life' was commonly expressed.

(Male): Being on the streets taught me more than school ever did . . . where to get food, where to get drugs, anything. 'Cause on the street you don't need maths.

(Male): School was shit . . . You learn more out of school than you do in school. Umm, yeah, just learning out of books, not of the real thing . . .

Whereas those still at school often reported that they had received at least some support from their families, those in the unemployed groups often reported having received little or no support. Even those still living at home sometimes seemed to receive little guidance and had been left to decide for themselves what route to take in life.

(Female): Uhh, my mum did not want me to leave school, but what can she do? Nothing! I'm not gonna go if she tries to make me.

(Female): My mum doesn't have any control. Basically she's just a friend now. Not my mother.

Only one-third of the young unemployed had parents who were still living together, and three-quarters of them no longer lived with either of their parents. The circumstances which led so many to leave home varied – some left of their own volition, others were kicked out by parents or by a parent's new partner – and there were some reports of unresolved and generally bitter conflict. On occasion, the move out of home led to homelessness, disrupted schooling, and a slide into unemployment.

(Male): I moved out of home at Year 7 . . . I was going from a friend's place to a friend's place . . . I never knew what couch I'll be sleeping on from day to day. Trying to keep up going to school was too much, and then I started going down hill.

(Male 1): I had a drug problem. My parents couldn't cope with me living with them.

(Male 2): My circumstances was basically family breakdown, no communication between the two of us, just bickering and fighting I guess.

Some of these young people saw no future for themselves. Tomorrow would be much like today – they just did not think about it. There was a resigned sense of fatalism, and it was sometimes difficult to see where any impetus for change was going to come from in their lives.

> *(Male): I don't see myself doing anything, for the rest of my life. That's not such a bad thing. Last seventeen years doing that . . .*

> *(Male): I have to fill in two job applications every four months now. Basically they just don't give a shit. If I can keep that up long enough I'll just be put on a pension.*

When they did have plans, they were often impractical and unrealistic. For some there was what might be described as a 'cargo cult' mythology that 'something would come along', or that 'at some point' they would move away and make a new beginning. But they had no clear vision of how all this might come about, and there was little sign that they were actually doing anything to make it happen, nor that they had the skills or resources necessary to bring it about.

> *(Female): I'm going to Queensland.*

> *(Question): What's in Queensland? What's the attraction for you?*

> *(Female): The weather . . . I'll just go up and find my own job.*

> *(Two females): We are going up to Queensland and we are going to start selling stuff in the local markets . . . There's more opportunities there because they are always hiring young people.*

Reinforcing this sense of drift was a pattern of regular, sometimes heavy, drug use (mainly marijuana) among some of these young people. A number of school students told us how they helped each other resist the local drugs culture, but unemployed substance abusers reported having gravitated towards a set of friends who helped to reinforce it. It is difficult to judge the extent of impairment caused by the high levels of substance abuse reported by some of the participants, but they themselves claimed that their habit prevented them from finding work or holding down a job.

(Male): You feel so high that you don't care. You don't care about what's going on, you don't care what you're getting yourself into, you just want to have fun and want to relax . . . motivation drops . . .

(Male): I spend all my money on chuff and I don't buy clothes, and because I don't have clothes I can't make the job interview. And because I can't make a job interview I can't get a job . . . So I smoke dope.

Some of those we spoke with seemed resigned to, and defensive of, their current life style.

(Male): All I see myself doing is mulling out smoking for the rest of my life . . . I don't want to handle it at the moment . . . Yeah, I'm happy. Fuck you, you know. I don't care what you think . . . I like where I am. Sort of like my life.

The work ethic and the dependency culture

We have seen that some of the young unemployed people in these groups express values and beliefs which are broadly consistent with many of the elements of a dependency culture as defined earlier. They have no serious intention to find and hold down a job, they are not interested in (or have unrealistic expectations about) training or gaining further qualifications, they have weak or non-existent support from their families, they are fatalistic, they have little or no future-orientation, and some of them are enmeshed in a debilitating drugs scene.

It was not possible in this research to determine whether these young people assimilated these values and behaviours from their parents, but we do know that many of them reported a fractured and fractious relationship with their parents, and that they sometimes expressed little regard or admiration for them.

(Male): My mum let me down in a way. My mum used to say, 'Go sit in front of the TV, don't bother me I've got stuff to do, shut up and don't annoy me'. She was high

most of the time. She didn't think that I would know, but I knew . . . If I had kids I wouldn't be like my parents. I would help them the best as I could and provide for them and everything, not like my parents.

(Male): If I had kids . . . I'd stay and help them until I die and not run off when I was four months old and not be a drug addict like my mum.

This pattern of weak or broken family ties, together with a general lack of parental guidance or meaningful contact in the lives of these young people, makes it difficult to see how a distinctive dependency culture could have been transmitted to them by their parents. The impression we formed was not that unemployed young people have learned a distinctive culture from their parents, but that family influence over their lives was weak – at least in regard to shaping educational and career aspirations. There is very little cultural heritage bequeathed to these young people from their parents which could be said to form the basis of a dependency culture – they seem to have grown up with little direction or guidance regarding their future economic participation.

This contrasts vividly with both the school student and worker groups where parents had generally played a supportive role, and where, in virtually every case, parents had apparently insisted that their offspring must either study or work. This suggests to us that young people may gravitate towards unemployment and welfare dependency almost as a default position, *unless their family directs them otherwise.* The reason these children had not drifted into unemployment and welfare dependency was because their parents (reinforced by teachers, peers, and even older siblings) had successfully set out to ensure that this would not happen.

It is precisely this influence which was missing in the backgrounds of some of those in the unemployed groups. Their 'culture' was defined, not by positive values learned from others, but by absences – the *lack* of a work ethic, *lack* of motivation, *lack* of parental support, *lack* of faith in the future. Their's is a culture of 'anomie' – a state of normlessness in which they fail to internalise either realistic expectations (goals) or appropriate forms of self-discipline (norms) – see Durkheim (1933).

If there is any intergenerational cultural transmission going on, therefore, it is most likely in the form of a work ethic being passed from parents to children, not a dependency ethic. If we go looking for a specific dependency culture as the explanation for why parents on income support tend to produce children who go on income support, then we are likely to end up chasing shadows. There is evidence for the existence of elements of a dependency culture among some unemployed young people, but this, we suspect, is the 'default position'. The real puzzle (and the ongoing remarkable achievement of so many Australian families) is how so many young people grow up seeking to engage positively in the worlds of education and employment.

Policy implications

Earlier, we outlined three hypotheses. The first – that the dependency culture is a myth – can now be discounted. We have seen that at least some aspects of such a culture exist in the values and attitudes of some unemployed young people, although we cannot estimate how widespread this may be.

The other two hypotheses cannot so easily be evaluated, for both accept that a dependency culture exists, and our evidence is therefore consistent with both of them. Where they disagree is in the analysis of why it exists. Hypothesis II sees culture as an independent cause of long-term reliance on income support (people's values lead to dependency), while Hypothesis III sees it more as a dependent effect (people's reliance on income support comes to shape their values).

One way in which we might begin to unravel this chicken-and-egg conundrum is by analysing what happens when new opportunities are offered to those exhibiting strong elements of a dependency culture. If it is true, as Hypothesis III suggests, that these young people's fatalism and lethargy are a reflection of their situation, then it should be possible to counter some of the effects of this culture by offering training or jobs that provide the prospect of an improvement in this situation. If, on the other hand, Hypothesis II is correct in arguing that the culture is the principal cause of the problem, then we should not expect new training or job schemes to have any impact at all on these young people's attitudes and behaviour.

We have seen that some unemployed young people have responded positively to the opportunities offered by participation in JPET schemes. For them, provision of training and education opportunities makes sense, provided, of course, that they are linked to authentic employment opportunities. These are the people for whom Hypothesis III seems to have validity.

However, some other young, unemployed people appear resistant to the opportunities offered by such programs. They may fulfil the minimum attendance criteria necessary to qualify for continued receipt of full income support, but they make little serious attempt to improve their skills or qualifications, they disrupt classes for those who do want to learn, they resent having to attend courses, and they show little or no inclination to find employment when the courses end. This negative reaction to enforced training is not surprising, perhaps, when we remember that these same young people had only recently escaped from a schooling environment which they had often experienced as alienative and irrelevant.

These are the people for whom Hypothesis II seems to have some validity – in their case, simply making opportunities available has had little effect. What, then, should be done about them?

One possibility is to do nothing. They may be a very small proportion of the unemployed youth population – we simply have no idea from this research how numerous they are – in which case they could be left alone. Perhaps there will always be a small rump of 'unemployable' people under any policy regime. Alternatively, if their numbers are small, their needs could perhaps be addressed through individual casework.

If, however, something is to be done to counter the various elements of a dependency culture when they are encountered among unemployed youth, then this study can offer three pointers to help inform future policy in this area.

First, opportunities to engage in work programs may be more suitable than the offer of training for some unemployed young people. Recent research has found that training schemes throughout the OECD countries have rarely been effective in providing youth pathways into work (Kalisch 2000; Martin 2000; see also Peter Dawkins' chapter in this volume), and our own study demonstrates that some young people on JPET training schemes are simply going through the motions and are deriving little obvious benefit from these schemes. All this suggests that we need to find ways of determining whether a work requirement may be more suitable than offering a training option for any given claimant.

Second, if we are correct in believing that young people need to learn a positive work ethic from their parents in order to counter the 'default position' of a dependency culture, then we should probably try to ensure that children grow up with one or more parent in regular employment. As Mead (1992: 164) writes: 'If the parents signal by their withdrawal that life is futile, no program is likely to teach the children otherwise.' To achieve this, it would be necessary to enable lone parents to engage more fully in the labour market.

Finally, it is clear that for some young people, the chronic failure to find and hold down a job is linked to other problems including family disruption, homelessness, educational failure and substance abuse. In the longer term, therefore, action designed to assist young people to move into the labour force will also need to address these related issues, and this probably means early intervention in high-risk families and through the schools.

Notes

1. This chapter draws on research undertaken by the authors for the Commonwealth Department of Family and Community Services and included in a report to the Department entitled *Transgenerational income support dependency: findings from a study of young Australians' values about work, unemployment, education and family life*. The Department of Family and Community Services funded the research and retains the intellectual property rights in it. We are therefore grateful to the Department for permission to use in this chapter some of the theoretical/conceptual ideas, as well as some of the

empirical research findings. We also gratefully acknowledge the contribution to the research of various colleagues at the Australian Institute of Family Studies who worked with us on the project. Further information about the research is available from the Department of Family and Community Services (Director, Participation Projects Section), Box 7788, Canberra Mail Centre, ACT 2600.

2. Some of the elements in the ideal type are not themselves aspects of a dependency culture, but are behavioural correlates/indicators of it.

3. The research also addressed the second, and subsidiary, question of whether there is any evidence that the kinds of values, attitudes and beliefs associated with a dependency culture might be passed from parents to their offspring. This was addressed through separate telephone interviews with parents and their 16–18 year-old children designed to test the degree to which the children's attitudes to issues relevant to our ideal type of the dependency culture correspond to those of their parents. This part of the research was inconclusive – the results were not inconsistent with the hypothesis of inter-generational transmission, but the number of cases was insufficient to provide an adequate test – and the results are not discussed here.

4. These statistics are compiled from Table 2 of the final report to the Department of Family and Community Services and refer to individual-level data rather than the group-level data computed in Table 3 of that report.

Chapter 7

Passive welfare and the destruction of indigenous society in Australia

Noel Pearson

Aboriginal society in Australia's Cape York Peninsula today is not a successful society. These are just some of the signs that our society is not functioning: our people die more than twenty years earlier, on average, than other Australians; our health is by far the worst of any group in the Australian community; our people suffer from diseases that other Australians do not have; we are vulnerable to new health threats such as HIV; our children do not participate in the education system anywhere near as successfully as other Australian children; we are over-represented in the juvenile justice system, the criminal justice system, and the jails; and there is more violence amongst our people than in other communities in Australia.

Whilst other communities and groups in Australia and in the world experience many of these same problems, the degree to which our society suffers from such problems is extraordinary. In a number of key areas our situation has deteriorated over the past thirty years. Probably the clearest indications of this are the decline in life expectancy, and the fact that the per capita consumption of alcohol in Cape York Peninsula is the highest in the world. This social deterioration occurred despite the vast improvement since 1970 in the material circumstances of our communities resulting from the government resource transfers that came in the wake of our citizenship and the recognition by the Australian state of our material poverty.

Despite the fact that ours is one of the most dysfunctional societies in the world today, none of the current discourses on the subject gives me any satisfaction that the underlying issues have been grasped, let alone confidence that the right measures are being taken to change this situation.

Even as our traditional society was ruptured by colonial invasion, our ancestors struggled to keep our Law alive. Our traditional values and relationships shielded us against loneliness and provided sustenance during desperately mean times. They still do. But when we look at our society in Cape York today, and the nature of our problems, we see our traditional values and relationships unravelling before our eyes.

I contend that it is passive welfare that has caused this social dissolution.

Aboriginal people's sad inheritance from the welfare state

Transfers from federal and state budgets to individuals and families without reciprocation is the principal source of income of Aboriginal society in Cape York Peninsula today. It has become common usage to equate welfare with such unconditional cash pay-outs to needy citizens of whom nothing further will be required. I have coined the term 'passive welfare' in order to distinguish between this narrow usage of the word and the full scope of 'the welfare state'.

In the wider sense, the term 'welfare' includes, for example, universally accessible health care and compulsory education. In most modern industrialised countries the state has assumed an overall responsibility for these domains, even if there is a mixture of state and private enterprise in these sectors of the economy. In the welfare state, working taxpayers collectively finance facilities aimed at their own wellbeing, development and security. Welfare in the wider sense does redistribute resources from richer to poorer citizens, but it also redistributes the resources of the individual over her or his own life cycle.

During the end of the nineteenth century and for most of the twentieth, all highly industrialised countries developed into welfare states to at least some degree. Why did this happen?

During this period the lower classes consisted mainly of a huge, homogenous industrial army and their dependents.

Since they lived and worked under similar conditions and were in close contact with each other, they had both the incentive and the opportunity to organise themselves into trade unions and struggle for common goals. They possessed a bargaining position through collective industrial action.

At the same time it was in the objective interest of the industrialists to ensure that the working class did not turn to radical ideologies, and that the workers were not worn down by the increasing speed and efficiency of industrial production. Health care, primary education, pensions, minimum wages, collective bargaining and unemployment benefits created a socially stable and secure working class, competent to perform increasingly complex work in industry and able to raise a new generation of workers. Workers with an income above the minimum required for survival and reproduction also constituted a market for the immense collection of commodities that they themselves produced.

These two factors – the organisation of the workers and the objective interest of the industrialists – produced an era of class cooperation: the welfare state. Thus it was in Australia during the long period of bipartisan consensus that Paul Kelly calls 'the Australian Settlement', established by Deakin at Federation and lasting up to the time of the Hawke and Keating governments in the 1980s.

Now this has changed. The modern economy of the developed countries is no longer based to the same extent on industrial production by an homogenous army of workers. The bulk of the gross domestic product is now generated by a symbol and information-handling middle class and some highly qualified workers. These qualified people have a bargaining position in the labour market because of their individual competence, whereas the workers in the manufacturing-based economy were interchangeable and depended on organisation and solidarity in their negotiations with employers.

The lower classes in developed countries have lost much of their political influence because of the shrinking and disorganisation of the only powerful group among them, the working class proper. The shift in the economy away from manufacturing, and economic globalisation, which makes it possible to allocate production to the enormous unregulated labour markets outside the classical welfare states, has deprived the industrial workers in the developed countries of their powerful position as sole suppliers of labour for the most important part of the world economy. The lower classes are therefore now unable to defend the welfare state. Nor is there any longer any political or economic reason for the influential strata of society to support the preservation of the welfare state.

Employees who have important functions in the new economy will be employed on individual contracts, and will be able to find individual solutions for their education, health care, retirement and so on, while the majority of the lower classes will face uncertainty. The welfare state will increasingly be presented as an impediment to economic growth.

It therefore seems likely that great changes will be made to the welfare systems which are the major source of income for Aboriginal communities. One might argue that it would be politically easier to defend welfare schemes specifically aimed at dispossessed indigenous peoples, but this is far from certain. Aboriginal Cape York Peninsula cannot continue to rely on support systems with such a precarious future.

But there is a further compelling reason why the current passive welfare dependency of Aboriginal communities in the Peninsula must be reversed. I will argue that passive welfare is in itself a destructive influence on Aboriginal society. Further, that unless our passive welfare dependency is soon addressed, it will inevitably cause the disintegration of our communities and the annihilation of our culture.

Economic and social history of Aboriginal Cape York Peninsula

In order to understand why we in Aboriginal Cape York Peninsula are now totally dependent on passive welfare, and to understand the contended relationship between our social problems and passive welfare, one needs to know our history. In particular, one must understand the difference between 'real' economies and the artificial economy of passive welfare, and our experience of these different economic systems throughout our history.

In real economies there is a correspondence between what we consume and what we produce. Broadly there are three kinds of real economies that we know of in Cape York: the *traditional subsistence economy,* the institutional *modern subsistence economy,* and the *market economy* of white Australia.

Hunting, fishing and gathering has been practiced within our communities in Cape York Peninsula throughout our modern history. Traditional subsistence activities continue to contribute a significant proportion of the food consumed by the people of Cape York. A valuable feature of this practice is that traditional subsistence activities revive the social values of responsibility and reciprocity, which have been eroded by our passive welfare dependency.

During the 'protection' phase of our colonial experience, our grandparents were removed to missions to live in what I call the institutional modern subsistence economy. The state established an elaborate system to regulate relations with the outside mainstream economy and sanctioned a system of unequal pay. All income was managed through the administration of missions and government settlements.

Within the missions the authorities and their inmates developed community ventures in the fishing industry, cattle and various agricultural experiments, which were supplemented by traditional subsistence, and by raising domestic animals and maintaining food gardens.

Our colonial dispossession is the ultimate historical cause of our welfare dependency. Upon our dispossession, the traditional economy of our ancestors was ruptured and we were dragged into the colonial economy for purposes of exploitation. Our ancestors managed to survive at the bottom end of the market economy doing whatever work was available. Our official and actual place until 1967 was in the underclass. Aboriginal people have therefore participated in the market economy for most of Australia's colonial history.

The welfare-based economy of Aboriginal society came about as a consequence of our official incorporation as

Australian citizens and the assumption of responsibility for Aboriginal Affairs by the Federal Parliament after the 1967 referendum. The great tragedy of Aboriginal history in the last decades was the Australian failure to remove the discrimination that our people suffered in the mainstream economy, *and keep us there.* We got the right to equal pay but on those terms we were no longer able to find employment. Aboriginal people withdrew from participation in the real economy.

The impact of the equal wage decision on Aboriginal labour in the cattle industry was decisive. People lost their place in the pastoral economy and were forced into the increasingly artificial economy of the former missions.

The Aboriginal peoples of Cape York are now firmly embedded in the passive welfare economy. Most economic activity, including the operation of community enterprises, occurs within the passive welfare economy, and is reliant upon government transfers. We share many problems with rural Australia generally, such as the decline of rural industries and the lack of infrastructure. When these difficulties are compounded by our social disintegration, our lack of resources and education, and by the low expectations the wider community has of us, it is difficult to see how a real market economy could replace this passive welfare economy.

Passive welfare has corrupted our society

Passive welfare has several aspects, which together constitute what I call the 'passive welfare paradigm'.

First, passive welfare is *an irrational economic relationship*, in which transactions between the provider and the recipient are not based on reciprocity. Unlike commercial transactions, no mechanisms promote rational and constructive behaviour either on the part of the recipient or on the part of the provider, which is usually the government. As Kant (1798: 87) observed: 'Welfare, however, has no principle, neither for him who receives it, nor for him who provides it, one will place it here and another there.'

Second, welfare is *a method of governmental action,* or governance. The welfare mode involves a superior power having all of the rights and responsibilities to both make decisions and take actions on behalf of relatively powerless people. People on the ground are seen as passive recipients or clients. Whilst clients may be 'consulted' and the bureaucrats talk frequently about 'community ownership', the welfare mode invariably concentrates all initiative and resources at the discretion of the people who are supposed to save and serve the hapless and the helpless. Welfare as a method of governance is increasingly becoming a method of managing marginalised groups at minimal cost, without even maintaining the fiction that a lasting solution to the problems is sought.

Third, welfare is *a mentality*. It is a mentality which accepts the principles underlying the economic relationship and the method of governance described above. This mentality is internalised and perpetuated by recipients who see themselves as victimised or incapable, and having a *right* to assistance without reciprocation. But the mentality is also held by people in power, white and black.

This passive welfare paradigm has been particularly destructive in the governance of Aboriginal society. The notion that passive welfare is an important right of citizenship, and the fact that alternatives to the welfare economy of the communities of Cape York Peninsula are so difficult to conceive, let alone achieve, has meant that passive welfare has been at the centre of Aboriginal policy and economy for the past thirty years. Passive welfare is almost seen as the Aboriginal way, part of the culture. Recipients of passive welfare are far removed from the real economy and have been for a long time now. Children who have grown up in this environment have little understanding of and have never experienced life in the real economy.

One reason why passive welfare has been so devastating is that it was introduced into a society with a highly sophisticated and complex system of social relations, which placed high value on the sharing of resources and concern for the wellbeing of other members of the group. In the communities of Cape York Peninsula, prior to the impact of passive welfare, the exchange of resources within the community followed the traditional patterns of rights and obligations between people who were socially connected. 'Cadging' – borrowing food from people when one is out – was common and occurred on a reciprocal basis between community members. People who did not have resources now could provide for others when they did.

Passive welfare has distorted these cultural arrangements, and the traditional balance between the rights and responsibilities of our people in our society has been corrupted. Whereas the traditional system had reciprocity as a fundamental principle, the passive welfare-based Aboriginal society has removed responsibility and left obligation in place (on the part of others). Exploitation of weaker members of the society is now a strong feature of the system of social relationships amongst our people.

The economic is the social

My central thesis is that it is the economic issue of passive welfare dependence that continuously corrupts Aboriginal social relationships. If we do not get rid of this continuous source of social corruption, whatever good changes people try to make through social programs are simply not going to work.

The way in which economic resources circulate in the community has a clear impact on social relationships. Whilst in theory there tends to be a general acceptance of the relationship between economic issues and social problems, in practice economic issues relating to Aboriginal policy tend to be relegated to the 'too hard basket'. To date, effort has been focused on specific health problems or behavioural problems such as domestic violence. But we cannot defer tackling the fundamental issue of the economic structure of our society. There has been too much of a separation of the social from the economic in both analysis and policy.

It is the *nature* of passive welfare that explains our social crisis. It explains the phenomenon that even as our material condition improved over recent decades, our social condition deteriorated. The nature of passive welfare has come to be the dominant influence on the relationships, values and attitudes of our society in Cape York Peninsula.

The influence of passive welfare on our relationships, values and attitudes soon came to be directly at odds with our traditional relationships and values. Invariably the outcome of the ongoing conflicts between our traditions and the nature of the economic base of our society, is that our traditions succumb and are eroded daily. We are now at a stage where the traditions we purport to follow are too often merely self-deceptions (that we care for each other, that we respect our elders, that we value our culture). The 'traditions' which we do follow are in fact distortions of our traditional values conditioned by the pathological social situation to which passive welfare has reduced us (that we sit around in a drinking circle because we are Aboriginal, that you are trying to be a flash white fella if you refuse your brother money for grog).

Why is the impact of passive welfare so decisive? The answer lies in Kant's observation, that welfare has no inherent principle. The resources of passive welfare are fundamentally irrational. Whereas the dollar earned through a commercial or labour transaction has a rationale, the dollar given as a matter of course has none. Everyone in a passive welfare economy is susceptible to irrational (mis)appropriation and (mis)expenditure of money, because that is the very nature of the money. Money without principle is expended without principle.

When people have only one means of existence the nature of that income obviously influences their whole outlook. The irrational basis of our economy has turned us into a wasteful, aimless people. Like other people who can not see any connection between their actions and their circumstances, we waste our money, our time, our lives. We neglect our material possessions, our education, our social and economic development. We do not seize opportunities that arise. There always comes another day and another cheque. No one feels the need to use a sum of money for a meaningful investment or to use a day to build something that lasts.

The worst consequence of this lack of purpose is that it has compounded the effects of dispossession and trauma in making us susceptible to an epidemic of grog and drug abuse. In turn, this epidemic now has its own momentum and has made it inevitable that our scarce resources increasingly finance irrational and destructive behaviour. We must now deal with both passive welfare dependency and substance abuse simultaneously as these two problems feed off one another and undermine any efforts toward social recovery.

Limited space prohibits me from discussion of how we are going to fight the grog and drug epidemics in our communities. Suffice to say that if we are to get anywhere with these problems it must be clearly understood that the notion underlying most discussion about substance abuse, the theory that substance abuse is only a symptom of underlying social and psychological problems, is wrong (Bejerot 1978: 13).

Addiction is a condition in its own right, not a symptom. An outbreak of substance abuse is a psychosocially contagious epidemic (Berjerot 1978: 17) which breaks out in societies where there are people psychologically susceptible to trying the substance, and then spreads rapidly among people who did not use the substance at first, as it becomes less and less a breach of social norms to do so. Of course our history (including dispossession, genocide and the introduction of passive welfare) has indirectly caused the epidemic of grog and drug abuse in the sense that it made many of us *susceptible* to start using alcohol and drugs, and made many of us too weak to resist being sucked in. But the epidemic of substance abuse is now established in our society and independent of the original causes of the outbreak.

Achieving recognition of our land rights, improving our social conditions, treating our individual and inherited traumas, that is, doing something about the factors that made it easy for grog and drugs to spread, will not automatically end the abuse of grog and drugs, for two reasons: First, the addicts will simply use any improvement in our circumstances to facilitate their abusive lifestyle. Second, it is evident that, for most addicted people now, the critical factors that made them start using grog and drugs were the availability of the addictive substance, a modest income, time available and the example of others. It was not psychological or social problems.

Not even changing the passive welfare economy to an economy based on reciprocity will remove our grog and drug abuse, it will only make it easier to prevent new out-breaks of substance abuse once we have cured the current epidemic.

Passive welfare alone would probably not have caused our social disaster. But passive welfare dependence and the drink and drug epidemic reinforce each other and will, if not checked, cause the total breakdown of our traditional social relationships and values. The intrinsic force in the epidemic is now stronger than the force of our traditional social norms and values. What (when people are not drinking but hunting) is an obligation to share food resources with countrymen, is turned into an obligation to share grog. But now mutuality only occurs between people who are engaged in exploitation. Whilst the relationships between adults drinking might involve mutual obligation, these are the only mutual obliga-tions that are honoured. The non-drinkers are also expected, and ultimately forced, to contribute resources to the drinking circle. And feed the families – including those who have spent their money on grog.

Drink and drug abuse coupled with an outlook determined by a passive welfare economy has proven to be fatal. People highly motivated by their addictions now regard and treat other people in our society in the same way as the passive welfare resource: these people (wives, girlfriends, parents, grandparents, children, relatives, friends) are no longer valued and respected. They will always be there and the addicts do not have to take any responsibility for them. These people are simply another source of resources (money, shel-ter, food, comfort and care) and they are treated accordingly.

Racism, dispossession and trauma

I have suggested that the nature of the passive welfare economy is reflected in our social relationships, and that it is passive welfare dependency which has corrupted Aboriginal society. But this is counter to the prevailing explanation of Aboriginal social problems in contemporary policy discus-sion. Our social problems are most often interpreted as a legacy of the experience of 'colonisation'.

Who is right? Obviously the impact of the 'colonial experience' on our society has been immense. I will need a very strong argument for my interpretation of our history, in order to challenge the established view. Before I present my argument we need to consider the prevailing explanations of our social breakdown.

In discussions of our historical legacy there are three general themes that arise: racism, dispossession and trauma. These are said to explain our position in Australian society and are seen as the origin of the problems which this paper is seeking to confront.

Racism is a fundamental theme. Racism played a decisive role from the moment Europeans set foot on the continent and has never abated as a key issue for black people since then. When people talk about racism today they usually have discrimination in mind. Not official racism by the state, but informal discrimination caused by attitudes and expectations remaining from the days of legally endorsed discrimination.

Dispossession is also a fundamental theme. Much discussion has rightly centred on the dispossession of Aboriginal peoples from their traditional homelands. One of the features of the struggle for Land Rights however is that, in its discussion of dispossession, it has largely focused on the historical events which accompanied the process of dispossession: the acts of bastardry and shame of our frontier history. The discussion is also very strong on the psychological and spiritual effects of the alienation of Aboriginal peoples from their homelands (and this is of course related to the trauma which I will next discuss). The emphasis has arisen from the spiritual relationship of Aboriginal peoples with their land.

However, when one considers the dialogue regarding dispossession in the Australian context, one is struck by how little focus there is on the *economic* effect of dispossession on Aboriginal society. Whilst the loss of livelihood and access to hunting grounds is mentioned in discussion, the economic aspect of colonial dispossession is largely passed over. Of course dispossession is seen as not just a matter of history, it has a continuing legacy.

Trauma is the third theme. The process of dispossession and the operation of racism throughout history has resulted in trauma which is also rightly seen as a major issue in our people's history and our contemporary society. Trauma is both historic and continuing. As well as the trauma associated with alienation from homeland, trauma is seen as affecting individuals and families who have experienced particular episodes of abuse (such as the taking of children from their families). The contemporary social problems experienced by individuals and families (alcohol and drug addiction, domestic violence and so on) are seen as related to past trauma. These social problems in turn create their own traumas: a ripple effect. Trauma is not just seen as an issue for individuals and families – it is seen in the context of communities (the community is traumatised) and indeed Aboriginal peoples are rightly seen as a sector of the population for which trauma looms as a large issue.

Our recent history can be seen as a sequence of phases characterised by the roles dispossession, trauma and discrimination have played at different times. Initially we were for a brief period simply formally dispossessed. This followed upon the (discriminatory) judgement that we were inherently less capable of using this land for the good of ourselves.

A phase of traumatic confrontation necessarily followed: murder, sexual enslavement and abductions. The effect of these crimes was compounded by the spread of diseases against which we had little resistance.

Official discrimination was the dominant aspect of the third phase of our confrontation with racism: the recent period after the breakdown of traditional society when we became a 'protected' people. The survivors of the traumatic confrontations were held down as an underclass. It was during this phase that institutionalised discrimination became the dominating aspect of racism. An enormous legal and bureaucratic apparatus was developed to manage the remnants of the beaten peoples. This system regulated the smallest movements and events in our lives, and we were still being traumatised, but more often through administrative decisions, for example in relation to the removal of children, and less so by violent assaults.

Today, during the current phase of our confrontation with racism, after the abolition of official discrimination, dispossession is still in place. Traumatic decimation of our people and disruption of our culture and families is the dominating factor of our collective psychology, and trauma is daily recreated in our dysfunctional communities. Whether today's unofficial discrimination is just a regrettable residue of past official discrimination, or if it fulfils the same function of holding us down, is a matter of dispute. But it is there.

In the light of all this it is perhaps understandable that racism, dispossession and trauma are the prevailing explanation for our present difficulties.

I want to emphasise that I do not belittle the debilitating effects of racism and the trauma associated with the history of our dispossession. Racism is a major handicap – it results in Aboriginal people not having access to opportunities, in not recognising opportunities when they arise, in not being able to seize opportunities when they arise, in not being able to hold on to opportunities when they have them. Trauma is an especially difficult issue to come to terms with because its personal manifestations can be incapacitating. The many Aboriginal people with personal traumas caused by separation of family members and by abuse and violence are often truly incapacitated.

However, it is my view that we need to look more carefully at the economic effect of our dispossession. One reason for this is that it is a structural issue that we can actually do something about. This might be dismissed as mere pragmatism. But it can easily be demonstrated that my interpretation of our history reveals the origin of our problems and enables us to attack them at the root in a way that the prevailing, racism-focused interpretation of our history does not.

It is a widely held misconception that the egregious social problems suffered by our people in Cape York Peninsula today have been with us since our traditional society was ruptured. This is not the case at all. Anybody who knows the history of our communities knows that the kind of social problems that afflict our society today – and their severity and extent – were not always with us.

The abuse and neglect of children today does not resemble the situation in the Cape communities of the 1960s and earlier. The numbers of Cape York people in prison and juvenile institutions today are unprecedented: these are statistics that started to emerge in the 1970s. There was not one Hope Vale person in prison in the early 1970s. At any time today, there are up to a dozen or more people in prison. The same dramatic differences apply to the other communities in the Peninsula. Alcohol abuse in Cape York communities developed into the huge problem that it now is, only in these same recent decades. Petrol sniffing amongst children and youth in Cape York Peninsula was unknown until recently. The bashing of old people for money for grog was inconceivable in Cape York communities in earlier times.

Even if there is a range of reasons why these social problems have emerged in the last three decades of the century, it is certainly significant that the emergence of these problems coincides with the period when passive welfare became the economic basis of our society.

And yet the 'service deliverers' ignore the fact that the nature and extent of our social crisis is of recent origin, and their entire policy proceeds from this ignorance. This is hugely problematic for at least three reasons.

First, it obscures the fact that our society was once functional – not just back in the long distant pre-colonial past, but only a bit more than three decades ago. We have ourselves internalised this forgetfulness and we therefore lose hope. Second, the (racist) assumption of the service deliverers is that our social problems are endemic to our society. They proceed with their programs as though we were subhuman. Third, by ignoring the historical development of our problems, this assumption reinforces further misconceptions about their source: the erroneous assumptions that our social problems are the legacy of racism, dispossession and trauma and that our chronic welfare dependency is the end result of these social problems.

This generally accepted causal chain – racism, dispossession and trauma create social problems which create passive welfare dependency – is wrong. Both steps in the reasoning are wrong. Firstly, prior to the 1970s, even though racism was state sanctioned, dispossession had been well effected, and trauma was still fresh and ongoing in our society, we did not have the kind or degree of social problems we experience today. Secondly, our social problems did not come before our passive welfare dependency – rather our social problems arose out of the economic condition of passive welfare dependency.

Of course racism, dispossession and trauma are ultimately the explanations for our precarious situation as a people. But the point is: they do not explain our recent, rapid and almost total social breakdown. If we build our ideology and base our plan of action on our justified bitterness about what has happened to us we will not be able to claim our place in the modern economy, because our current social dysfunction is caused by the artificial economy of our communities and by the corrupting nature of passive welfare.

Why have we missed this insight? It is because the service deliverers, who do not know our communities and our history, have obscured these basic facts in their domination of Aboriginal policy. They have confused our earlier poverty with social degeneration. We have allowed Aboriginal policy to forget that our parents, grandparents and great grandparents struggled mightily to preserve our families and communities – our society, our laws and values – against great and constant attack, and we survived. Whatever our material deprivations, whatever our poverty, we had a strong if bruised society.

Our social degeneration in fact accompanied the vast improvement in our material condition from our earlier poverty over the past thirty years. We are socially poorer today despite vastly improved material circumstances.

It should not be necessary for me to say that I am not urging poverty as a solution to our social predicament. Rather I am seeking to draw the distinction between material poverty and passive welfare dependency. It is the latter which harbours the seeds of social destruction. The argument in this chapter is that poverty needs to be overcome via the development of real economies for our society and that we should

utilise our welfare resources to develop an economic foundation to our society that is based on real principles. Anti-
poverty programs based on passive welfare have only
produced 'opulent disasters' and this is now surely plain to see.

Principles for a solution to the welfare dilemma

The central thesis here is that we have suffered two cata-
strophic disruptions: first dispossession and then the introduction of the passive welfare economy. Is, then, welfare bad?
Not necessarily. Our problem is that we have been
impacted by one aspect of the welfare state, namely unconditional assistance. Our experience of welfare undermines our
traditional values and stops us from developing the attitudes
necessary for successful participation in the modern economy. Our situation is a dilemma in the true sense of the word:
a choice between two alternatives which both have disastrous
consequences. We cannot remain on passive welfare, but we
need welfare support for our immediate survival.

The solution does not lie in government abandoning its
responsibility for the provisioning of resources to the Aboriginal communities of Cape York Peninsula. To say that passive
welfare corrupted our society, is not to say that the resources
embedded in passive welfare provisioning are not valuable.
But when delivered as passive welfare, these resources are
useless. If these resources were properly applied on real economy principles, they would not generate the problems which
passive welfare has generated over the past thirty years. They
could in fact ultimately facilitate our participation in the real
market economy.

Why is it the government's duty to provide resources for
the development of our society? Some people have argued
that cash pay-outs are compensation for dispossession, a kind
of rent. But even if you accept this argument, the rent is not
paid in a form that benefits us and we cannot live in an artificial economy indefinitely. No, the government's responsibility
is simply its usual responsibility to coordinate and facilitate
the solution of an urgent social crisis. It has the responsibility
to facilitate our return to the real economy.

But the government can only facilitate a solution, it cannot solve the problem. It also follows from what I have said that the government's responsibility is only transitory, or at least not indefinite.

The reality is that we are not going to develop self-reliance in the short term. We are now 95 per cent reliant on the welfare economy, and our communities are not going to make even modest inroads into self-sufficiency in the next few years. We are for the moment stuck with government being the provider of these basic resources. Our focus must therefore be on how we can fundamentally change the *nature* of welfare while improving our engagement in the real economy.

Economic development is a generational challenge. This is because of the lack of resources and the need for education and training, in addition to all of the problems that attend economic development in remote Australia. Remote Australia is not an easy place to get economic enterprises going. The least skilled, least resourced people are living in the areas of Australia where it is hardest to get economic development going. That is our predicament.

The first step in leeching out the poison from passive welfare is to ensure that government stops interacting directly with individuals in our society, by sending cheques in the mail. It is the direct corruption of individuals through the provision of resources via the government's welfare mode that is the source of the problem. Reciprocity and responsibility must be built into all government-financed programs in Cape York Peninsula, the first aim being to stop the corruption of our society, with the longer term goal being to develop a modern economy.

I am conscious that this proposal may appear to go against the grain of the Aboriginal struggle as many people conceive it. It will be seen as discriminatory not to deliver passive welfare to Aboriginal Australians on the same terms as other citizens receive these benefits. But welfare reform is being discussed (and this book is being published) largely because of the negative effect passive welfare is seen to have on the lives of the relatively small marginalised group in the wider

Australian community. A support system that has such a negative impact on the recipients obviously cannot be allowed to form the basis for the economy of an entire people.

If it is going to be possible to deliver the available resources on principles of reciprocity and achieve real development, a new interface between Aboriginal society in Cape York and government must be created. This needs to be established by complementary state and federal legislation so that all agencies of government – state, federal and the Aboriginal and Torres Strait Islander Council (ATSIC) – are involved in the interface. Government agencies, with their resources, need to sit on one side of the interface, and Aboriginal representatives of Cape York need to sit on the other side. All government programs and inputs must be coordinated through this regional interface. In the regional interface the people of Cape York Peninsula and the government representatives will jointly develop policies which move beyond the passive welfare paradigm. The question we must ask about each program is whether it will promote empowerment and economic independence in the long term.

The right to a real economy

It is said that we Aboriginal people have a right to passive welfare. Indeed, it is an entitlement which flowed from the recognition of our citizenship in 1967. Aboriginal leaders routinely defend access to passive welfare as a fundamental indigenous right.

But this is wrong thinking. We have (as all citizens in this country have) a right to an economy. Passive welfare does not offer our people a real place in a real economy. Nor does it enliven or energise recipients to take a real place in the real economy. Our failure to properly distinguish between passive welfare dependence and the real economy has seen us pursue, advocate, design and deliver policies which have more usually exacerbated problems than solved them.

Unconditional cash transfers were originally only a minor aspect of the welfare state which developed in the market growth economies. This was just intended as a temporary safety net. In white society passive welfare has become the only source of income for a small minority. Aboriginal people on the other hand have collectively lost their foothold in the real economy.

Yes, we have always said that we do not want welfare as a permanent destination for our people. But we have been living in passive welfare dependence for three decades now and the social consequences of this condition are devastating, as anyone who understands these communities knows. Aboriginal and non-Aboriginal communities that have not experienced full-body immersion in passive welfare dependence do not appreciate how devastating it is. But look hard at the social problems in Cape York Peninsula. If my analysis is correct, passive welfare has caused some of the worst social disasters the world has known.

Our struggle for our rights is far from over. Nothing I propose casts any doubt on the correctness of our struggle for rights – including our unique position as the original people of this country. But ever since the Whitlam Government introduced the language of self determination into official Aboriginal policy, we have never been agreed as to its meaning. There is still interminable musing about the 'powers' and 'rights' which self determination should afford to Aboriginal people – but no clear idea, let alone consensus.

We have a right to an economy. We have a right to the resources currently tied up in passive welfare. We need to apply these resources on real economy principles to lift us out of the passive welfare economy. This is the right we have. We have the right to demand of government that we have access to resources for a real economy.

However, we have to be as forthright and unequivocal about our responsibilities as we are about our rights. Otherwise we will eventually get all of our rights and our society will have fallen apart in the meantime. The critical insight for those concerned with Aboriginal policy, at the highest levels and at the grassroots, is that in claiming the right to self determination, we are claiming the right to take responsibility.

Chapter 8

Mutual obligation: what kind of contract is this? [1]

Anna Yeatman

Mutual obligation has become a key concept in contemporary social policy. The obligation to make an active contribution to society is set against what is portrayed as passive welfare dependency. Obligation is seen to be a condition of citizen rights, and, thus, obligation is set against ideas of automatic entitlement. While defenders of social citizenship in T.H. Marshall's (1950) sense of this term generally reject what they see as this substitution of obligation for rights in social policy, the idea of mutual obligation commands at this time wide consensus amongst political leaders. In the Australian case, this includes leaders of both major political parties (Howard 1999b; Swan 1999) as well as prominent Aboriginal political leader, Noel Pearson (1999, and chapter 7 in this volume).

Such consensus on a value would be unlikely to occur without there also being a convergence on mutual obligation in the agenda-setting social policy literatures, as indeed there is. Third Way or revisionist social democrats (Giddens 1998), the new paternalists (Mead 1997, and chapter 2 of this volume), and contemporary communitarians (Etzioni 1995) are all offering intellectual defences and specifications of the idea of mutual obligation.

Mutual obligation is an idea that seems to capture an element of populist commonsense: that individuals should make a contribution to society in exchange for the support society gives them. This old axiom is brought to bear especially in contemporary social policy discourse on welfare recipients. In populist mutual obligation rhetoric, as used by most politicians, it is taken for granted that the focus should be on the welfare recipient's obligation to 'society', not the other way around. This translates into the idea that the welfare recipient should either work for welfare, or receive welfare on condition that s/he seeks work.

Whether mutual obligation as an idea also draws upon the liberal concept of the social contract depends on whether its application to welfare recipients is said to enhance their freedom or not. Champions of mutual obligation for welfare recipients argue that its primary purpose is to push and support these individuals in moving off welfare dependency into self-reliance. To the extent that self-reliance denotes market-based contractual freedom of individual action, these champions are invoking both the populist axiom and the liberal concept of political obligation.

Political rhetoric is one thing, and it should not be confused with policy. When we turn to the *policy* rhetoric of mutual obligation, we find a denser and richer set of specifications of mutual obligation than is suggested in the populist-political rhetoric. It is at this point that those who advocate mutual obligation have to think seriously about its policy specification and implementation. In this chapter, I want to suggest that, as policy, mutual obligation is an idea that has a substance and complexity which demands critical evaluation.

Mutual obligation and the new paternalism

While mutual obligation as policy rhetoric has been adopted in the Anglo democracies of Australia, New Zealand, the United Kingdom and the United States, most references to the policy discourse of mutual obligation follow the American literature. This is because the policy of mutual obligation – its rationale, goals, implementation and evaluation – is most elaborated in that literature, and this being so, this literature has become influential across all these jurisdictions. For instance, Lawrence Mead's championship of mutual obligation provides a ready source for ministerial speech writers and policy makers in the Australian jurisdiction. However, it is important to understand that the same general invocation of mutual obligation across national jurisdictions means different things according to the specific traditions of political culture and welfare statism, as well as the structure of the labour market, in each of these jurisdictions.

For instance, Mead (1986: 71) suggests that 'job seekers often choose to remain jobless rather than take the jobs most accessible to them,' even though these may be very low-paying jobs which turn their holders into the 'working poor'. Such a proposition may be more persuasive in the context of the United States, where the idea of a fair and basic wage has never taken root, in contrast to the institutional history of labour relations in Australia. In the United States, the structural and cultural legacy of slavery, as well as the history of mass immigration, means that there is a largely unregulated, low-pay labour market targeted to Afro-Americans, Hispanics and illegal immigrants. Moreover, the American assumption that there is nothing especially problematic about directing mutual obligation to mothers of young children has yet to find a resonance in the Australian policy jurisdiction where there is still an attachment to the idea that mothers should be available to their children when young. When critically evaluating the concept of mutual obligation we should be careful to clarify whether the criticism relates to the policy in general or a specific jurisdictional version of it.[2]

If the policy of mutual obligation is effectively implemented, it represents a serious effort to use the authority and resources of government, as well as the commitment and creativity of good case managers, to compel individuals to become self-reliant. This is a peculiarly late twentieth-century version of the paradox of paternalist contractualism that Rousseau offered in *The Social Contract*: namely, that individuals have to be 'forced to be free'. Instead of a nineteenth-century distinction between those who would be self-reliant if they could be (the 'deserving' poor) and those who choose to be wastrels, spongers, thieves and vagrants (the 'undeserving' poor), the new discourse of self-reliance is non-discriminatory and egalitarian in its assumption that each individual would prefer to be self-reliant if they could be.

This is a discourse informed by the disciplines of sociology and psychology because it assumes that an individual preference to be self-reliant cannot become effective if the individual in question lacks the training, disciplines, skills and worldly experience on which effective self-reliance depends. In this sense, self-reliance is not merely a moral disposition, but a reciprocally reinforcing bundle of competences, skills and psychological capacities. The latter fundamentally depend on a self-regard that has been socially cultivated and supported.

The policy of mutual obligation is a pro-government orientation because it assumes that government is responsible for the development of this capacity for self-reliance in individuals whose welfare dependency is taken to indicate they lack this capacity. Advocates of this policy are not only pro-government, but are also serious about how such a policy might be effectively implemented. Such advocates make it clear that effective implementation means a government that is willing to make the necessary degree of expenditure to make a program an effective intervention. It also means a government that commits to evaluation of the program so that information is generated about how the program might be improved and made more effective. Finally, effective implementation depends on giving this process of social reform time to work. It takes time to get new systems and approaches up, time to permit the new learning that is involved in such innovation, time to evaluate and disseminate, and time to 'mainstream' the efforts of the innovators and entrepreneurs within the new reform process.

Thus in discussing the idea of mutual obligation, we need to make a distinction between broad rhetorical usage of this idea on the one hand and, on the other, the more careful policy specifications of this idea. Generally, the latter turn out to be a set of recommendations for an elaborate as well as costly social policy. In this sense, the policy advocates of mutual obligation represent a new argument for what it is that government can and should do that the market cannot do. These advocates are 'new paternalists' because they argue that government has an active role in the re-shaping of the behaviour of welfare recipients. As Mead (1997a: 11) recognises: 'It is a conservative policy in that it focuses on changing how the poor live rather than on improving their benefits or opportunities . . . But paternalism is also a liberal policy because it is pro-government. Far from reducing the welfare state, paternalism expands it.'

The new paternalists reject conservative pro-market recommendations that welfare should be abolished, leaving people no alternative than to work and support themselves. They reject the assumption in the conservative position that those who have been dependent on welfare already know how to be self-reliant, and argue instead that individuals are not always capable of exercising free choice in self-regarding and socially responsible ways. Instead, they claim that society has to play a part in developing and sustaining people's capacity for self-regarding and socially responsible choice. For reasons of family history, poor schooling or generally disadvantaged backgrounds, individuals and the communities they comprise can lack the 'moral education' (a Durkheimian term used by Etzioni 1995) necessary for the development of this capacity. This being the case, agencies which act on behalf of society need to step in and offer the direction and structure that permit individuals to acquire the capacity and skills for self-regarding and socially responsible choice. These agencies will act in accordance with the policies laid down by governments.

The policy rhetoric of mutual obligation, then, can be said to represent a rediscovery of the social in the face of the specific kind of market failure that occurs when, for whatever reason, individuals cannot choose in self-regarding and socially responsible ways. However, as we shall see, this is a particular conception of the social, one that is radically individualised.

In what follows, first, I specify the various different values which underpin the idea of mutual obligation. Second, I discuss the contractualist features of mutual obligation when it is translated into a service delivery relationship between publicly-funded service providers and individual clients. Here I enquire into the distinctive kind of paternalism that is involved in this particular neo-Durkheimian version of Rousseau's paradox: the necessity of 'forcing individuals to be free'. I conclude by raising some of the issues that are implicated in the policy of mutual obligation.

Mutual obligation as a cluster of values

The idea of mutual obligation indicates a cluster of values which centre on the obligations of adult individuals to be self-reliant, where it is assumed that, by being so, individuals are making a contribution to the society from which they derive a range of benefits and supports.

There are five specifications of this idea of self-reliance which, taken together, bring out the particular historical nature of this version of self-reliance. These are in turn: the rejection of dependency; a non-discriminatory conception of the self-reliant individual; the conception of the individual as the site of the social; the pairing of individual freedom with social obligation; and, finally, the reduction of the idea of making a social contribution to participation in a market economy.

Rejection of dependency

The rhetoric of mutual obligation begins with a *rejection of dependency*. Dependency is associated with both passivity and a long-term, self-destructive reliance on unearned economic support, or 'welfare'. It is self-destructive because long-term dependency of this kind for adults is seen as cultivating a particular social psychology that makes it virtually impossible for individuals to be sufficiently self-regarding to do what is necessary to move off welfare in the direction of self-reliance. Employment, part-time or full-time, is seen as the primary means by which individuals acquire self-esteem, confidence in handling problems, skills, and the regard of others. In the OECD discourse of the active society that was adopted by the Labor Government in Australia from 1986 until its demise in 1996, employment is the gateway to citizenship understood as full membership of society. Dependency, read as persistent unemployment and dependence on public income support, is defined as incongruent with citizenship, where citizenship is assumed to reside in the kind of active membership of society that self-reliance makes possible through stable patterns of employment, domestic partnership, parenting, and involvement in voluntary associations.

The wholesale condemnation of dependency for adults is something quite new in the history of modern capitalist societies as Fraser and Gordon (1997) have argued, and it represents a distinctive feature of post-industrial social formation. Until very recently, it was not just socially legitimate but normal for wives to be dependent on husbands as the breadwinners for the household/family. This was reflected in the state's readiness to take over this breadwinning function in cases where women lacked a husband. Indeed, previously the non-commodified work of women as wives, mothers, carers, and contributors to socially valuable volunteer work of various kinds was valued as the distinctive contribution that women make to industrial society. Now that market liberalism has assumed an equal opportunity form, the most common type of social contribution as a market-based one is extended to all adults regardless of their sex. While private dependency of wives on husbands persists, it no longer has normative status. And when women lack husbands they are expected to become both economically active and earners in their own right.[3]

At the same time, post-colonial moral standards have banished notions of some races being less evolved and thus more dependent on the leadership and benevolence of civilised races. As Fraser and Gordon (1997: 135) summarily put it: 'With all legal and political dependency now illegitimate, with wives' economic dependency now contested, there is no longer any self-evidently "good" adult dependency in post-industrial society.'

Non-discriminatory conception of the self-reliant individual

The second specification of the rhetoric of mutual obligation follows from the first, and it resides in its *non-discriminatory character*. All adult individuals, regardless of their differences, are expected to be self-reliant. It is not just women. The same expectation is made of indigenous people: they are to become self-reliant both as individuals and as communities – which is why Mead (1997a: 22) calls these paternalist programs 'a post-racial social policy'. Adults with disabilities are also expected to become economically active, the level and nature of their disability permitting.

Conception of the individual as the site of the social

The third specification of mutual obligation rhetoric concerns *the status of the individual*. In this rhetoric, the primary dynamics of social life are played out in terms of individual behaviour, motivation, competences and skills. Where economists derive the dynamics of the market economy from individual choice, considered as an unproblematic feature of individuality, in this case the whole domain of individual choice is problematised. It is not enough that in a formal sense an individual is capable of exercising a preference or choice. Rather, the emphasis switches to whether the individual is morally educated in ways which make him/her capable of the kind of choice that can sustain both him/herself and society. This is the neo-Durkheimian component of the rhetoric of mutual obligation. Durkheim (1933) argued that the voluntary dimension of contract (choice) can work on behalf of social order only to the extent that it is informed by a normative adherence to the behaviours on which social order depends.

The social is viewed as immanent in individuals, so whether society is well ordered or not depends on how these individuals are functioning. If society is reduced in this way to individual psychology it is only because individual psychology itself has become imbued with the social. Thus, social intervention of various kinds now targets the individual. Institutional design is conceived and implemented in terms of individual motivation and capacities. The institutional and corporate features of society are no longer assumed to have an existence independent of how individuals think and behave. It is this radical individualisation of social life that explains the salience of the contract metaphor in contemporary rhetoric. Because how individuals think and behave are the driving forces of how their relationships, connections, interdependencies and institutional life operate, it becomes supremely important that individuals 'contract into' their social engagements and commitments. It is on the extent and quality of the willingness of individuals to assume such obligation that social order depends.

Pairing of individual freedom with social obligation

The radical individualisation of social life that is presupposed in the rhetoric of moral obligation helps us to understand the fourth specification of this rhetoric. Namely, mutual obligation means that individuals understand that they are *obligated to contribute to and to sustain society,* and that they cannot expect society to contribute to and to sustain them without their assuming this reciprocal obligation. As Etzioni (1995:19), deploying a communitarian rhetoric of mutual obligation, puts it: 'At the heart of the communitarian understanding of social justice is the idea of reciprocity: each member of the community owes something to all the rest, and the community owes something to each of its members.'

One of the most difficult features of the rhetoric of mutual obligation for traditional social democrats is that the reciprocity (or mutuality) involved in the obligation seems always to emphasise to what it is that individuals are expected to do for society, not the other way around. Or, to refer to arenas where government is already positioned as the provider of funds or income to individuals or groups, the contractual specification and sanctions of what is owed in this relationship seem to be directed at what these individuals or groups do, not to the adequacy of the level or nature of support provided by the government.

This is not an entirely accurate perception of how the rhetoric of mutual obligation works. The specification of obligation on the government side is made in terms of how the publicly-funded service in question is provided to individuals. That is, on the government side, the specification of obligation is made at the level of service provision. Thus there is an elaborated set of bureaucratic, professional and technical discourses that bear on the conduct of the agencies to which government contracts responsibility for delivering the service. If the implementation of the government's side of mutual obligation is specified in terms of service provision, it is because policy, as Mead (1997a: 21) proposes, has become 'administrative' – see also Bardach (1997), who makes the same point in a way that resonates with new public management discourse. Because social policy now works through individuals, its method of implementation must be one of individualised service delivery. Social policy is dependent more than ever before on how it is implemented by those responsible for the direction, monitoring and supervision of the behaviour of these individuals. 'Case management' becomes the inevitable term for government-delegated management of the individual to direct service deliverers. Just as there is a strong tension between the normalisation and individualisation of social action, there is a parallel tension in service delivery between 'managing cases' and responding to individuals.

The societal subject of this relationship of mutual or reciprocal obligation with the individual remains shadowy. If the Keynesian welfare state assumed a hierarchical, centralised presence in people's lives, there is, in this case, no comparable corporate presence. The state is 'hollowed out' because, first, the social becomes immanent in individual psychology, and thus individualised, and second, the state's presence as government becomes a rather indistinct one, at least from the standpoint of the individuals whose welfare is at stake. For these individuals, government no longer appears in the form of a standardised, one-size-fits-all bureaucratic approach. Instead, individuals become 'customers' for whom government policy is mediated by agents who adopt a flexible, customised approach toward them.[4] The client will be more aware of a case manager's presence in the governance of his/her individual case than s/he will be of the larger role of government in framing this policy domain.

If government makes individuality possible by forming and developing the capacities to be an individual (see Yeatman 1997), the presence of government is delegated to a host of agents of governance. These include schools, families, and non-government welfare agencies. It is for these reasons that 'the community' is invented to represent this now nebulous sociality that makes individuality possible.[5] Individuals are exhorted by the advocates of 'the community' to be aware of what it is that they owe to all the other individuals taken together to constitute this community. The exhortation is all the more urgent now that the social is seen to depend on who individuals think themselves to be – indeed, specifically on whether their individualism is healthily or unhealthily narcissistic.

Social contribution to participation in a market economy

The fifth specification of mutual obligation rhetoric resides in the association of the kind of individuality that can assume mutual obligation – that is, an individuality which is socially connected with and socially responsible to *market participation*. Responsible individuality on this approach depends on active participation in the market economy – and specifically, on earning sufficient to achieve a base-line of economic independence. Increasingly, governments are suggesting they are prepared to redesign social policy so as to provide income support that tops up low-wage earning activity rather than to continue a social security-tax regime that makes dependence on public income support more attractive than low-wage earning. The emphasis on self-reliance is the feature of the discourse of mutual obligation that marks its continuity with the regularly recurring and traditional populist-capitalist themes of individualistic self-help and self-improvement (see Lasch 1995).

A paternalist contractualism?

The most evaluated and obvious instance of the contractual nature of mutual obligation is what American public policy calls 'welfare-to-work', or the requirement that individuals who are on welfare move into jobs. In the American context, welfare is different from social security. Social security is a social insurance system where people in employment contribute to a public fund to insure themselves against the risks of unemployment, sickness, and retirement. Welfare refers primarily to what used to be called Aid for Families with Dependent Children (ADFC), most of which are headed by non-working single mothers, of whom many are Afro-American (see endnote 2).

Having already accepted in the early 1960s a general policy of equal opportunity regardless of both gender and race, in 1967 the US Congress adopted a Work Incentive program. According to Mead (1997b: 43): 'WIN had authority to require welfare mothers, if employable, to participate in work or training or face a sanction, a reduction in their grants.' The direction since then has been progressively to tighten this requirement and to limit the discretion of state welfare departments in applying it. In 1996, Congress changed AFDC to Temporary Assistance to Needy Families (TANF) and, also in 1996, adopted the Personal Responsibility and Work Opportunity Reconciliation Act which 'requires adult recipients to work within two years of accepting aid, and demands that states move half of them into work activities by 2002' (Mead 1997b: 45).

Thus in the United States, at this time, participation in a work program is mandatory for welfare recipients, although it is accepted that a small percentage of them will be unemployable, and the 1996 Act permits states to exempt one-fifth of their case load from the five-year limit to families staying on the welfare rolls (Mead 1997b: 45).

Mead argues that compulsory participation is more effective than voluntary programs, and that the evaluation data support this argument. It seems a contradiction in terms to compel people to be self-reliant, to force them to be free, and critics of the policy argue that for participation in employment to become an effective means of self-reliance and active citizenship, it needs to be voluntary. Mead's response is that a voluntary policy ends up putting government resources behind individuals who are already self-motivated to find employment, and leaves the poorest and most vulnerable individuals effectively excluded.

Leaving this argument aside for the moment, it is important to understand that paternalism of this kind does not seem to rule out making employment services contractual. Indeed, to the extent that they are individualised (that is, customised to the wants and circumstance of the individual participant), this is required. As I understand the evaluation data presented by Mead (1997b) and Bardach (1997) on the

American work programs, the more effective services are those that involve persistent, personalised contact and intense interaction between staff and clients (Mead 1997b: 62).[6]

It is in the contractual requirement that the job seeker be active in efforts to become effectively self-reliant that the peculiar individualism of moral obligation resides. Considerable effort can be put into contractual protocols of negotiated agreements between service providers and individual job seekers. These protocols engage clients in the evaluation of what it is they need to do to become employable, in the identification of their hopes and aspirations for work futures, and in the specification of the next steps that they need to make in order to move towards employability.

The contractual features of such protocols are three-fold in nature. The first contractual feature is the direct engagement and participation of the individual in making decisions about and planning for his/her future. In this particular and limited sense, he or she gets both choice and voice. To be sure, the nature of this contract is directive: the individual client is directed to be a self-reliant individual, but this cannot occur without the individual being actively engaged in this process of learning to be an individual. It is for this reason that Bardach (1997: 260-261) distinguishes between the acceptable paternalism of the case manager's direction to the individual client to get a job, and an 'inappropriate' paternalism where the case manager substitutes 'their own wisdom and sophistication for the client's.' Citing evidence from one of the most successful Californian JOBS program agencies, Bardach (1997: 260-261) comments: 'The best line workers said the . . . director of staff development and training were not rescuers but pragmatic counsellors . . . Another worker in Riverside said, "Yes, they do face these barriers, and they can be hard. I am sympathetic, but I do not propose solutions. At least not right away. I say, Yes, you are right, that's a real problem, I can see that. How do you think you might solve it?"'

The second contractual feature follows from the first. The service provider's guidance and direction have to be offered so that, as far as possible, they work with, rather than against, the client's voice and choice. A service provider will be likely to offer direct feedback on whether an individual's aspirations are realistic or not (see Bardach 1997: 256), but 'because nothing motivates people so much as their own goals, even in the most paternalist of programs, effective case managers respect those goals as much as possible, as long as the goals involve moving the recipient toward eventual employment' (Bardach 1997: 255). The second contractual feature can be summed up in the requirements of the service delivery relationship that it be dialogical in orientation, and that, as far as is possible, decision outcomes reflect a negotiated agreement between the case manager and individual client.

The third contractual feature resides in the explicitness of the transaction between service provider and client. Each is drawn into a process whereby expectations, goals, decisions, processes and outcomes are made explicit. Mead (1997b: 58) emphasises the critical importance of welfare employment agency staff making their expectations of clients crystal clear: 'The effect of making expectations clear was not to repel the clients but to involve and motivate them.' Explicitness of this kind provides a framework for the relationship on which both parties can rely.[7] Such explicitness, also, cannot exist without being accorded symbolic expression, and thus not only entering into, but also underwriting the dialogical nature of the interaction between the service provider and client. Finally, with such explicitness the reciprocity of the exchange is defined. Without such explicitness, neither party could be aware of when or if reciprocity is breached by the other.

The contractual features of this service-delivery relationship, to the extent that they exist, are real even though they are contained within a hierarchical, disciplinary relationship. There is some evidence (Bardach 1997) that when they are practised in an ethos of provider commitment to their importance, they lead to individual clients becoming more self-confident and effective in seeking employment. It is no argument against these contractual features to point out that service providers have the power of using the sanction of taking away their benefit if clients are deemed to have broken their side of the agreement. To be sure, this is a peculiar kind of contract. It is a contract not between equals, as is presupposed in classical market exchange contracts, but a contract between unequals where the function of this inequality is to provide a paternalistic direction to the individual, who is thus positioned as the client of the more powerful party to the contract.

In the past, paternalistic relationships of service provision were not contractual in nature except to the degree that a client could exercise rights of choice and exit in buying or not buying the service in question. Client right of this kind did not enter into the internal substance of the relationship which was conducted in terms of an old-fashioned paternalism where the professional knew what was best for the client and directed him/her accordingly. When a paternalistic relationship of service provision is contractualised, it means that the individual client is invited to participate actively in how this service provision operates. In this way, paternalistic service provision is individualised.

It would not be the first time paternalism has been harnessed to work on behalf of individualisation. Learning and assessment contracts offer further examples of a paternalist contractualism. Contemporary parenting practice also uses contractualist methods of the kind described above. In these contexts, paternalism is to function on behalf of the development of an individual's capacities for self-reliance and autonomy.

In historical context, this is a distinctively modern type of paternalism. Historically, paternalism denoted both given and permanent relationships of dependency for those types of person who were for reasons of sex, race, or social station, deemed incapable of contractual freedom. John Stuart Mill (cited in Lown 1990: 96) distilled the nature of this type of paternalism: 'The lot of the poor, in all things which affect them collectively, should be regulated for them, not by them. They should not be required or encouraged to think for themselves, or give to their own reflection or forecast an influential voice in their own destiny. It is the duty of the higher classes to think for them . . . The relation between rich and poor should be . . . affectionate tutelage on the one side, respectful and grateful deference on the other.'

Reconciling paternalism with individualisation?

What kind of paternalism can it be, then, that can foster individualisation? And how can paternalism be reconciled with contract? These are two versions of the same question.

Goodin (1995) suggests an answer to this question in his carefully considered defence of paternalism as a means of securing the interest of individuals, even if this runs counter to their freedom to choose. The kinds of examples he has in mind are interventions on behalf of an individual's interest where their right to choose leads them to engage in self-destructive behaviour in instances where the decision may either be seriously detrimental to their life prospects, or irreversible. Examples might be smoking, leaving school early without any marketable skills or credentials, or engaging in what is called 'problem gambling'.[8]

According to Goodin, paternalism – in this case making decisions for the individual – is warranted only in such circumstances of high stakes and where it can be supposed that the individual either weakly agrees with this restraint on their choice, or will agree with it later. Essentially, the rationale for such paternalistic intervention is the individual's own interest as evaluated by authoritative others where it is assumed that the individual either currently knows this to be his/her interest, or realises it was so later. As Goodin (1995: 125) puts it: 'That is to say, public officials are engaged in evaluating your surface preferences ["choices"], judging them according to some standard of your deeper preferences.'

In the employment service setting, the argument made by Mead (1997a, b) and Bardach (1997) is similar. Most welfare recipients want to work, this is their deeper preference. But their lack of positive work experience, together with the non-work-oriented structuring of their everyday existence, mean that they find it hard to act on their 'deeper preference'. Mead (1997b: 57) writes: 'Why do requirements cause recipients to participate and work when simply offering them the chance usually does not? Most staff of welfare employment programs I have interviewed say that participation in a work program must be mandated to get recipients' attention. Most adults on welfare would in principle like to work, but they are preoccupied with day-to-day survival. Few will make the effort to organise themselves for regular activity outside the home unless it is required. Starting to work or look for a job must also be enforced, many staff members say, because recipients are often reluctant to seek work on their own. They may want to work, but they have usually failed to find or keep jobs before, especially good jobs, and they fear to try again. Many prefer education and training because it is less threatening. It postpones the day when they must reckon with the labour market. Meanwhile, remaining on welfare is secure.'

Both Mead and Bardach make it clear that paternalism of this kind goes along with 'high expectations' of clients which are sustained by means of a close and constant monitoring, as well as Mead's (1997b: 62) 'personalised attention' to them. 'Contact! . . . once a week, twice a week, there's no such thing as too often', said one Riverside supervisor, 'it reminds them that you care and that you're watching' (Bardach 1997: 269).

The combination of case manager direction, care, and monitoring with the active engagement of clients in their own 'individualised' program of employment activity is not a peculiar one. It is often to be found in contemporary classroom teaching, and it also characterises the early stages of postgraduate supervision relationships. Empirically, then, the harnessing of paternalism to contract in order to foster the individualisation of clients is not an uncommon phenomenon.

Mutual obligation evaluated

Mutual obligation in welfare policy is a defensible approach only if its stated assumptions are true. These are: (a) most welfare clients want to work and to be self reliant, and should be assisted in this; (b) employment is the best antidote to poverty; and (c) their children will do better on all social indicators if their parents work and are self-reliant.

Recalling that most welfare clients in the American context are mothers, it is important to appreciate the complexity of their situation. There is a good deal of empirical evidence collected by social scientists over the last fifty years that adult women want to work, but there is also considerable evidence that they want to *combine* their parenting responsibilities with work in ways that permit them to fulfil both of these obligations.

As policy makers, employers and social scientists know, this is why so many women when they are mothers of young children make themselves available for part-time as distinct from full-time work. Even were professional child care services to be cheaply available, a proposition that is increasingly evident as a contradiction in terms, it is not obvious that long day care for five days a week is the best option for infants and young children even though it permits their mothers to work full-time. Thus, a policy that forces welfare mothers to work full-time is not necessarily a wise policy from the standpoint of their interest as mothers and the interest of their children.

In this context, the evaluation of American welfare reform since 1996 by Jencks and Swingle is apposite: 'Strictly economic considerations aside, two facts stand out. First, almost all mothers who are working tell interviewers that they prefer work to welfare. Second, many working mothers report problems finding satisfactory child care. There is a lot of anecdotal evidence that young children are being left alone for long periods. These reports suggest that welfare reform could end up helping parents [as self-reliant individuals, but not in their parenting role] but hurting their children. Because we have no reliable system for monitoring children's wellbeing, we will probably never know how welfare reform affected them' (Jencks and Swingle: 2000: 40, interpolation added).

OECD policy papers talk up the importance of government support for flexible and equitable combinations of market participation (paid employment) and different forms of social participation (parenting, education, volunteer work, etc.) in ways that do not impoverish individuals when their market participation drops or ceases. However, governments in the Anglo democracies still pursue policies that make full-time labour market participation the norm for social adulthood and effective economic self-reliance.

This point should make us aware that public income support does not necessarily have to promote dependency. Public income support can be designed in ways which both foster and support different combinations of economic and social participation (see as an example the Interim Report of the Reference Group on Welfare Reform 2000, discussed by Peter Dawkins in chapter 11), but this would require a rethinking of what it means to be a self-reliant individual.

What self-reliance might mean for individuals who make active but non-market contributions to care and to community and/or civil development (anything ranging from neighbourhood building to the development of voluntary associations that make a social contribution of some kind) needs to be thought through. Tacit assumptions about what kinds of social contribution are appropriate for adults at different stages of the life cycle need to be made explicit, and their rationale considered, before there can be a well-considered approach to mutual obligation for all adults.

Finally, let us return to what kind of contract a policy of mutual obligation may be. What I earlier termed the axiom of populist commonsense – namely that individuals should contribute to society in return for society's contribution to them – is, unless qualified, an old and illiberal idea. It is based in what Weber (1968) calls patrimonial authority, a type of authority structured by the exchange of a master's or ruler's protection and support of his dependents in exchange for their obedience.

As I have shown, mutual obligation is intended to work on behalf of individual self-reliance and against the perpetuation of dependency. In this way, mutual obligation is decidedly not a re-invocation of patrimonial authority, and, in fact, is directed toward the contestation of patrimonial authority. Self-reliance is a value that makes sense only to the extent it is tied to an individual's freedom to be his/her own individual. To this extent, mutual obligation follows the logic of the social contract. Government has the authority to compel individuals to do certain things only as long as two conditions are operative. The first of these is that government is acting on behalf of the interest of all – understood as the public interest – and not on behalf of any particular or private interests. The second condition is that whatever the individual is compelled to do does in fact advance his or her freedom.

In this connection, we must ask whether being compelled to enter employment on the terms of today's labour market necessarily advances individual freedom. This is a large topic that cannot be addressed here. Suffice to say that employment will not advance individual freedom if (a) wages for fulltime work are so low they cannot permit individuals to move out of poverty, and (b) employees are subjected to a patrimonial type of employer authority at work.

Notes

1. This chapter is a substantially revised version of 'Mutual obligation: What kind of contract is this?' in S. Shaver and P. Saunders (eds) *Social Policy for the 21st Century: Justice and Responsibility. Proceedings of the National Social Policy Conference*, Sydney, 21-23 July 1999, Social Policy Research Centre, University of New South Wales, 1999.

2. Growing concern in both Australian and United States jurisdictions has been directed at increasing numbers of sole, mostly female, parents dependent on public income support, and both jurisdictions have adopted a policy designed to create incentives for these women to re-enter the labour market. In the United States, where 36 per cent of 'welfare mothers' are African-American and 20 per cent Hispanic, the approach has been one of compulsion, but in Australia the approach has been one of facilitation of voluntary re-entry for women with children under the age of sixteen. Across all of these national jurisdictions, however, the private dependency of wives for income support on husbands continues to remain unproblematic, and is likely to attract tax privileges for the husband's earnings.

3. In the American case, the new paternalists argue that it was the increased rate of dependency of welfare mothers that provoked 'policies to promote employment' (Mead 1997b: 42). Mead (1997b: 42-43) comments: 'Thus policies to promote employment were inevitable. They might have taken many forms. Congress first enacted welfare work programs in the early 1960s. These programs were voluntary, offering to help welfare mothers to work without requiring them to do so. But few welfare mothers participated or took jobs on their own. Accordingly, later programs applied increasing pressure to require participation and work.'

4. In Australia, these agents are not just the case managers delivering intensive assistance types of employment services but also the direct

service staff of Centrelink who are now expected to offer one-to-one customer service, and to broker the range of services Centrelink offers to fit the individual case. Centrelink is the one-stop-shop government agency responsible for the assessment and delivery of the various types of public income support.

5. To be sure, communitarians such as Etzioni (1995) and Bellah (1995) revert to Durkheimian formulations of the social as something that is both transcendent to and independent of the individuals whose well-being it makes possible. Thus Bellah (1995: 49) declares against the 'contractualist' and expressivist traditions of radical American individualism: 'What both types avoid is the notion that there is any objective normative order governing the relationship, any transcendent loyalty above the wishes of the individuals involved, any community that is really there independent of the wills that compose it.' However, this reversion to a corporatist conception of the social is an exercise in nostalgia which is declared in the use of nineteenth-century concepts of voluntary association, civic virtue, and the family to give substance to the idea of community.

6. Effective programs, according to Mead (1997b: 61-62): 'use case managers to resist the tendency of clients to avoid programs or withdraw from them. When recipients assigned to work programs fail to show for orientation or drop out after entering, case managers pursue them to find out what their problem is . . . In leading programs this follow-up is relentless. Case managers help overcome obstacles such as breakdown of services or a family crisis, but they also levy expectations, pointing to consequences if expectations are not met. In strong programs they struggle persistently to get even troubled recipients into the program and keep them there. At its best, like good parenting, case management combines help and hassle.'

7. Mead (1997b: 63) states that mainly, case management is rule enforcement, and argues (1997b: 62) that the discretionary features of case management are constrained by this rule-oriented contractualist approach: 'Observers might fear that case management could be personal in an invidious sense, that caseworkers might decide client obligations in the arbitrary way that was common before the welfare rights era began in the 1960s. They might demand on their own authority that clients change their lives – for instance, by avoiding men – if they are to get aid. In today's work programs, however, discretion is limited by program policies, which are much more explicit and detailed than they were forty years ago. Congress or state legislatures decide which groups of recipients have to do what.'

8. The example of problem gambling is a good one according to the Australian Productivity Commission's Report on Gambling just released (Allard and Murphy 1999: 1). While four out of five Australians report that they gamble,'75 per cent, including most of those who bet once a week, regard it as doing more harm than good . . . and more than 90 per cent say they do not want more gaming.'

Chapter 9

A sorry tale: welfare against the family[1]

Lucy Sullivan

The English-speaking countries are engaged in a shared alter-cation concerning the need to curb welfare spending and are reassessing the belief that government provision is the best way of providing people with economic security. The United States has led the way in asserting and delineating the problem. The liberalisation and growth of Aid for Families with Dependent Children (incorporating the equivalent of Australia's Sole Parent Pension) three decades ago has been identified by Charles Murray (1994) as a key element in the creation of a new American 'underclass' of social and moral incompetents. The obligation-free provision of income for mothers and children meant that women no longer needed to take care to secure husbands to support them in the care of their children, and men no longer felt obliged to provide for the economic needs of their offspring. The fatherless families which resulted raised children, particularly boys, who exhibited high rates of criminality, promiscuity and unemployment.

The solution proposed, and to some extent implemented, has been on the face of it straightforward and to the point: abolish the hand-outs that caused the problem; force fathers, where identifiable, to pay for, if not live with, their families; and oblige mothers without husbands to go to work to support themselves and their children. The state of Wisconsin has implemented these reforms most patently and with apparent success. Mothers are off the welfare rolls, but it remains to be seen whether men will return to the family and start civilising their sons.

But if the social or moral aspect of the problem has been solved, the economic one, which is probably of more concern to Britain and Australia, perhaps has not. It is very expensive getting women back to work, for the state must organise and subsidise both employment and child care, which can be just as costly as providing income directly.

The conception that loss of 'obligation' and of 'responsibility' is central to the welfare problem has been picked up by Prime Ministers Howard and Blair, of Australia and Britain respectively, but in these countries, each with a century's experience of a many-stranded Social Security system, the terms obligation and responsibility have taken on a rather different complexion. Whereas in the United States the obligation is to take the responsibility to provide for oneself, in Australia and Britain it is, rather, the obligation to behave responsibly in exchange for the provision of welfare, and to apply genuine effort to moving out of dependency by such means as persistent job applications and working for the dole. In comparison with Wisconsin, the requirements here are trivial – a few hours on an environmental project or attending instruction in literacy and a dozen or so job applications a month. To enforce more would merely add to the expense of a system whose chief tangible fault at present *is* its expense.

Reform of the welfare system in Australia, as in Britain, is not a relatively simple matter of rolling back a single, comparatively recent and obviously disastrous innovation, as it is in the United States. 'Welfare' here is a parasitic growth on a deeply rooted and fundamentally indigenous plant, and it is the unacknowledged recognition of this fact that has prevented any real espousal of the American treatment. Our only immediately achievable option in Australia is to excise the growth, not uproot the plant. In historical terms, this means a return to *social security* and the eschewing of *welfare*.

Self-reliance and the Australian welfare system

No Australian political party could hope, in the foreseeable future, to be elected to government on a platform of abolishing our Age Pension, our Disability Pension, our Widows Pension and our Unemployment Benefit. They have been the prized backdrop to our sense of nationhood for the lifetime and beyond of almost all Australians. The Liberal/National

Coalition failed to gain office, despite a general antipathy to the policies of the Labor government in power, for as long as it threatened to severely curtail our system of pensions and benefits. When Howard finally announced, dramatically at the Australian Council of Social Services Annual Conference of 1996, that the Coalition would leave Australia's Social Security system intact, his party was swept to power with a landslide victory.

The attachment of the Australian electorate to its social security heritage was interestingly revealed in a survey of voters' opinions taken before the 1987 Federal election (McAllister 1991). It found that both Labor and Coalition voters favoured the Coalition position on almost every issue, from industrial relations to multiculturalism to the environment. Only on social security (but not welfare) was the Labor position favoured, and it was favoured by voters from both sides of politics. Yet two more elections passed before the Coalition came to government. Its disapproved position on social security appears to have been sufficient to outweigh its advantage on all other issues. Clearly, any planned welfare reform must contrive not to offend this belief system.

What is the difference between social security and welfare in the Australian mind? In the above survey they were differentiated in the approval given to the item, 'spend more to reduce poverty', but at the same time a majority agreement with the apparently contradictory, 'too many rely on government hand-outs' and 'reduce taxes, not spend more on social security'. This is no transient phenomenon. A large survey taken in the late 1970s (Laydon 1979) showed a strong commitment to institutions of social security such as pensions and superannuation by *both* union and business respondents. It also found that *neither* group supported such provisions as being there for the asking, but rather wished them to be integrated with participation in employment. The underlying philosophy appeared to be one of maintaining personal responsibility through individual effort, while providing support should the ability to exercise that responsibility fail.

The Australian system of social security has embodied this philosophy – of taking independence as far as it will go but providing for mishap – in a manner which distinguishes it from its equivalent in Britain and other western European countries. The Old Age (now Age) and the Invalid (now Disability) Pensions, introduced in 1909 and 1910 respectively, were not attempts to compulsorily organise the whole population into prudential saving. It was assumed that the majority of the population would provide for their own

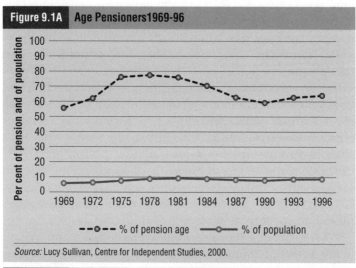

Figure 9.1A Age Pensioners1969-96

Source: Lucy Sullivan, Centre for Independent Studies, 2000.

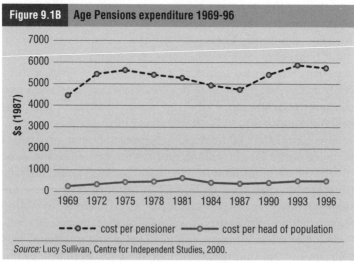

Figure 9.1B Age Pensions expenditure 1969-96

Source: Lucy Sullivan, Centre for Independent Studies, 2000.

retirement via saving or insurance, at a level suited to their condition in life. Only those whose standard of living made such provision difficult were expected to access the Old Age Pension, and it was set at a level which made it unacceptable to those whose standard of living was generally above a minimum sufficient for frugal existence. It has always been a flat-rate pension, available to all who have not made better provision for themselves. Government-sponsored support for private superannuation via the introduction of tax exemptions in the 1950s continued this approach, and even the compulsory partial superannuation of the 1990s has not entirely dismantled it.

The Old Age Pension was conceived as an 'earned right'. The major eligibility requirement (other than lack of income) was initially twenty-five years residence in Australia, but eligibility could be lost for criminal or socially irresponsible behaviour (such as drunkenness or desertion). Figures 9.1A and 9.1B show recipience and cost of the Age Pension from 1969 to 1996. Uptake of the Pension among those eligible was somewhat higher at the end of the period, rising from 56 per cent in 1969 to 64 per cent in 1996, while the percentage of the population receiving the Pension rose from 6 per cent to 9 per cent.

The large rise in recipience which occurred between 1972 and 1975 is accounted for by the temporary withdrawal of the means test for persons aged over seventy, which was later reversed. The average value of the Pension per recipient rose by 29 per cent over the total period, while the average cost per head of population doubled. While these rises are substantial, they do not represent a major change in the conception and functioning of the Age Pension, which in essence remains well-accepted by the community.

The Australian Old Age Pension system made it impossible for a respectable and long-standing member of the community to be without income in old age, while nevertheless supporting the principle that individuals should provide for themselves wherever possible. This approach was replicated for Invalid (now Disability) Pensions in 1910, and for Widows Pensions and Unemployment Benefits when they arrived half way through the century.

Figure 9.2A shows Disability Pensions as a percentage of the population from 1969 to 1996. The number of claimants remained fairly low until the late 1980s, but has escalated in the 1990s, for reasons which will be discussed later. The cost per pensioner, following a moderate rise, fell to about 10 per cent lower in 1990 than in 1975, while the cost per head of population rose 30 per cent (Figure 9.2B). In 1996, it was only

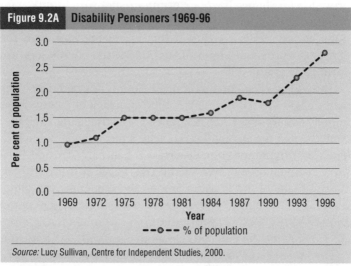

Figure 9.2A Disability Pensioners 1969-96

Source: Lucy Sullivan, Centre for Independent Studies, 2000.

Figure 9.2B Disability Pensions expenditure 1969-96

Source: Lucy Sullivan, Centre for Independent Studies, 2000.

slightly above its highest earlier level of cost per pensioner, but due to the rapid rise in the number of pensioners, the cost per head of population has risen by 80 per cent in just five years.

The distinction between a Pension and a Benefit was considered an important one, the latter applying in circumstances in which temporary need had the potential to develop into long-term malingering. The fear that an Unemployment Benefit would encourage free-riding was partly responsible for that measure arriving so late in the piece. The income it provided was set at a much lower level than the Pensions to emphasise the fact that its role was to provide emergency assistance in a situation which should not last long.

Social security becomes welfare

The introduction in 1973 (under the first Labor government for twenty-two years) of the Supporting Mothers Benefit (which became the Supporting Parent Benefit in 1977, and later the Sole Parent *Pension* when it was combined with the Class A Widows Pension in 1989) opened a major new field for recruitment to social security dependency. It marked a wholesale and conspicuous breach of the 'earned right' tradition of Australian social security, and our re-characterisation as a Welfare State.

The post-war immigration program had produced some weakening of the old eligibility criteria with a reduction in the residence qualification to ten years for the Age Pension, and even less for the Invalid Pension and Widows Pension. But the Supporting Parent Benefit differed in that it was specifically directed at claimants who had no earned right to support and, as unmarried mothers without partners, were disqualified from the Widows Pension under the old requirement (by then becoming dormant) of 'responsible character'. Moreover, it indirectly benefited equally irresponsible males whose behaviour was similar to that of deserting husbands.

At much the same time, and just as critically, a similar breach was made within the Unemployment Benefit system. In its dying days (in 1972) the Liberal/Country Party raised the Unemployment Benefit to a level close to the Age Pension, almost doubling it in lower age brackets. Then, in its first year in office, the new Labor government extended the damage by abolishing entirely the lower rates for unmarried youths aged less than twenty-one. The Unemployment Benefit now available to this age group was more than the weekly earnings of apprentices in some trades.

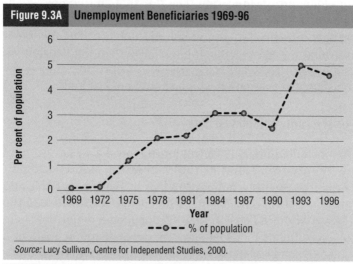

Figure 9.3A Unemployment Beneficiaries 1969-96

Source: Lucy Sullivan, Centre for Independent Studies, 2000.

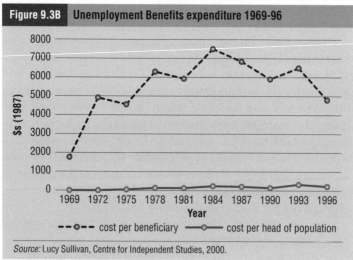

Figure 9.3B Unemployment Benefits expenditure 1969-96

Source: Lucy Sullivan, Centre for Independent Studies, 2000.

Figures 9.3A and 9.3B show the number of Unemployment Beneficiaries per head of population and the cost per beneficiary and per head of population. The increase in recipience which followed hard on the heels of its increase in value is dramatic. Expenditure per beneficiary rose by close to a factor of three between 1969 and 1972, and the number of beneficiaries as a percentage of the population rose by a factor of 14 between 1972 and 1978.

The enticing effect of a liberal Unemployment Benefit can be judged by the dramatic rise in the percentage of the unemployed actually taking the Unemployment Benefit, which rose from 20 per cent in 1972 to 70 per cent in 1975. The generous Benefit offered to the young was particularly important in effecting this change. In 1973, the unemployment rate was 1.8 per cent, with the rate for 15–19 year olds 7.7 per cent and for those aged 35 and over, 0.7 per cent. In 1975, the overall rate was 4.6 per cent, with that for teenagers 15.6 per cent, but for older workers only 2.3 per cent.

The Australian community went into what was well-nigh panic mode at this flouting of their long-term belief system of earned social security for responsible citizens. Their concern was undoubtedly exacerbated by the concurrent appearance of the first significant levels of unemployment in the post-war period, although this latter was at least partially created by making the Unemployment Benefit attractive to the young. In the lead-up to the 1975 Federal election in which the new Labor government unexpectedly lost power, tabloid newspapers and commercial radio ran many, perhaps exaggerated, exposés of young people living in idle luxury on the dole (for example, a front-page photograph showed a group of young people supposedly on Unemployment Benefit reclining by the private pool of an expensive Gold Coast apartment). Nevertheless, these changes were here to stay and only minor reforms of the worst opportunities for abuse were imposed by the returned Liberal government.

In 1976, the Supporting Parent Benefit found a new role which soon overshadowed its initial one in cost to the taxpayer, although not its elicitation of public disquiet. It slotted neatly into place to provide for the veritable explosion in numbers of divorced wives and their dependent children which followed the introduction of no-fault divorce under the Family Law Act 1975. Its existence, together with new notions of male and female equality, meant that little effort was made to ensure that fathers continued to support their children after divorce. The Supporting Parent Benefit absolved these deserting fathers.

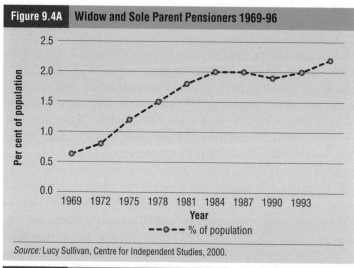

Figure 9.4A Widow and Sole Parent Pensioners 1969-96

Source: Lucy Sullivan, Centre for Independent Studies, 2000.

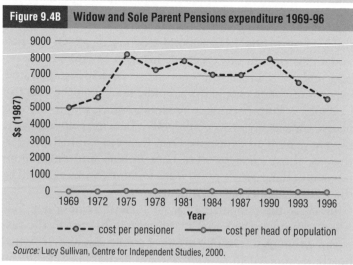

Figure 9.4B Widow and Sole Parent Pensions expenditure 1969-96

Source: Lucy Sullivan, Centre for Independent Studies, 2000.

Figures 9.4A and 9.4B provide beneficiary/pension and expenditure data from 1969 to 1996 for all widows, with and without children (classes 'A' and 'B', respectively), and single, divorced and separated parents (Supporting and Sole parents), as these identities were variously separated, combined and renamed over the years. The large rate of rise produced by the introduction of the Supporting Parent Benefit decelerated only slightly before the mid-1980s, flattened, but took off again in the 1990s.

The cost per recipient rose markedly between 1972 and 1975 as the proportion of recipients with children rose, then stabilised. The apparent fall in the 1990s is an artefact of changed categories of payment, as will be discussed later. The cost per head of population of supporting women and children with living but non- or inadequately contributing fathers (the major element in the increase) rose 340 per cent between 1972 and 1990.

This situation was not remedied, and then fairly ineffectually, until the introduction in 1988 of the Child Support Scheme, which takes a modest contribution from the minority of fathers earning above a moderately generous threshold. The reasonable concern is, of course, to allow these men to start new families, since most incomes cannot satisfactorily support two households.

Excoriating the intact family

The notable growth in social security spending and welfare dependency which occurred in the first half of the 1970s, largely stabilised in the 1980s, although the benefits showed more continued growth than did the pensions. In that more of the population had become dependent, the burden fell the more heavily on those who remained productive. The Hawke Labor government of 1983 was concerned to contain the costs of social security and welfare, which had necessitated large rises in tax rates and were seen to be affecting the stability of the economy.

However, the New Left welfare lobby would not brook incursions into the achieved values of pensions and benefits, which were largely maintained during a period of high inflation. Beyond this, there was pressure to remove the pension/Benefit distinction both conceptually and as regards rates of payment. While this was not achieved for the Unemployment Benefit (which remains slightly lower than the Age and Disability Pensions, and is now called an Allowance but still not a Pension), the distinction between widows and other lone parents was finally removed in 1989. The Sole Parent Benefit was converted into the Sole Parent Pension and Class 'A' widows (with dependent children) were included under the same category, thus eliminating any acknowledgment of an 'earned right' distinction between the unmarried mother and the widow.

As the value of pensions and benefits was not to be allowed to fall, savings had to be made somewhere, and this was achieved at the expense of the conventional family.

Maintenance of family income at a level adequate to the living costs of a couple with dependent children had remained largely external to the social security system throughout the century. In keeping with the dominant Australian approach to financial viability, the choice had been to establish conditions which allowed the family to provide for itself. For the first half of the century this was achieved by the imposition of a basic wage for adult men sufficient to support a couple and three children in 'modest comfort'.

From 1941, this was topped up with Child Endowment, a universal (no income ceiling) payment per child of quite generous proportions in relation to the basic wage of the period. In the 1950s the preferred method was again non-welfare in character, and consisted of generous tax deductions and rebates based on the number of dependents reliant on an income and recognising expenditure on health, housing and education. These measures largely protected an average family on an average wage from payment of any taxation at all.

The first steps towards dismantling the tax exemption approach to protecting family income were taken in 1976 under the Fraser Coalition government. The tax rebates for dependent children were abolished and an upgraded Family Allowance replaced the by then vestigial Child

Endowment. This process was completed in the early 1980s, when the last specifically child-related tax exemptions were withdrawn. The Family Allowance was a return to a flat rate of assistance per child instead of the higher returns at higher income levels which accrued under the tax deduction system, and was justified in terms of equity. But it also meant much less in the total value of income protection for families.

Over the next half decade the Family Allowance was allowed to fall drastically in value with inflation. In the absence of tax rebates and deductions for families, horizontal equity as between family members and single earners without dependents at similar income levels all but disappeared. As a result, middle and higher income families found themselves in straitened circumstances, and lower income families were plunged into genuine poverty. Child poverty suddenly became an issue, and the Labor government, whose policies had contributed to its persistence and spread, announced its commitment to a program for its elimination by 1990.

Revenue gains and budget savings at the expense of families began with this abandonment of horizontal equity as a universal measure of family income protection. With an enhanced social security orientation to the poverty line, maintaining family income was re-defined as a welfare matter, and increases in Family Allowances were now directed exclusively towards the lowest family incomes. The terminology has changed several times over the years, but basically the original Family Allowance has remained minimal (with a ceiling for eligibility at about double male full-time average weekly earnings), while additional Family Payments are much more generous, but are selective (targeted, with very modest income ceilings). Having reduced many families to poverty by over-taxing them, the government then uses welfare payments to raise their incomes to a standard provided by the Unemployment Benefit and Sole Parent Pension for a family of the same composition.

But because Family Payments are tapered as income rises, higher levels of earnings do not immediately result in incomes above the Unemployment Benefit and Sole Parent Pension level. Any gains are largely lost by a commensurate reduction in the Family Payments received. Families across a substantial range of earnings are trapped at around the value of the family Unemployment Benefit income, and any efforts to improve their position by working extra hours (including maternal employment) are largely defeated by further loss of benefits as earned income rises.

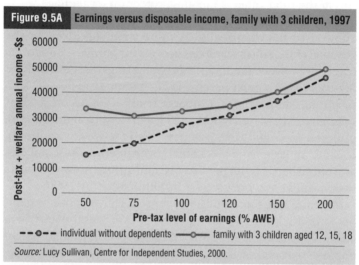

Figure 9.5A Earnings versus disposable income, family with 3 children, 1997

- - ○ - - individual without dependents ——○—— family with 3 children aged 12, 15, 18

Source: Lucy Sullivan, Centre for Independent Studies, 2000.

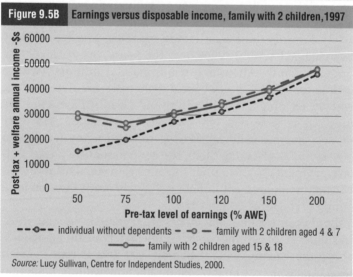

Figure 9.5B Earnings versus disposable income, family with 2 children,1997

- - ○ - - individual without dependents - -○ - family with 2 children aged 4 & 7
——○—— family with 2 children aged 15 & 18

Source: Lucy Sullivan, Centre for Independent Studies, 2000.

Figure 9.5A shows the level of final (post-tax +welfare) income for a family with three children aged 12, 15 and 18 at various levels of initial earnings expressed as a percentage of 1997 Average Weekly Earnings. It can be seen that final income remains virtually unchanged between 50 per cent and 120 per cent Average Weekly Earnings – that is, between initial earnings of about $18,000 (probably part-time work) and about $43,000. A family on full Unemployment Benefits receives a somewhat lower income of about $27,000, but also has access to indirect benefits of considerable value not available to families with similar earned incomes, besides being spared the costs of employment. With fewer dependents, families can, with rising earnings, exceed the welfare level of income for their family size slightly sooner. A family with two children, pre-school or older, can begin to improve its position as earnings pass Average Weekly Earnings (Figure 9.5B), and with a single child there is an improvement above 75 per cent Average Weekly Earnings (Figure 9.5C).

This system was introduced in the middle period of the 1980s, and despite minor efforts at reinstatement of universal family tax exemptions since 1996 (subsequently reabsorbed into the Family Allowances system), it is still in place. All

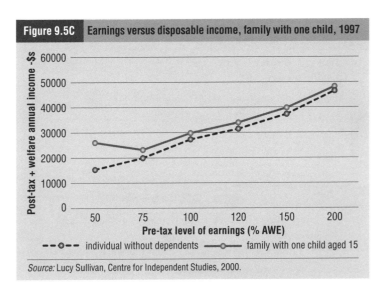

Figure 9.5C — Earnings versus disposable income, family with one child, 1997

y-axis: Post-tax + welfare annual income -$s

x-axis: Pre-tax level of earnings (% AWE)

– – ○ – – individual without dependents   —○— family with one child aged 15

Source: Lucy Sullivan, Centre for Independent Studies, 2000.

three graphs show the loss of horizontal equity, the small difference between final income for a family earner with several dependents and an individual earner with none at Average Weekly Earnings and above. Yet welfare planning continues to treat families on $45,000 or $50,000, regardless of number and age of children, as wealthy, as if on a par with individuals without dependents on these incomes. The

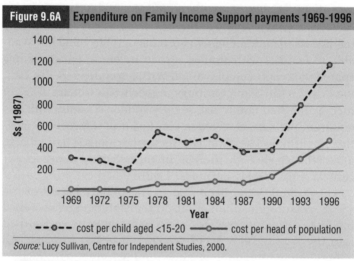

Figure 9.6A Expenditure on Family Income Support payments 1969-1996

Source: Lucy Sullivan, Centre for Independent Studies, 2000.

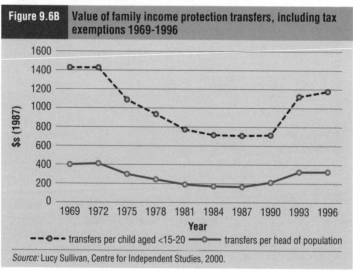

Figure 9.6B Value of family income protection transfers, including tax exemptions 1969-1996

Source: Lucy Sullivan, Centre for Independent Studies, 2000.

situation will not be altered greatly by the GST reforms whose extra family benefits are designed to be largely balanced out by the extra costs families will accrue in the purchase of goods and services.

We have noted the increases in expenditure on Social Security for the elderly, disabled, unemployed and sole parents in the period 1969 to 1996. Figure 9.6A shows budget expenditure on the various forms of family income support – Child Endowment, Family Allowances, Family Payments – as cost per child aged less than fifteen from 1969 to 1987 and aged less than twenty from 1990 to 1996, recognising the large increase in retention in education and therefore in dependency which occurred across the decade of the 1980s. (In 1980, 35 per cent of youths were still in school in Year 12, compared with 76 per cent in 1993.) The graph indicates a moderate rise between 1975 and 1978 (when Family Allowance replaced Child Endowment), and a dramatic increase from 1990 through to 1996.

This, however, is misleading as an indication of the levels of family income protection across the period, as it omits the value to families of tax exemptions in the earlier period, which also were deductions from revenue. The real value of family income protection is shown in Figure 9.6B. Comparison of Figure 9.6B with Figures 9.1B, 9.2B, 9.3B and 9.4B shows that when the real value of tax exemptions is included in the sum of transfers to families, *family income protection is the only category of social security in which the value of expenditure per beneficiary and the cost per head of population was lower in 1996 than in 1969.* Moreover, loss of family income protection has been greater than the graph indicates for, as we shall see later, the apparent rise in the 1990s is a record-keeping, not a real, effect.

Family strategies for income betterment

The growth of social security and welfare spending in the last three decades has fallen heavily on families, which now pay tax at similar rates to those without dependents. High taxation reduces the incomes of earning families to welfare levels, which prompts their transfer to welfare itself, which then results in higher taxes to fund a larger dependent population, which then draws the next level of families down to the welfare level, and so on. This is a situation of implosion.

The almost flat gradient of income for families with three children on 50 per cent to 120 per cent of average weekly earnings, and on 50 per cent to 100 per cent of average weekly earnings for families with two children, means that such families are as well or better off semi-employed or even unemployed. Full Unemployment Benefits can be retained with earnings of about $3,000 per annum for a couple, and the value of indirect benefits (concessions on council rates, electricity, telephone, transport, free car registration and license, payment of rental bond, etc.) can amount to several thousands of dollars per annum in value. Such families are also spared the major costs of earning an income, estimated at $2,000–$3,000 per annum.

A family on average weekly earnings and above can be much better off if the couple ostensibly separate, for the husband's net income scarcely diminishes, and the wife can claim full Sole Parent Pension for herself and the children. For example, a family with three teenage children, even accounting for the additional rent of a separate domicile for the husband, can be $10,000 better off, with a total income of about $42,000 per annum compared with $32,000 if they live together. A family with two young children on 120 per cent of average weekly earnings is also about $10,000 better off 'separated', with a total income of $45,000, compared with $35,000 if they live together.

Family welfare equal in value to earned family incomes has made husbands redundant, for mothers and children can be as well off proportionally without a resident father as with a moderately earning one. In Australia, marriage rates are now much lower for men and women of lower socio-economic status, where men are least likely to be able to offer more income than is provided by Sole Parent Pensions and Family Allowances (Birrell and Rapson 1998).

The withdrawal of family income protection can also be seen as lying behind the fall in the Australian birth rate to well below replacement level, which is beginning to be recognised as cause for concern, not least in regard to funding the welfare of the future. The decision not to have children is understandable when one considers the sacrifice and the relative poverty it now implies for middle and higher income earners.

Suppose the members of a couple without children are earning $43,000 and $36,000 respectively per annum. After tax they have an income of $59,000 to share between them, or $29,000 each. If the couple decide to have a family, their savings, if they have been prudent, will see them over the first few years, but will only last so long. Ten years further into the life cycle, with two children (still not enough on average for population replacement), the husband is earning $55,000 and the wife $18,000 in a part-time job, which, with the care of the children, stretches her resources of time and energy. But in today's welfare discourse, this is a really wealthy family with a total income of $73,000, double average weekly earnings. Their disposable income, shared between four, is $55,000, and this amounts to $18,500 for each partner, if $18,000 is deducted for the costs of the two children (as estimated by Harding and Percival 1999).

Perhaps this sounds reasonable, but a single person with the same disposable income of $18,500 after tax (earnings of about $25,000) would by the same welfare authorities be considered low income. And if the couple have a third, younger child who keeps the mother at home, the family will have a disposable income of $41,000 and the parents only $10,500 each after allocating $20,000 for the expenses of the children.

On the other hand, should they decide to remain childless, ten years on in the life cycle they are earning $55,000 and $43,000 a week, respectively. Their income after tax is $69,000, or $34,500 each, double that available to them if they had two children, and more than three times that if they had three children. The emotional rewards of having children are great, but so, often, are the costs. Given genuine choice, it is not surprising that in the conditions we have established for families today, many of the most talented are choosing against establishing families.

Obfuscation of the new escalation

The sacrifice of intact employed families to welfare growth in other areas is creating the explosion in welfare dependency in the 1990s, seen in Figures 9.3A, 9.4A and 9.5A, and the rising welfare expenditure seen in rising Disability Pensions, Unemployment Benefits and Sole Parent Pensions. Reference back to the various graphs of social security/welfare recipience and expenditure reveals that, after the deceleration of the 1980s, a massive increase in dependency and costs began again in the 1990s. The set of dysfunctional motivations described in the last section was largely in place by the late 1980s and plays a leading role in determining the character of the current welfare crisis.

The fates of the Disability Pension, Unemployment Benefit, Sole Parent Pension and Family Allowances in the 1990s can only be understood, and therefore must be considered, in conjunction and interaction with each other because of the category shifting which has occurred over this period, both as regards recipients and the recording of expenditure. The Age Pension, by contrast, plays little part in this drama, although the rise in the value of the Age Pension between 1969 and 1996 is not inconsiderable and indirect benefits to the whole elderly population have become an increasing cost to the working taxpayer.

The improvement in the economy and the steadying of the divorce rate produced some levelling in Unemployment Benefit, Sole Parent Pension and Disability Pension recipience at the end of the 1980s (in the late 1980s, Sole Parent Pensioners with a youngest child aged sixteen or over were transferred to the Unemployment Benefit). The recession of 1993 was accompanied by rises in all three. With the end of the recession, the Unemployment Benefit rate of recipience fell somewhat but the rates of Disability Pension and Sole Parent Pension recipience continued to rise, suggesting that welfare dependency was to some extent being fuelled by the availability of these pension payments.

It is generally accepted that there has been a shift of long-term unemployment beneficiaries to the Disability Pension in response to the job seeking requirements imposed in the wake of the Social Security Review of the late 1980s and the attraction of an extra $20 or so a week ($1,000 per annum), compared with the Unemployment Benefit. (In 1999, 25 per cent of people in the pre-retirement years, aged 60–65, were Disability Pensioners.)

The percentage of the population on the Disability Pension rose from 1.8 per cent in 1990 to 2.8 per cent in 1996. The rise has continued to 3.2 per cent in 1999, nearly doubling in the course of a decade. The percentage of the population on the Sole Parent Pension (that is, not including widows without children) rose from 1.5 per cent in 1990 to 1.9 per cent in 1996, and continued to rise to 2.1 per cent in 1999. Despite the fall in the percentage of the population on the Unemployment Benefit between 1993 and 1996, there was a large overall rise from 2.5 per cent in 1990 to 4.6 per cent in 1996. In 1996, Unemployment Beneficiaries numbered 106 per cent of the unemployed – that is, the total number receiving the Unemployment Benefit was greater than the total number of unemployed. This indicates the presence of numbers of Unemployment Beneficiaries topping up their welfare payments with part-time work and perhaps achieving higher incomes than they would receive by working full-time.

The costs per pensioner/beneficiary and per head of population show somewhat different patterns, due to changes in the recording categories for payments on behalf of the dependents of recipients. Between 1990 and 1993, payments for the support of the children of unemployed, disabled and sole parents were recategorised from the Unemployment Benefit, the Disability Pension and the Sole Parent Pension to the Family Allowance system as Additional Family Payments. And between 1993 and 1996 payments for the support of dependent partners with children also were transferred to the Family Payments system (as the Basic + Additional Parenting Payment). This explains the rise in Family Allowances/Payments expenditure across this period and demonstrates the spuriousness of any generalised claims that income support for families was greatly improved under Labor in the first half of the 1990s.

The 10 per cent rise in the cost per Unemployment Beneficiary between 1990 and 1993 occurred despite the transfer of the costs of children of unemployed parents to the Family Payments system. This suggests that there must have been an increase in the percentage of beneficiaries who were men with families and who received a married rate of benefit (as we have seen, a sensible strategy). The changes in accounting also

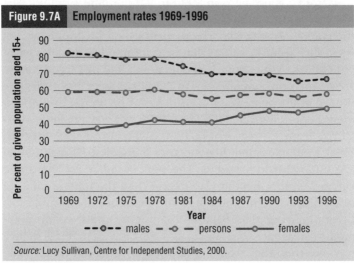

Figure 9.7A Employment rates 1969-1996

--○-- males - ○ - persons ──○── females

Source: Lucy Sullivan, Centre for Independent Studies, 2000.

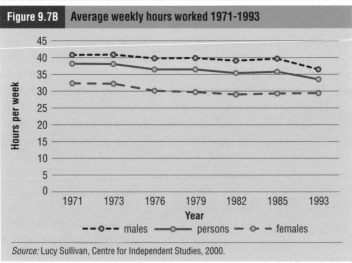

Figure 9.7B Average weekly hours worked 1971-1993

--○-- males ──○── persons - ○ - females

Source: Lucy Sullivan, Centre for Independent Studies, 2000.

explain the modest rise in cost per Unemployment Beneficiary compared with the more than doubling in cost per head of population between 1990 and 1993 (as the transfer of child support to Family Payments neutralised the added cost of an influx of families) and the disproportionate fall in cost (by about 30 per cent) between 1993 and 1996 (as the cost of dependent partners with children was transferred to Parenting Payment).

The cost per Sole Parent Pensioner fell sharply, but the cost of Sole Parent Pensions per head of population only slightly, between 1990 and 1993, again due to the transfer of support costs for children to the Family Payments system together with rising recipience. The continuing fall in cost per pensioner between 1993 and 1996 may reflect the transfer of rent allowances to the Family Payments system in this period. The second change explains the fall in cost per Disability Pensioner between 1993 and 1996, while an increase in single as well as married Disability Pensioners would have maintained a rising cost per head of population.

The role of men in minimising welfare dependency

There have been large changes in the workforce participation of men and women over the period of the parasitic growth of

Figure 9.7C Women in the labour force 1969-1993

Source: Lucy Sullivan, Centre for Independent Studies, 2000.

welfare on the social security system. Figure 9.7A shows changes in the participation rates of men and women from 1969 to 1996. While the percentage of females aged fifteen and over in employment rose from 36 per cent to 49 per cent over the period, the percentage of males fell from 83 per cent to 67 per cent.

Figure 9.8A | **Non-working males 1969-1996**

Source: Lucy Sullivan, Centre for Independent Studies, 2000.

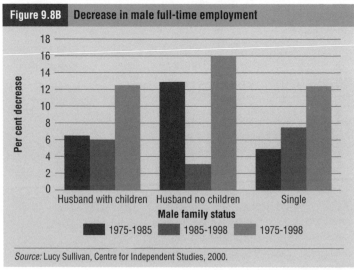

Figure 9.8B | **Decrease in male full-time employment**

Source: Lucy Sullivan, Centre for Independent Studies, 2000.

Interacting with these changes is the fact that more women than men work part-time. The average hours worked by men and women in the period 1971 to 1993 is shown in Figure 9.7B. Average hours worked fell by about four for men and about three for women. The major drop in the average occurred for women between 1973 and 1976 when mothers first joined the workforce in considerable numbers (see Figure 9.7C), and for men between 1985 and 1993, over the period when Family Payments began to be used to raise family incomes, regardless of initial level of earnings, to around the net family income retained on average weekly Earnings. Women's rising employment is not a substitute for men's falling employment, because it results in more incomes which require topping up by welfare.

Figure 9.8A shows the increasing absence of men from employment over the period of growth in welfare dependency, almost doubling from 17 per cent in 1969 to 33 per cent in 1996 as a combination of unemployment and detachment from the labour force. Figure 9.8B shows the percentage fall in male full-time employment from 1975 to 1985 to 1998 in three categories of family status – husband/partner with dependent children, husband/partner with no dependent

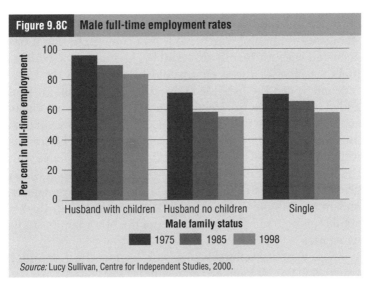

Figure 9.8C Male full-time employment rates

Per cent in full-time employment (y-axis)

Male family status (x-axis): Husband with children, Husband no children, Single

Legend: 1975, 1985, 1998

Source: Lucy Sullivan, Centre for Independent Studies, 2000.

children, and unattached male without dependent children (male sole parents, a very small percentage of the population, are not shown).

Falls in all categories were substantial, in the region of 15 per cent. Male unemployment rose from 3.2 per cent to 8.7 per cent between 1975 and 1984, and this accounts for much of the decrease in full-time male employment across the first time span. But it has stabilised since, and a large further fall in male full-time employment should not have been expected on these grounds.

Among husbands with no children, the major decrease occurred in the earlier period (1975 to 1985), reflecting, as well as unemployment, an epidemic of early retirement, which began in that period among holders of superannuation policies which permitted retirement from the age of fifty-five (and was therefore without immediate social security repercussions): the proportion of 55–64 year old men in employment fell from 85 per cent to 57 per cent between 1969 and 1984, but not greatly thereafter. Among single men with no children, by contrast, the decrease was greater in the later period, and this reflects the increased retention of young men in education which occurred in the early part of that time span.

Among husbands with children the decrease of the first period continued across the second period, despite the stabilising of unemployment. This is of concern in that it has occurred without readily discernible extenuating considerations, as most of these men would be neither in the early retirement nor the extended education stages of life. It is of added significance in that the non-full-time employment of such men is likely to imply social security or welfare support for more than one person – the man's wife and children as well. As Figure 9.8C shows, this is the category of males with the highest attachment to the full-time workforce, so that a given percentage decline represents the loss of more labour, and more independence in population terms, than does a similar percentage change in either of the other family status categories.

These figures graphically illustrate, as does the continuing rise in Sole Parent Pension recipience (Figure 9.4A), what has been argued above – namely, the necessity for protection of earned family incomes as a foundation of the social security system. The result of its abandonment has been to turn the availability of Family Payments into an inducement to under- or unemployment in fathers of families and to the establishment of separate households by mothers and their children. This must be recognised as a key factor in the most recent spurt of vigorous parasitic growth on the various limbs of our social security system. There is no sign of abatement in this development, and until realistic protection of earned family income on a universal basis is reintroduced into the system it will continue.

Moral degeneracy or unfair temptation

I do not believe that Australians have lost their traditional sense of the desirability of a society which assumes self-help and independence in the majority of the population, merely underpinned, not scaffolded, by collective assistance in cases of genuine need or misfortune.

In the early 1970s, these values were undermined in two areas by the seductive offer to the young, yet unformed in character, of agreeable incomes without the need to work (Unemployment Benefit) or to make personal provision for their needs (Supporting Parent Benefit). In the 1990s, the values and behaviour of the parenting age group are slowly being forced from their true character by the government's failure to enact universal family income protection. The social security system's proper targets for stringency versus reasonable assistance have been translocated, and the apparent inability of the academic and bureaucratic elite, and of the left-wing media, to perceive the moral distinction between welfare and social security – a distinction which is so easily if inarticulately recognised by ordinary Australians – puts public discussion of these issues at cross purposes and explains the almost total divide between public opinion as expressed on the ABC and on commercial talkback radio.

The American model of reform cannot help us greatly in the immediate task ahead, which is to re-establish the distinction between legitimate social security support and irresponsible 'welfare', not to dismantle our social security system, to which the American system overall bears scant likeness. The essential first step is to return to universal and equitable family income protection, whether by tax exemption, Child Endowment or both, so that the family can again be responsible for its members as far as possible. Only this reform can halt the drift of families onto Unemployment Benefit, Disability Pension and Sole Parent Pension.

Further, if the family is allowed to retain resources on a par per capita with those available to couples and individuals without dependents, it will be able to provide for its young adult members during their higher education and while they establish themselves in employment. This will remove the need for the payment of welfare benefits (Unemployment Benefit and Youth Allowance) to the younger population.

An expectation has been engendered in young men and women by the Sole Parent Pension, that the state will provide for the support of their offspring on 'credit' but without the obligation for repayment, should they choose to renege on what we now realise is the only viable course for the raising of children in independence, namely the two-parent family. This expectation must now be disabused. It may possibly best be done, without leaving its present victim/beneficiaries in the lurch, by indeed treating the Sole Parent Pension as a loan which must be repaid by both parents when their children reach independence and their incomes return to a level above their needs. Similar conditions of repayment could be instituted for young people who make use of the Unemployment Benefit or Youth Allowance prior to the age at which family responsibility ceases – currently at twenty-five.

The welfare industry points to large increases in expenditure on the totality of Family Allowances in recent years, but, as the above analysis makes clear, a major part of this (in fact diminished) expenditure is welfare provision for children in semi- or unemployed families and should be categorised as Unemployment Benefit or Sole Parent Pension rather than generalised as family income support. More than 60 per cent of families in 1996 received only the token basic Family

Allowance, while one-fifth of all children are now said to be growing up in jobless households which receive the full complement of Unemployment Benefit and Family Payments.

To prevent this masking of realities, a separate recording category of Family Income Protection external to social security should be established to track accurately what is being achieved for earning families in terms of horizontal equity, proportional to the number of children they support.

The growth in parasitic welfare in the 1970s prompted the neglect of the just deserts of families in the 1980s, and today, nearly two decades on, the balancing of the budget is still being done at their expense. From their condition of relative powerlessness, parents are taking unanticipated action to protect themselves. Unless their needs are attended to, the welfare crisis will not be resolved.

Note

1. All the data in this paper, other than family income figures, are derived from the Australian Bureau of Statistics collection. The graphs are my own. T.H. Kewley's *Social Security in Australia 1900-72* (Sydney University Press 1973) and *Australian Social Security Today:Major Developments from 1900 to 1978* (Sydney University Press 1980) were a constant resource for historical material up to 1978; thereafter the papers of the Social Security Review and Department of Social Security material. The views expressed in this article are the author's and do not represent those of the Centre for Independent Studies.

Chapter 10

Families, work and welfare

Fiona Macdonald and Don Siemon

How helpful is the concept of welfare dependency, with its implication of a 'culture of dependency', as a diagnosis of the problems associated with being a sole parent, having a disability, or being unemployed? Any judgement must be made in the light of what we know about the realities of people's lives and about the broader economic and social factors affecting them.

Sketches of the lives of two families who might be described as welfare dependent are presented below for illustrative purposes. Both these families are participants in the Brotherhood of St Laurence's Life Chances Study – a longitudinal study that has been following the lives of 160 or so children since 1990.[1] At particular points in time during the 1990s, both families could be said to be 'welfare dependent', since they were reliant on government income support payments for long periods.

The first family, the Trans, experienced long periods during which neither parent had paid work and the family's only income was social security payments. Prior to entering full-time 'self-employment' the father, Huong, received unemployment benefits for almost three years. During that time both he and his wife had bits and pieces of casual and part-time work.

In the second family, Sandra Miller relied on a single parenting payment (at that time called a sole parent pension) as her only income for over two years following separation from her husband. In the following year when she had paid work, Sandra continued to rely on parenting payments as a major part of her income.

Two families

The Tran family, a couple in their thirties with three school-aged children, migrated to Australia from Vietnam in 1985. Soon after their arrival here, Huong obtained work in a car manufacturing plant as a machine operator. He worked there for five years, eventually becoming a team leader. While Huong worked night shift his wife Nga worked full-time during the day as a machinist in a clothing factory.

Huong lost his job in early 1990 following an argument with his foreman. The family had a new baby and Nga had left her job. Eighteen months later both Huong and Nga were looking for full-time work. Both had some irregular casual work for a clothing manufacturer. Huong had recently lost his full-time factory job of several months when the business failed. The family's main source of income was social security payments.

In 1993 Nga was looking for permanent part-time work while she continued to get irregular casual work in a clothing factory from which she earned little income. Huong had been unemployed for almost two years. During this time he had undertaken further English language training and picked up occasional casual work in a clothing factory. Nga worried that she and her husband would find it hard to get employment because they were getting too old – she was 36 and he was 38. The Trans lived with their four children in the inner-city high-rise flat where they had lived since their arrival in Australia. Nga wanted to move because the flat was too small. Huong said being unemployed made him 'sometimes depressed and . . . irritable'. He wanted full-time work 'to provide my family all the things they need, and to get self-respect'.

In late 1995, the Trans had moved to a rented house in the suburbs and they were no longer receiving unemployment payments although their income was still low. Huong had regular part-time work in a clothing factory and Nga had frequent casual work as a machinist working from home.

In October 1996 Huong was self-employed as a home-based contractor sewing clothes. He worked 60 hours a week and Nga helped him. The family's income was still low and they had considerable financial difficulties. Huong worried about their financial situation and said the family 'just live day by day' and that they 'hardly make ends meet'. His business was 'unstable'. He said: 'I am very concerned about my family's future. If my business goes down I can't find a job elsewhere because of my old age.'

Sandra and John Miller had a six month-old baby girl in 1990. Sandra had part-time waiting work and John was employed full-time as a fitter. By 1993 the couple had separated and Sandra had moved with their daughter to a regional city where she had been brought up, and where her family still lived. The advantages of returning to the country were cheaper housing, support from her family, and a better environment for her child. The family relied on social security payments as their only source of income as they had no contact with John and did not receive any child support from him.

In 1996 Sandra started working part-time as a kitchen hand. She worked three days a week from 8 a.m. to 3 p.m., hours which enabled her to collect her daughter from school and to participate in school activities, such as classroom reading and helping in the canteen. A babysitter looked after her daughter for three hours a week and at other times Sandra's mother provided child care.

During school holidays Sandra relied on her mother, her sister and her neighbours to care for her daughter. She said working 'makes it hard to be organised and babysitting is a problem, but otherwise it's better for me'. With a combination of her wages and a reduced sole parent payment, Sandra found money was still a problem. While she had 'just enough to get by', she found it difficult to afford clothes for her daughter and she had not been able to pay some school costs.

These two stories are included here for what they might remind us about families reliant on social security incomes for long periods, things which are sometimes overlooked in some discussions of welfare dependency. They remind us in particular of the extent of diversity and change. We know families are not the same and they are not static, and that their members are active in bringing changes to their lives. Some experiences will be common, such as the struggle parents have to provide for their children on a low income, while others will not. If we mean something other than reliant on social security incomes when we say these families are 'welfare dependent', if we mean personally deficient in some way – inactive, lacking in motivation, passive beings with few aspirations for their families – then it is a very poor description of the situations of these two families. And from what we know about the lives of most families on low incomes in Australia it is likely to be a very poor description of their situations as well.

The statistics tell us there are large numbers of people in Australia receiving social security payments and that their numbers have increased. However, neither the statistics nor the label 'welfare dependent' helps us to understand or address the various aspects of this problem, the most serious of which is that many of these people will be living in poverty or on very low incomes, often for long periods.

The recent discussion paper of the Minister for Family and Community Services has defined the problem of welfare dependency as one of finding ways for families to 'mov(e) beyond reliance to self-sufficiency' (Newman 1999b: 2). The two family sketches hint at some of the individual, social and economic factors which can constrain families from achieving 'self-sufficiency' despite their desires to do so and despite the hardships of low incomes. Many of these constraining factors lie largely outside the control of the people receiving income support payments and outside the control of the social security system. For example, the experience of the Tran family points to the failure of the labour market to provide full-time jobs for all who want them, while it also suggests employment may not be as secure a pathway out of poverty as is often supposed.

Poverty, low income and being unemployed

Australian research consistently points to the strong associations between sole parenthood and poverty and between unemployment and poverty (McClelland 2000). In a recent study Harding and Szukalska (1999) have identified the children in Australia most at risk of poverty in 1995–96 as:

those living in families headed by a female, in sole-parent families and in larger families; those with no parent in paid work; those in families whose main source of income was government cash benefits; those living in public rental accommodation; and those living in families whose head was born overseas – especially the Middle East, North Africa and Central America.

Recent studies using different methodologies have arrived at very different estimates of the overall extent of poverty.[2] However, reviewing the findings relating to child poverty in Australia, McClelland (2000: 31) concludes that: 'a cautious estimate would be that between one-third to one-half of Australian children with no parent in paid work were in families with below-poverty line incomes in 1996 (with the difference depending on the impact of housing costs).' In the same paper McClelland reviews the research findings on the impacts of poverty on children and summarises these as: hardship and stress; isolation and exclusion; and adverse effects on health, development and education.

The Brotherhood of St Laurence's research over many years has found that, for families with low incomes, the hardship and stress resulting from trying to meet basic costs and balance competing demands is often acting together with stress from other problems including unemployment:

'Unemployment benefits are not enough for a family to live on. As he hasn't got a job my husband gets angry with the children when they cry or are noisy.' (Taylor and Macdonald 1998: 61)

'It just makes me sick. It is so frustrating, and it has such socio-economic boundaries. It dictates where you can live, it dictates how much rent you can pay, it dictates how much you can spend on your kids' birthday presents, and it dictates your life . . . It obsesses you. It owns you. Unemployment owns you.' (Jackson and Crooks 1993: 9)

Housing costs and availability are significant problems for people with low incomes and can contribute to isolation. Housing choices can be limited to outer areas with few services and difficult transport, or low-income families can become isolated in concentrations of public housing or in caravan parks (Fegan and Bowes 1999). Isolation and exclusion can impact on children in families with low incomes. The Life Chances Study found that, at ages three and six years, the children in low-income families were less likely than other children to participate in a range of services and learning and social activities (Taylor and Macdonald 1998).

The isolation and exclusion accompanying poverty can be intensified for unemployed people by a sense of being marginalised, of not being valued in a society where paid work continues to be the major means by which people achieve a sense of self-worth as well as social status and legitimacy (Jackson 1996):

'The thing is too, when you're not working you're sort of out of the mainstream. You feel like you're just on the outskirts of everything. You feel as if you're on the edges of things.' (Jackson and Crooks 1993: 10)

'I've worked hard and solid for thirty years and I'm just being discarded.' (Jackson and Crooks 1993: 10)

'It costs money to do things so we stay home and do the same old thing every day.' (Jackson and Crooks 1993: 14)

Contraction of personal networks and social life can arise not only from financial constraints but, for unemployed people, from the loss of a base of common experience on which their relationships with friends had been built:

'You're out of the main swim so you don't have that thing in common with them any more, do you? . . . And you've got to try and make new friends, and if you're home with no job it's very hard to make new friends.' (Jackson and Crooks 1993: 14)

'Your social life changes . . . You can't afford to waste money on going out socially so then your contact with people diminishes and the friends you have can't understand why you don't want to go out with them.' (Jackson and Crooks 1993: 15)

For many men the role of paid work remains inextricably linked to the role of breadwinner or provider as it is for many women, particularly sole parents. Unemployment means inability to fulfil that role:

> 'Like a bird with a nest you look after your wife and have children. Without a job you can't do that properly.' (Probert with Macdonald 1996: 22)

> 'I now know how important a job is. A man's reason for being on earth is to work ... For each individual person, that's your identity – for example, electrician. Once your job's gone, you're a nothing.' (Probert with Macdonald 1996: 18)

Welfare reform, to the extent it is limited to changes to the social security system, should be directed to solving problems of poverty. Levels of income support are critical to the living standards of low-income families, and useful strategies for income support will be ones that address these living standards. In Australia, positive changes in government assistance during the 1980s and early 1990s made real differences to the levels of child poverty, and the family tax initiative introduced in 1996 has also been important for low-income families (McClelland 2000). An effective system of income support needs to be able to respond to an increased diversity of individual and family circumstances and needs as well as to frequent changes in these in both the short term and over the life cycle.

While social security arrangements must be capable of ensuring people are supported as they seek more secure and adequate incomes through the labour market, it must also be able to support people who need to rely on combinations of earnings and social security for what may be lengthy periods, and it must be able to support those engaged in caring for others and for whom labour market participation is not currently an option.

There are limits to what we can expect to achieve through the social security system, however. Along with adjusting the tax system we can seek modifications to ensure employment is supported. However, the current concentration of attention paid to the 'incentive effects' of the transfer and tax systems seems to have shifted the focus of some discussions about the role of income support to a point where it is seen as some kind of inducement to be given or taken away as required to change the behaviour of poor people.

Understanding the limits of income support means recognising some of the realities of the social and economic context in which couples and sole parents make decisions and work to build secure lives for their children

Social and economic change

The most striking of the social and economic changes which have contributed to increases in reliance on social security by people of workforce age over the last few decades is *lack of full-time employment*. High levels of unemployment and long-term unemployment have been persistent features of the Australian labour market for much of the 1980s and 1990s. For most of the 1990s unemployment remained over 8 per cent, only dropping below this level in 1999. While rates of unemployment are high among young single people, unemployment is experienced by many family breadwinners. More than one in four unemployed people is a parent with a child under fifteen, while one in six families with a child under fifteen has no family member employed (ABS 2000).

Alongside persistent unemployment, the nature of jobs has changed significantly over the last two decades with much of this change in Australia occurring since the mid 1980s. Global changes have seen a decline in full-time blue-collar and manufacturing-based employment in many industrialised and wealthy nations, including Australia.

The proportion of jobs that are part-time, temporary and casual has increased dramatically. Between 1985 and 1997 half of all additional jobs created have been part-time and almost two-thirds (62 per cent) have been casual (Quinlan 1998). The greatest increase has been for males, with a 115 per cent increase in casual employment and a 2 per cent decrease in non-casual employment in the ten years to August 1998 (Productivity Commission 1999). More than one in four employees is now employed on a casual basis and more than one in four workers is employed part-time (ABS 2000).

Along with the increase in part-time employment has come an increase in underemployment with one in four part-time workers wanting to work more hours – currently more than half a million people (ABS 2000).

The majority of income support recipients are not receiving unemployment payments and most would not be among those counted in official estimates of unemployment. However, many income support recipients, including sole parents, disability support pensioners, and older jobless people in receipt of mature-aged and other allowances will be among the hundreds of thousands of 'hidden unemployed'. The Australian Bureau of Statistics (ABS 1998b) estimated the size of this group at more than 900,000 in September 1998. The growth in reliance on social security incomes is clearly correlated with the persistence of unemployment, and particularly with longer periods of unemployment (long-term unemployment declines more slowly during the recovery and expansion phases, as does social security recipience).

Significant social changes have accompanied changes in labour demand over the last few decades. Most apparent have been the *increase in women's labour force participation*, particularly that of married women, and the *increase in sole-parent families* (the latter is mainly the result of separation and divorce, not because of an increase in teenage pregnancy which remains low in Australia compared with Britain and the United States). Sole-parent families now account for one in every five families with children under the age of fifteen (ABS 2000).

These changes have contributed to a polarisation of employment among families. While some families appear to be 'work-rich' with both parents in paid employment, others are 'work-poor' with no adult employed. During the 1980s the proportion of families with one parent in paid work declined while the proportion with two parents in paid work increased. Growth in families with no parent in paid work occurred mainly during the 1990s. While this was partly due to an increase in the proportion of couples with neither parent in paid work, it was mainly due to growth in sole-parent families without jobs (Gregory 1999).

While the majority of employed women with children are in part-time jobs, there has been a substantial increase in married women's full-time participation in the labour force so that 43 per cent of employed women in couples with dependents have full-time jobs. The labour force participation of sole mothers is lower than that of partnered mothers while unemployment rates are much higher, an indication of the disadvantaged position of sole parents in the labour market. Unemployed (as opposed to 'jobless') sole parents make up over a quarter of all unemployed parents with children under fifteen (ABS 2000). Low incomes from government pensions along with high rates of unemployment contribute to high rates of poverty among sole-parent families.

Employment as a pathway out of poverty?

While employment is seen as the major pathway out of poverty for most of the working-aged population and their families, it appears to be a less secure route than is often supposed. Many unemployed people may only gain short-term and intermittent work while poverty in families with paid work appears to be a result of low levels of pay as well as underemployment.

The risk of a child living in poverty is much lower in families where one or both parents are in paid work. However this does not mean that paid work protects all children from poverty. In fact, the majority of children in poverty in Australia live in families with at least one parent in work. Harding and Szukalska (1998) have found, while many of these families have parents who are self-employed, a quarter of all children in poverty live in families in which at least one parent is a wage earner. Most are low-paid wage earners (earning $10 an hour or less in 1995–96) while low weekly earnings for others is probably attributable to reduced hours of work. One recent study (Eardley 1998) found an increase in poverty between the mid-1980s and 1995–96 in families with a worker in full-year full-time employment. The same study found casual and contract work also contributed to a growth in family poverty.

Low-paid jobs have often been seen as providing a foothold in the labour market – a stepping stone to a better, higher-paid job. However, in the mid-1990s evidence from an OECD Study (OECD 1996) indicated many workers were getting stuck in low-paid employment, or going through the revolving door back into unemployment – or out of the labour force all together. In Australia, findings from a recent Australian Bureau of Statistics survey (ABS 1999a) show the prospects of finding *secure* work following unemployment are very poor, with unemployed job seekers generally having short periods of employment in between lengthy periods of seeking work with no improvement in the situation over time. While 70 per cent of unemployed job seekers in a longitudinal study (ABS 1997b) worked at some time in an eighteen-month survey period, two-thirds of the jobs they started were casual and 89 per cent lasted less than twelve months.

Low-paid work, particularly short-term, casual and contract work, now appears less likely to provide an entry point to better paid and more secure work than it has been in the past. While this is due in part to compositional shifts (from manufacturing to services employment), in Australia contracting out and down-sizing by large organisations, particularly government enterprises, have also contributed to an increase in short-term, casual and contract work, and to a decline in entry-level jobs which have traditionally provided opportunities for advancement through internal career paths (Wooden 1998; Wooden and Hawke 1998).

At this point is it worthwhile returning to the experiences of Huong Tran. Along with another twenty-four of the fathers in the Brotherhood of St Laurence's longitudinal Life Chances Study, Huong was unemployed in the early 1990s, at a time when Australia was in recession and unemployment was at its highest ever recorded level. Like most of the others who were out of work, Huong had been employed in a full-time waged job in the manufacturing sector in Victoria during the 1980s. By the end of 1996 Huong was one of a very few of the twenty-five fathers who had full-time work. For Huong this was very low-paid, so-called 'self employment', as a contracted outworker in the clothing industry. Most of the others had similar experiences over the study period – a series of temporary, casual and part-time employment, including low-paid contract and on-call work with few industrial protections and no job security. Employment that was intermittent, low-paid or both had not led to more secure or higher-paid work and families continued to depend on low incomes, mainly combinations of social security and earnings.

While this is a small group of men, many of whom were recent immigrants from non-English-speaking countries, the similarities in their experiences are striking. Their stories are those of 'prime working-age' fathers in families with pre school-aged children, active in the labour market, but over long periods unable to obtain secure employment with adequate hours and income to support themselves and their families. More than one man looked to the solution of 'buying' himself work through self employment after facing months or even years of rejection. More than one went into considerable debt to do this, including one family who lost their home (Macdonald 2000).

These stories do not sit comfortably with a characterisation of the problem as one of welfare dependency. Rather, along with what we know about the range and nature of work opportunities at the end of the twentieth century, they point to a labour market without enough full-time jobs for those who want them and characterised by diminished prospects for those whose labour and skills were at one time in demand. They also highlight the insecurity of the pathway offered by employment for some people seeking to support themselves and provide for their families.

Similar arguments apply in the case of lone parents. In Australia, we have seen employment as a key means for sole parents to escape poverty. Recognition that long periods outside the paid work force are likely to reduce employment opportunities – with the risk of locking single mothers into poverty in the long term – has been one of the major reasons for the support and assistance provided to sole parents to return to work, such as through the Commonwealth government's Jobs, Education and Training (JET) scheme. However, in Australia we have not expected or demanded that sole mothers be in paid work, as is the case in the United States. While we know that the opportunity to participate in paid work continues to provide the best means for many sole parents to avoid long-term poverty, policy approaches need to take into account at least a couple of other things we know. The first, discussed above, is that if opportunities for a person to get stable and reasonably paid work are limited then employment is not a reliable pathway out of poverty. The second is that employment is not an absolute end in itself. This is something of particular importance when considering the choices and options for parents who are caring for children alone.

From the research undertaken by the Brotherhood of St Laurence and others we know that sole mothers have the same aspirations in balancing the needs of their children and the need to work as other parents.[3] However, the context in which they must make decisions about whether or not to engage in paid work is different from that of other parents. This should not be overlooked. The labour force participation of other mothers should not be seen as the appropriate yardstick for setting expectations for sole mothers' participation, as appears to be the suggestion in Minister Newman's discussion paper (Newman 1999b: 21).

Like Sandra Miller, who returned to live in a depressed regional city with high unemployment so she could have the support of an extended network of family and friends, most sole parents are attempting to build a secure family life after separation from a partner. Their choices and success in the labour market will partly reflect their prior experiences in couple families. For some, this will have been out of the labour force altogether while for others it will have been as the family's 'secondary' earner – whose engagement in paid employment depended on it fitting in with caring and other responsibilities in the household.

The choices and successes of sole mothers will also reflect the fact that it is harder for them to work and look after their children than it is for partnered mothers. Finding work, keeping work, and getting a financial return from work will be more difficult. On average, sole mothers receiving parenting payments have less education or marketable skills than other mothers (Wilson et al. 1998). We also know many will have difficulty affording child care and finding work opportunities with demands that can be managed while parenting alone. In addition, many will face very low returns from paid work when child care and other work-related costs are taken into account.

Given these facts it would be surprising if sole mothers did not have lower levels of workforce participation than partnered women. If the purpose in encouraging them into the labour force is to reduce their risks of long-term poverty then this must be done in ways which accord with what we know about their lives and aspirations and about the sorts of labour market opportunities available to them. Work or activity-testing sole parents would be a poor way of assisting them improve their employment prospects. Indeed, insisting that sole parents enter the labour market while supporting the choices of other families to have a parent at home itself sends contradictory messages to women about what it is to be a good mother.

From what we know of the situation of sole parents, the most significant barriers to labour market success are not attitudinal but lack of real opportunities. As noted earlier, already one in five sole parents is unemployed. The belief that changes to social security conditions or income tests are likely in themselves to lead to noticeably higher employment levels (and therefore less spending on income security) is implausible. The belief that reducing or limiting benefits will bring about a reduction in welfare spending without lowering living standards is also implausible.

What actually helps?

In the United States, the Centre on Budget and Policy Priorities found that the incomes of the poorest families, those headed by single women, have fallen since the introduction of welfare reforms in that country. The same study indicated that levels of government assistance have dropped far more dramatically than poverty rates (*The Economist*, 'Off welfare but poorer', 28 August 1999: 23). While belief in the success of the American reforms is based on the high take-up of employment by sole parents, this increase has occurred during a time of significant economic growth and low unemployment (Curtain 1999).

For unemployed people in Australia the emphasis of changes to payment arrangements under the Coalition government has been on strengthening the 'mutual obligation' requirements they must meet. Introduced at the same time as funding for employment assistance was substantially cut, these changes do little if anything to improve job prospects while they make life harder for those people who are unemployed. Under the previous Working Nation arrangements, the government's side of the obligation was a commitment to ensuring long-term unemployed people a place in work, education or training. This commitment has gone and resources for assistance have been downgraded while the demands and the extent of compulsion have been increased.

In a detailed comparison of mutual obligation arrangements in the United States, the United Kingdom and Australia, Richard Curtain (1999: 26) concludes: 'What is notable about the operation of Australia's mutual obligation arrangements is the emphasis on the requirements or obligations without any strong focus on the purpose for doing so. Mutual obligation is primarily a set of administrative hurdles presented to the job seekers to test their good faith in seeking work. The range of options available under mutual obligation are disjointed and are not focused on how to best meet the needs of the individual job seeker.'

The emphasis has come to focus on unemployed people 'giving something back' in return for their income support. This is the appeal for many in the community of the centrepiece of mutual obligation – the Work for the Dole scheme for young unemployed people. Work for the Dole appears to provide unemployed people with an opportunity to contribute to society, to be useful and to give something back in return for their social security benefit. However, at the same time, it sends the message that the problem is understood as solely one of unemployed people lacking motivation. It encourages the view that unemployment is in some way due to unemployed people not trying hard enough, through laziness or lack of a 'work ethic'. In short, it promotes the view that unemployment is a result of individual failure. It is difficult to believe that this was not the government's intention when naming the program given the likely strong association between the terms 'dole' and 'dole-bludger'.

While the community might expect that unemployed people should be required to demonstrate they are actively seeking work, no amount of strengthening of the obligations on unemployed people will increase the number of jobs. It makes life harder for unemployed people who already are dealing with a social security system that is not easy to negotiate. It should not be forgotten that the Australian income support system is already tightly targeted – benefits are not easy to get, nor are they easy to keep.

The evidence that unemployment is not good for people rests largely on the fact that poverty is not good for people. Added to this may be a sense of isolation, of being apart from the rest of society, of being unable to fulfil a role as provider, or of not being a valued member of the community. Policies such as Work for the Dole that reinforce the message that the rest of the community does not place much value on the time, labour, choices or hopes of people who are unemployed can only worsen this situation. We know that there is no evidence to show compulsion will improve the lives of the parents or the children in unemployed families.

We see little evidence of 'dysfunctional' behaviour or of a 'culture of defeat' among the vast majority of families receiving social security payments in Australia. At the same time we know that many unemployed people, early retirees and mothers at home feel that the contributions they make to their families and their communities (for example, the unpaid work many mothers like Sandra Miller do in their children's schools), while enormously rewarding, are not valued as paid work is (see Probert with Macdonald 1996). Positive support for those who want employment must be balanced with greater recognition of the unpaid work that keeps families and communities going.

The extent to which employment will be able to provide a pathway out of poverty for families will depend more than anything else on the number and nature of jobs we can generate. Training and education can prepare people for work and a responsive welfare system can support people as they balance different combinations of employment and other activities over the various stages of their lives.

Over the last decade in particular some Australian communities have experienced a significant erosion of their social infrastructure. We know that the existence of a range of supports and services can ensure opportunities for people to participate in their communities and can contribute to raising the living standards of those on low incomes. In discussions of welfare reform a narrow focus on employment and on income support arrangements can mean we do not pay enough attention to the potential for broader community-building strategies to improve people's lives.

If our aim is to support families now, while also ensuring opportunities for children in the future, we must remember that education, health and housing matter too. Concerns about the inter-generational transmission of welfare dependency should lead us to examine the resources within communities as well as those within families.

Notes

1. The employment experiences of some of the families in the Life Chances Study, including the two case studies provided here, are reported in Macdonald (2000). The names of those in the case studies have been changed to ensure anonymity. The two families discussed here are not intended to be statistically representative of all unemployed families, but their stories are included in order to provide a greater depth of understanding about how people may come to require income support, what their lives are like while claiming income support, and the way people's circumstances change over time.

2. Poverty in Australia, conceived in relative terms, is defined not as lack of sufficient resources to meet basic needs, but as lack of resources necessary to permit 'participation in the lifestyle and consumption patterns enjoyed by other Australians' (Saunders 1996: 227). The most commonly used measure is the Henderson Poverty Line (see Saunders 1996), while more recently a median income poverty line (set at half the median of equivalent family income) has been used to estimate the extent of poverty and its incidence among different groups.

3. Relevant Brotherhood research has investigated the role and meaning of work in people's lives (Probert with Macdonald 1996), the role of parenting in young women's decisions about work and parenting (Probert and Macdonald 1999), the experiences and aspirations of low-income sole parents with older children (Brotherhood of St Laurence 1999), and the affordability of child care (Tasker and Siemon 1998).

Chapter 11

Labour market issues in welfare reform[1]

Peter Dawkins

In September 1999 the Minister for Family and Community Services, Senator Jocelyn Newman, established a Reference Group on Welfare Reform which presented its Interim Report in March 2000. I am a member of this committee. This chapter refers to the Interim Report and its appendices,[2] but the views expressed are those of the author and may not necessarily be shared by other members of the Reference Group.

The central thrust of the Interim Report (Reference Group on Welfare Reform 2000), is the case for re-orienting the social support system to be a 'participation support system', with a strong emphasis on encouraging economic and/or social participation. In this chapter I focus on economic participation, which is essentially about participation in the labour market, and issues of social participation are not discussed. My focus is on 'welfare to work' policies, and in discussing these issues, a supply and demand framework is adopted.

Some historical background

In 1966, Ronald Henderson carried out a study in Melbourne in which he first used what has become known as the 'Henderson poverty line' in order to measure the extent of poverty in the community. He later went on to chair a Commission of Inquiry into Poverty in the 1970s which pointed to the fact that poverty was still a significant problem in Australia despite the establishment of a welfare state in the post-war period. The establishment of the Henderson poverty line, for all its limitations, was also a significant step in helping us to monitor how much of a problem this was over time, and also in raising the awareness that poverty has a relative as well as an absolute dimension.

With this heightened awareness of the problem of poverty, in the mid-1970s the Australian government made significant steps to reduce the incidence of poverty by, for example, increasing unemployment benefits and age pensions. From that time on, however, the welfare system has been battling to deal with a growing number of challenges.

First, unemployment became a major problem. Unemployment had been very low in the post-war period, until the mid-1970s. Since then it has averaged about 7.5 per cent which, for such a prolonged period, is very high by historical standards. Second, before the 1970s the typical couple income unit had one breadwinner who was male. Since that time, there has been a growing diversity of working arrangements and types of household composition. Female labour force participation has grown strongly, as has part-time employment. A large proportion of part-time jobs have been taken up by people in households where there is at least one

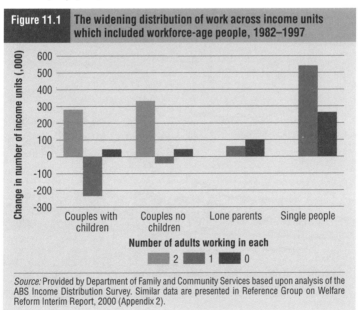

| Figure 11.1 | The widening distribution of work across income units which included workforce-age people, 1982–1997 |

Source: Provided by Department of Family and Community Services based upon analysis of the ABS Income Distribution Survey. Similar data are presented in Reference Group on Welfare Reform Interim Report, 2000 (Appendix 2).

other employed person, typically full-time. Third, social and demographic trends have led to a growth in lone parents and to a growth in the number of people claiming disability support. Families have also needed to support their children for more and more years as education participation has increased. Fourth, globalisation and technological change has made the labour market more difficult for unskilled workers and operated in favour of skilled workers thus tending to widen the distribution of employment opportunities and increase the inequality of earnings.

These changes have given rise to an increasing concentration of employment into 'job-rich families' and 'job-rich communities', and of joblessness into 'jobless families' and 'job-poor communities' (Dawkins 1996; Miller 1998; Gregory and Hunter 1998).

Figure 11.1 shows how the number of income units in Australia with no job has increased substantially between 1982 and 1997, as have the number of income units in which there are two jobs holders, illustrating this widening distribution of jobs. The only type of income unit where there has been a

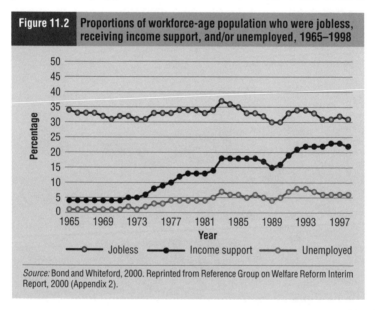

Figure 11.2 Proportions of workforce-age population who were jobless, receiving income support, and/or unemployed, 1965–1998

Source: Bond and Whiteford, 2000. Reprinted from Reference Group on Welfare Reform Interim Report, 2000 (Appendix 2).

substantial growth in just one person working, is the single adult (without child) income unit.

In this increasingly challenging world, successive governments have increased the scope of the welfare safety net, while at the same time seeking to maintain a high degree of cost effectiveness by attaching means tests to each of the various benefits. The result has been a highly complex system that is very difficult to understand. As a result, the effect of any single policy change is hard to predict and may be counter-productive.

One aspect of this problem has been high effective marginal tax rates. The combination of the withdrawal of means tested benefits and the increase in income tax paid, results in many low income families retaining only a small proportion of any extra income earned from entering or increasing their employment. Another aspect of the problem has been the rigidity of the social security system. The growing array of benefit types over this period, has brought with it a compartmentalisation of the welfare system where the benefit types are associated with different payments, different means tests, and different expectations of the benefit recipients with respect to their employability.

Meanwhile, although the employment to population ratio has risen in Australia (and the proportion who are jobless has fallen), over the last twenty-five years the proportion of Australians of working age receiving income support through the social security system has more than quadrupled (Figure 11.2). This has led to a substantial growth in the proportion of GDP being devoted to such income support payments. And although there has been a strong growth in employment since the end of the last recession, which has led to a reduction in unemployment, this has not translated into a reduction in the number on income support over the same period.

Figure 11.3 presents analysis by Bond and Whiteford (2000) of how this growth in income support has been distributed between different categories. It can be seen that over the over the last thirty years, there has been an increase in the numbers of people on disability/sickness payments, the number of lone parents, the value of payments to partners, carers and parents, and the number of students receiving support, as well as a growth in unemployment. All of these have been driving the increase in income support payments.

Thus there has been a strong rise in the proportion of the workforce-age population receiving income support over the last twenty-five years. It is now between 20 and 25 per cent, about four times the proportion of the workforce-age population who are unemployed. Table 11.1 provides details of the main payment types that those on income support were receiving in 1999 and how long they had been on their benefit. It excludes Youth Allowance, Austudy Payment, Sickness Allowance, and Special Benefits, all of which tend to be for short periods. It can be seen that the largest numbers are in receipt of Newstart, Disability Support Pension, and Parenting Payment Single, and Parenting Payment Partnered.

One of the big questions for the Welfare Review is the extent to which we should be seeking to achieve the movement of people from welfare to work, or to increase the hours of work of people currently on payments other than Newstart, such as Disability Support Pensions, Parenting Payments, and

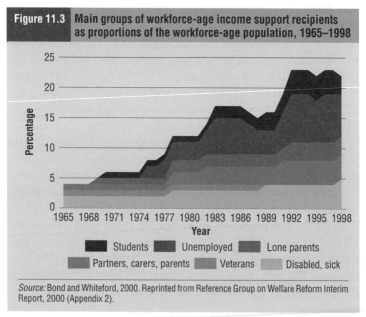

Figure 11.3 Main groups of workforce-age income support recipients as proportions of the workforce-age population, 1965–1998

Source: Bond and Whiteford, 2000. Reprinted from Reference Group on Welfare Reform Interim Report, 2000 (Appendix 2).

the variety of allowances for older jobless people. While it is clearly appropriate for a substantial proportion of those on Disability Support Pension and Parenting Payment not to be expected to seek employment, there are also many in these categories for whom part-time employment may be a very good idea. Indeed some do work on a part-time basis.

Another interesting feature of Table 11.1, is the detail provided on the length of time that income support recipients have spent, on average, on the different benefit types. Of those listed, clearly Newstart Allowance includes the largest proportion with relatively short durations. By contrast, those receiving the two other major benefit types listed, Disability

Table 11.1	Workforce-age income support recipients, by payment type and duration, both continuous and cumulative (bracketed), March 1999					
	Proportion (%) of recipients with duration of:				No (% of all recipients)	
Payment type, March 1999	Under 2 yrs	2 yrs or more	5 yrs or more	10 yrs or more		
Widow B Pension	2 (0)	98(100)	96 (98)	83 (84)	10,600	(0.4)
Wife Pension	3 (0)	97(100)	71 (73)	23 (24)	100,900	(3.9)
Disability Support Pension	20 (12)	80 (88)	49 (52)	23 (24)	568,200	(21.7)
Mature Age Allowance	38 (15)	62 (85)	6 (9)	0 (1)	45,400	(1.7)
Widow Allowance	52 (20)	48 (80)	13 (22)	4 (8)	25,200	(1.0)
Parenting Payment Single	42 (20)	58 (80)	25 (30)	7 (8)	362,400	(13.8)
Carer Payment	43 (30)	57 (70)	15 (20)	5 (6)	38,100	(1.5)
Partner Allowance	55 (39)	45 (61)	1 (2)	0 (1)	85,700	(3.3)
Parenting Payment Partnered	64 (35)	36 (65)	2 (4)	0 (1)	226,700	(8.7)
Newstart Allowance	73 (43)	27 (57)	4 (7)	1 (1)	720,400	(27.5)
TOTAL*	56 (38)	44 (62)	19 (22)	8 (8)	2,617,000	(100.0)

* Includes payments not mentioned separately – Youth Allowance, Austudy Payment, Sickness Allowance, Special Benefit. Receipt of these payments is mainly short term.
Source: Reference Group on Welfare Reform Interim Report, 2000 (Appendix 3). Constructed from Department of Family of Community Services, Longitudinal Dataset, 1 per cent sample.

Support Pension and Parenting Payment Single, have mostly been on these benefits for more than two years. In the case of Disability Support, about half have been on the benefit for five years or more.

While the Australian situation has its own peculiar features, many other OECD countries have been confronting similar trends and problems in their welfare systems. The rising trend in the proportion of the workforce-age population receiving income support, and the rising trend in government spending on income support, has given rise to an international interest in policies that can help to move people from welfare to work. At a conference in Australia, organised by the Reserve Bank and the Australian National University, Martin (1998) identified a number of principles that international experience suggests are important in designing labour market programs:

- integrate the referral to active programs closely with benefit and placement work;

- 'profile' new benefit claimants to identify those at risk of becoming long-term unemployed and provide the latter immediately with counselling and job-search assistance;

- make passive income support as 'active' as possible by using instruments like re-employment bonuses, in-work benefits etc.;

- enforce availability to work and job search tests;

- make continued receipt of income support conditional on agreeing to participate in active programs after a certain minimum duration of unemployment;

- ensure that participants in training and public sector employment programs continue to be available for work and actively seek jobs; and

- explore ways of making the public employment service more effective by giving greater play to the role of market signals.

In a more recent review paper about welfare to work policies, Martin (2000) concluded that in-depth counselling, financial incentives for those who get a job, and job search assistance can be the most effective strategies, especially when combined with increased monitoring and enforcement of the work test. He also argued that:

- training programs should be kept on a small scale and targeted to the needs of job seekers and the local labour market;

- early interventions for disadvantaged people, starting as early as pre-school, can be effective;

- steps to reduce premature school leaving and measures to improve the skills and competencies gained from school are also important;

- employment subsidies can help maintain an attachment to the labour market, but they should be of short duration, targeted and closely monitored, and will more than likely only produce modest net employment effects because of high deadweight loss and displacement effects;

- direct job creation in the public sector has had little impact in helping unemployed people get permanent jobs in the open labour market; and

- assistance to potential entrepreneurs among the unemployed population can be effective for a small niche group.

Some of these ideas are canvassed below, and related to the Australian case. In so doing I adopt a supply and demand framework.

Labour supply

While there has been a substantial growth in the numbers receiving income support (most of whom are jobless), the total of all jobless has fallen slightly over the last thirty years as a proportion of the workforce-age population. The major problem is that there has been an increasing proportion of the jobless who are concentrated into jobless families and job-poor communities.

We have noted the trends among those registered as unemployed in Figure 11.2. The remaining jobless are outside the labour force, of which some are 'hidden unemployed' and some completely outside the labour force (that is, they do not wish to work). Figure 11.4 presents trends in the two measures of hidden unemployment. It is an interesting question to what extent those on income support payments are in these various categories. People on Newstart are presumably mostly in the unemployment numbers, and some are working part-time. They are probably not to be found, much, in the marginally attached group.

Those on Parenting Payments and on Disability Support Pension and Mature Age Allowance could define themselves as job seekers, as marginally attached, or as completely outside the labour force. It is interesting to note that the number of marginally attached males has been significantly increasing. It seems likely that part of the growth in income support payments has been in this category.

Apart from the unemployed and the marginally attached, the other labour force category that has been rising strongly over the last twenty-five years is people in part-time employment. This increase in the number of people in part-time work is another reason why more people now claim income

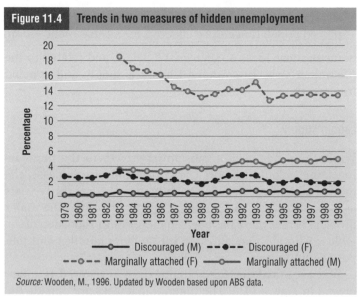

Figure 11.4 Trends in two measures of hidden unemployment

Source: Wooden, M., 1996. Updated by Wooden based upon ABS data.

support, for many part-time workers use income support to top up their earnings. As noted earlier, this applies to some on Newstart. It also applies to some on other benefits such as Parenting Payment Single. However, the growth of part-time employment can only explain a small part of the growth in the numbers of people on income support. In June 1998, only 18 per cent of workforce-age income support recipients received a part rate of payment because of other income (usually but not always from employment). Thus 82 per cent were on the maximum rate. (Appendices to Interim Report of Reference Group on Welfare Reform 2000: 9).

Many part-time employed wish to work longer hours, as do some full-time employed. Figure 11.5 suggests that this represents about 6 per cent of the labour force, or slightly less than one-quarter of part-time employees, (a higher percentage of male part-time employees and a lower percentage of female part-time employees). To the extent that these underemployed may be in receipt of income support payments, the fact that they report the desire to work more hours can give some encouragement to policy makers seeking to increase that tendency. It would require further research to identify

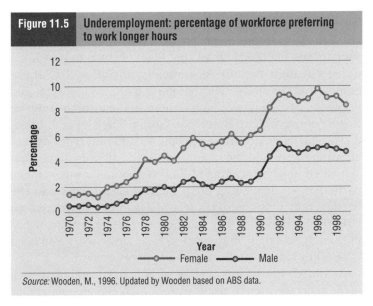

| Figure 11.5 | Underemployment: percentage of workforce preferring to work longer hours |

Source: Wooden, M., 1996. Updated by Wooden based on ABS data.

how many of the self-reported under-employed are in receipt of such payments.

One of the factors inhibiting the movement of a substantial proportion of all these potential suppliers of labour into employment (or more hours) is their level of *skill and job readiness.* The international evidence reviewed by Martin indicates a strong emphasis on early intervention, an emphasis on job search assistance (job search skills are for many people the skills they may need), an emphasis on targeted and small scale training programs aimed at the needs of job seekers and the local labour market, and a recognition that training and public sector employment programs should not distract people from continuing actively to seek jobs (any such active programs should be integrated closely with benefit and placement work). Thus labour market programs and the benefit system should have as their primary goals facilitating the movement into employment.

Another aspect of the welfare system is that there are some categories of workers receiving benefits for whom there is little or no expectation in the system that they will seek employment, yet who given the right encouragement may be willing and able to seek employment. This includes some older jobless people, some lone and partnered parents whose children are teenagers, and some people with disabilities. The kind of support and encouragement that is often given to people on unemployment benefits is typically not offered to these groups, and the suggestion that participation support should be offered to such people is an important theme of the Interim Report of the Welfare Reference Group. The aim is to break down rigid barriers between people on different types of benefits and to provide the type of service to all individuals that suits their needs in seeking to achieve economic and/or social participation, depending upon their circumstances and the barriers they may face. This recognises that not everyone on a particular benefit under the current system is alike or has like needs, and that 'individualised service delivery' will need to be a key feature of the any new support system.

As noted, the means testing of benefits, combined with income tax payments, result in very *high effective marginal tax rates* for many low income individuals and families as they move into employment or increase the amount that they work. This is especially a problem where there are overlaps in the tapers on benefits as they are withdrawn.

The tax reform package being introduced in July 2000 includes some improvements to incentives for low to middle income families. This results from a simplification of family benefits and reductions in their rate of withdrawal which, along with income tax reductions, reduce the effective marginal tax rates (the proportion of any increase in private income that is lost through benefit withdrawal and tax paid) for many families. However, while this has eased the problem, it has not eliminated it. The severity of these effective marginal tax rates varies considerably across individuals and families, depending upon their circumstances. Consider just two examples, one of a single person on Newstart Allowance, the other of a single income couple receiving allowance payments.

Figure 11.6 illustrates the case of a single person receiving Newstart Allowance, who experiences effective marginal tax rates of 67 to 81 per cent over an income range of $31 to $293 per week in private income. This results from the combination of the withdrawal of Newstart Allowance, the withdrawal

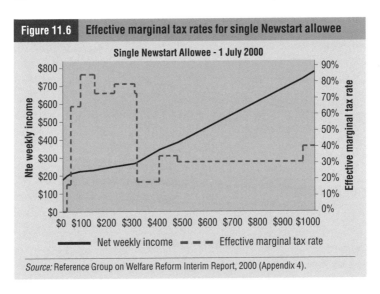

Figure 11.6 | Effective marginal tax rates for single Newstart allowee

Single Newstart Allowee - 1 July 2000

Source: Reference Group on Welfare Reform Interim Report, 2000 (Appendix 4).

of the Low Income Tax Rebate, reduction in the Beneficiary Rebate entitlement, the shading in of the Medicare levy, and ordinary income tax.

Figure 11.7 illustrates the case of a single income allowee couple with two young children. One is in paid work while the other looks after the children. They face effective marginal tax rates of between 61 and 104 per cent over a wide range of earnings. This results from the combination of the withdrawal of Newstart Allowance, of Parenting Payment and of Family Tax Benefit, of the shading in of the Medicare levy, and ordinary income tax.

Appendix 4 to the Interim Report also examines incentives facing other types of beneficiaries such as those on Parenting Payment Single and Disability Support Pensions as well as some other family types receiving Newstart. Each group has its own distinctive incentive stimulus which will need to be continually reviewed in the process of welfare reform.

It should also be remembered that there are other costs of job search and of employment that have to be factored into

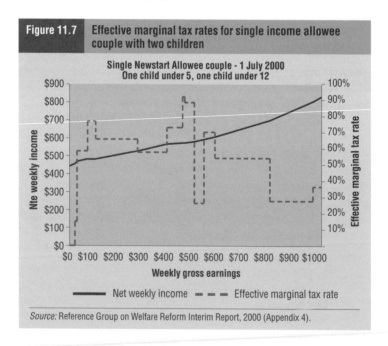

Figure 11.7   Effective marginal tax rates for single income allowee couple with two children

Source: Reference Group on Welfare Reform Interim Report, 2000 (Appendix 4).

these calculations. These include the costs of transport and child care which can diminish the advantages of moving from welfare to work. The Interim Report states that:

> The right incentives, with targeted assistance, need to be part of a systematic approach to helping people to move into employment. There should be strong and clear signals to people that there are financial benefits from obtaining employment. Consideration must be given to the costs of participation (such as child care, transport) as well as the amount of extra income obtained from employment. (Reference Group on Welfare Reform 2000: 39)

There are different possible approaches to improving work incentives. The Reference Group on Welfare Reform is of the view that the sheer complexity of the present system may lead to uncertainty about the benefits of work which can reduce the incentive to work for risk averse people. I have argued for a number of years that it would be a good idea to aim for a simpler tax-transfer system that eliminates the very high effective marginal tax rates that some income units face and greatly increases the simplicity of the system.

One radical solution to this problem would be the 'basic-income flat-tax system', often thought to be the purest form of 'negative income tax'. Under such a system everyone receives a basic income (which can vary according to circumstances such as the number of children) and then pays a flat tax rate on any private income. Such an approach would reduce the complexity of the system and eliminate the highest effective marginal tax rates.

However, it would not be possible to protect the current level of entitlements for people with no other income without increasing effective marginal tax rates for the majority of tax-payers. This was demonstrated by Dawkins et al. (1998). Further, the work incentive effects of moving to a 'basic-income flat-tax system' could be expected to vary significantly across different individuals and family types. While many would have more incentive to earn, others would have less, and the likely aggregate effect on work effort is therefore uncertain.

Furthermore, a basic income in its pure form would not carry with it any 'mutual obligation'. This would raise the danger of reducing the incentive for work for some people whose obligations would be less than under current arrangements. This problem would be avoided in a 'participation income' system proposed by authors such as Atkinson (1993), under which payments would be contingent upon economic or social participation, the nature of which could vary depending upon people's circumstances. The case for moving towards a Participation Income System, to increase the simplicity and transparency of the system, to remove the highest effective marginal tax rates, and to emphasise the importance of economic and social participation, has a lot of merit. I return to this below.

Meanwhile, the Interim Report of the Reference Group on Welfare Reform has identified a number of reforms that would be realistic to consider achieving, in the short to medium term, that would be consistent with such a long-term goal, and may have a significantly positive effect on work incentives.

One possible type of reform is that of *in-work benefits*, or what are sometimes called 'employment conditional benefits'. Examples of such policies from overseas include the Earned Income Tax Credit in the United States, and the Working Families Tax Credit in Britain. Employment conditional benefits can be administered either through the tax system or through the benefit system. The Reference Group on Welfare Reform saw some merit in this sort of policy but noted that care would need to be taken not to jeopardise the benefits flowing out of the government's new tax package and that a rigorous cost benefit analysis of such an approach would be needed before any such policy could be developed.

The Interim Report notes that:

> There is considerable research available on the potential impact of schemes such as the EITC [Earned Income Tax Credit]. Firstly, they can make a significant difference in encouraging income support recipients into work. This is especially the case for lone parents in the United States. Their impact on couples with children is less positive. Although they induce some people

to move from income support to work, they also reduce workforce participation by some second earners in a family as assistance is withdrawn at higher income levels. In the Australian context, it would be critical to integrate any such tax credit with the new Family Tax Benefit to ensure that the expected positive work incentive effects flowing from the government's new tax package were not compromised.

If a primary aim is to boost the incentives for people to secure full-time employment or a substantial number of part-time hours, there is some logic in a benefit that increases with hours of work or is conditional on a minimum number of hours. These are features of the tax credit arrangements in the United States and the United Kingdom respectively. The Reference Group believes that such a development in the Australian context would require rigorous cost benefit analysis. This analysis would need to take particular account of any adverse effects on incentives for people to take and/or declare part-time work. (Reference Group on Welfare Reform 2000: 44)

The Interim Report also notes that:

Employment conditional benefits could be a significant component of a strategy to boost employment opportunities by allowing the real costs of low skilled labour to decline, while maintaining or increasing the incomes of low-income families containing such low skilled workers. (Reference Group on Welfare Reform 2000: 46)

This idea has been put forward by the so-called Five Economists, of which I was one (see Dawkins 1999), and it was also proposed by the Business Council of Australia in its submission to the Reference Group on Welfare Reform. I return to this idea when discussing labour demand issues.

Another type of policy, which has a limited presence in Australia already, is that of *return to work benefits,* whereby cash rewards are provided to benefit recipients when they move into work. They have the advantage that if they are targeted at groups with weak work incentives and apply for only a limited period, that contains their cost, but may provide significant returns. This idea is well worth exploring. It is being experimented with in Canada for lone parents who move into full-time employment.

Another idea canvassed in the Interim Report is that of a *participation supplement*. The Interim Report states:

> *The broad idea is that people of workforce age on income support have the opportunity to accumulate a sum of money in a 'participation support account', which could be then drawn from when they participate in acceptable economic or social activities. This would be in addition to their basic allowance or pension.*

> *A participation supplement could compensate for some of the costs of economic or social participation and/or provide some additional financial incentives for economic or social participation. Acceptable activities that could fall within the scope of this proposal include education or training (including basic literacy courses), part-time work and job search outside a person's local labour market. Any accumulated balance could also be available to invest in starting a small business or to reimburse costs of relocating to a new area with better employment opportunities. The accumulated balance could also fund a return to work bonus, either in a lump sum form or payable over a period of time. (Reference Group on Welfare Reform 2000: 47)*

An idea of this kind has previously been put forward by Harding and Loundes (1999). In their version, the account could be drawn down as a return to work bonus at the same rate at which funds were paid into the account. This was designed to avoid the moral hazard problem of building up a substantial fund over a prolonged period and then drawing it down quickly after a return to work. The account could also be drawn down as a wage subsidy for an employer to help increase the incentive to hire the person. One of the major criticisms of wage subsidy schemes is that they may be used to subsidise employers who would anyway have employed the person in question. However, this alternative scheme may be more cost effective as employees who could obtain work without using their participation account in this way would not have to offer the funds to an employer as a wage subsidy. For example, where the funds may be more beneficially used to assist the job search process or pay for transport to work for a period of time, they could be used in that way.

There are three other very specific ideas canvassed in the Interim Report for improving financial incentives to work.

First, as noted earlier, the high effective marginal tax rates for those on Newstart Allowance, result in a low return to taking part-time employment. One idea canvassed in the Interim Report is to increase the amount that could be earned before the Allowance is reduced, along with a reduction in the current withdrawal rate of 70 per cent. It is noted, however, that the potential danger of such a policy is that it could reduce the incentive for some people to take full-time work. This requires further analysis.

A second issue is the treatment of casual earnings. It may be advantageous to encourage people to take short-term or temporary work, to help them get a foothold in the labour market, by allowing them to keep a greater proportion of the associated earnings without losing benefits in the way that they do under current arrangements. This is a similar idea to the return to work benefits discussed earlier.

Third, despite the reforms to family payments under the government's new tax package there will still be some families facing very high effective marginal tax rates. An outstanding case of this, identified in the Interim Report, is a middle income family with dependent children in both the Youth Allowance and Family Tax Benefit systems. This results from the overlapping of these two types of assistance. It is suggested in the report that there are a number of ways that this could be ameliorated by altering thresholds and/or taper rates.

All three of these proposals involve offering financial incentives or 'carrots', to provide stronger rewards for people moving from welfare to work. However, there appears to be a growing international consensus that incentives or carrots need to be combined with other policies which might be called 'sticks' and 'services'. Martin's review, for example, emphasises the importance of enforcing availability to work and job search tests; making continued receipt of income support conditional on agreeing to participate in active programs after a certain minimum duration of unemployment spell; and ensuring that participants in training and public sector employment programs continue to be available for work, and actively seek jobs.

Thus, the argument goes, there should be certain administrative requirements of benefit recipients that will vary according to their circumstances. Severely disabled people and lone parent with young children should not be expected to work. But unemployed people and perhaps lone parents with older children, and people with less severe disabilities (where, for example, part-time employment might be possible and in many cases desired) might be expected to undertake activities which will help them in due course to move from welfare to work.

The nature and extent of such requirements should be a matter for further discussion. In many cases, such mutual obligations may involve social participation rather than economic participation, but where economic participation is a reasonable prospect, there is a strong case for encouraging it.

The central thrust of the Interim Report is the case for re-orienting the social support system to be a *participation support system*. An important feature of this is the idea that income support payments should be increasingly viewed as 'participation support payments' and part of an integrated participation support system, where the financial incentives, services provided to those receiving payments, and the associated administrative requirements, all join together to promote economic and social participation. This has been advocated by Tony Atkinson (1993) in Britain, and in Australia Julia Perry (1995) has explored ways in which a 'conditional benefit system' could be introduced. This is essentially the same idea, whereby payment of benefits is made conditional upon economic and/or social participation.

In its simplest form such a participation income system could involve the same basic benefit for all working-age people, perhaps varying according to such things as the number of children and partner's circumstances, and subject to the same withdrawal rates. This would involve removing the distinction between allowances and pensions. From this basic model more complicated versions could be devised. For example, the participation supplement could be added to the basic benefit, with different rules about how the supplement can be drawn down according to how much one could reasonably expect somebody to seek and secure employment.

The difficult task is to work out how to move to such a system from the current much more complex system involving a wide range of benefit types and associated payments and withdrawal rates, without reducing any payments, but also without imposing too much fiscal stress on the government's budget. Such an approach would clearly have to be phased in over a number of years, but is an idea worthy of further development.

Labour demand

The policy ideas discussed above have focused on labour supply. The central idea is that policies are needed improve the job-readiness, job search and work skills of those on income support, and to increase their incentive to move from welfare to work.

But are there sufficient jobs for these people to do? If there is only one vacancy for every eight unemployed, so the argument goes, what is the point of welfare reform increasing the incentive to work amongst the unemployed, let alone others on welfare benefits who are not currently seeking work? According to this argument, the only important policy is to stimulate the demand for labour.

But this issue is complicated for a number of reasons. One is that supply side policies can improve the matching of the jobless with vacancies. When employment increases as a result, this in turn can further stimulate the demand for products and services and, in turn, for labour. Furthermore, there is considerable turnover in the Australian labour market, and there are always new job opportunities for some of the people who are currently jobless. Some of these jobs are not particularly secure, but for people who have been excluded a temporary job is better than never having a job.

Figure 11.8 is taken from an article by Elizabeth Webster (forthcoming). The grey line shows how the ratio of vacancies per unemployed person has varied between 0.06 and 0.16 over the last twenty years. It should be noted that since 1998 this ratio has moved further in favour of the unemployed, albeit still not strongly by historical standards.

The black line in Figure 11.8 presents Webster's estimates of the mean length of a vacancy, which has varied between five and fifteen days. This is much shorter than the mean length of an unemployment spell. Thus while an unemployed job-seeker may at any point in time be competing with, say, eight other unemployed job seekers (plus a number of employed job-seekers), over a period of five to fifteen days, there is another set of vacancies for which to compete. The following example illustrates this point.

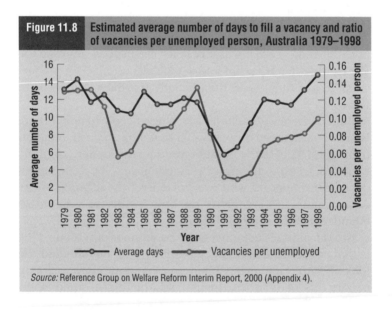

Figure 11.8 Estimated average number of days to fill a vacancy and ratio of vacancies per unemployed person, Australia 1979–1998

Source: Reference Group on Welfare Reform Interim Report, 2000 (Appendix 4).

If an average unemployed person is competing, in time period I, with an average of sixteen people for every job he or she applies for (say, eight unemployed and eight employed people), and that person is an 'average applicant', then he/she has a 6.25 per cent chance of obtaining a job in that period, or a 93.75 cent chance of still being unemployed after that time period. Then, in time period II (which begins after about fifteen days – the average length of a vacancy), if he/she is still unemployed, there is another 6.25 per cent chance of obtaining a job. Thus the cumulative probability of still being unemployed is 87.9 per cent after thirty days and so it goes on: 82.4 per cent after forty-five days, 77.2 per cent after sixty days, 72.4 per cent after seventy-five days, 67.9 per cent after ninety days, and so on through to 43.2 per cent after 195 days. In this hypothetical example, therefore, there is a greater than even chance that our average unemployed person will be employed before six months is up.

It is important to think about job search in this dynamic context. It leads to greater optimism about the prospects of the unemployed obtaining a job and, in turn, of the value of supply side measures to help them obtain a job. Another statistic, from the Australian Bureau of Statistics Survey of Labour Force Experience (ABS 1999b) is that while about 13.6 per cent of the labour force were unemployed at some time in the year to February 1999, only 2.0 per cent were unemployed for the whole year.

Of course, none of this is to deny that it is important to increase the number of job vacancies in order to facilitate the movement from welfare to work. However, it also illustrates the value of raising the competitiveness of those on welfare benefits in their job search process. The kind of supply side measures discussed earlier in this chapter have the potential to raise significantly the likelihood that a person on welfare benefits will move into employment. However, it would be wrong to underestimate the challenge for many of them, especially as they tend to be disproportionately among the unskilled.

On the labour demand side, there are two levels at which policy can be discussed. First, good macro-economic policy making, combined with micro-economic reform, can help to create sustained growth in aggregate employment. Second, there is an argument that it is worth exploring policies that are designed specifically to raise the demand for the less skilled since they are over-represented among jobless people on benefits.

One way of doing this is through wage subsidies, which reduce the cost of employing unemployed job seekers. This was an important plank in the Working Nation policies adopted by the Labor government in the early to mid-1990s, but it was to a large extent abandoned by the Coalition after its election in 1996. The movement away from large scale use of wage subsidies was based on evidence that suggests that many of the subsidised workers might have been employed anyway.

There would probably be general agreement that Working Nation placed too much emphasis on wage subsidies as the solution to the problem of long-term unemployment. However, there may be policies which involve the possibility of the wages of a person seeking to move from welfare to work being subsidised, perhaps in a more targeted and cost effective way. The idea of a 'participation account', discussed earlier, is one such possibility.

Interaction of supply and demand

John Freebairn (2000) has discussed the macro-economic effects of welfare reform policies (such as reducing effective marginal tax rates), within the context of a model that is widely used in modern analysis of the aggregate labour market. In so doing he talks about the kind of supply and demand influences that have been discussed above.

Freebairn shows how welfare reform can be expected to stimulate employment in a number of ways. First, by increasing search intensity it can be expected to improve the matching of supply and demand, such that for any given level of job vacancies a higher employment rate is achieved. Second, welfare reform increases the amount of labour that is supplied at a given wage rate. This takes pressure off the wage that needs to be offered in the wage setting system, which in turn leads to higher employment. Third, the increase in employment resulting from the two above effects in turn results in higher product demand from the new employees. This then increases the demand for labour. Thus, three factors join together to raise employment, and ongoing research at the Melbourne Institute is seeking to determine their relative effects.

The broad conclusion that follows is that such welfare reforms can be expected to increase the employment to population ratio and in so doing take the pressure off the income support system to the extent that the employment effects favour those on benefits whose labour supply has been stimulated. What the net effect would be on the unemployment rate (that is, the proportion seeking employment but not obtaining it) is ambiguous. It could rise or fall depending on the net effect of the changes of the positive increase in employment and the positive increase in labour supply. This is again an empirical question under investigation at the Melbourne Institute.

Summary and conclusions

The Interim Report of the Reference Group on Welfare Reform (2000) has proposed a re-orientation of the social support system towards a participation support system. In this chapter I have canvassed the labour market issues associated with such a welfare reform agenda.

An important focus is on ways in which incentives for people to move from welfare to work might be increased, and the associated problem of the complexity of the income support system reduced. As noted, however, such reforms to the income support system need to be married to other changes to the social support system associated with service delivery and administrative requirements. A multi-pronged approach is required.

On that note it is appropriate to list the five features of the proposed Participation Support System that the Welfare Reform Reference Group put forward in its Interim Report (2000: 6-7):

Individualised service delivery. Income support and related services should activate, enhance and support social and economic participation, consistent with individual capacities and circumstances. Service delivery would focus on meeting the needs of the individual and on helping them to identify and achieve participation goals. This would include a greater emphasis on prevention and early intervention to improve peoples' capacity for self-reliance over the course of their lives.

A simpler income support structure that is more responsive to individual needs, circumstances and aspirations. We envision a dynamic and holistic system that recognises and responds to people's changing circumstances over their life cycle and within their own family and community context.

Incentives and targeted assistance to encourage and enable participation. Social support structures would ensure a fair return from paid work, while maintaining fair relativities between people in different circumstances, and take account of the additional costs of participation.

Social partnerships. Governments, businesses, communities all have a role to play. Governments would continue to invest significant resources to support participation. Employers and communities would provide opportunities and support.

Mutual obligations. Income support recipients would be expected to make the most of opportunities provided by Government, business and community, consistent with community values and their own capacity.

This chapter has focused primarily on the case for a simpler income support structure and for stronger work incentives, while touching on the issue of mutual obligation and individualised service delivery. If all parts of the Australian community can be mobilised into assisting in this welfare reform process, building on and extending the kind of 'social partnerships' that already exist, this will further raise the prospects of a successful participation support system.

Welfare reform needs to be multi-faceted process, with mutually reinforcing policies.

Now is a good time to embark on welfare reform, with unemployment below its average for the last twenty-five years and the economy still growing strongly. There are good reasons to believe that the kind of welfare reforms being canvassed will raise the share of employment opportunities obtained by those on income support, and raise the employment to population ratio, as well as labour force participation. The net effect on the aggregate unemployment rate is uncertain, but it is doubtful that changes in the unemployment rate would be a very good indicator of the success of welfare reform directed at a wider range of groups than just those on unemployment benefits. The effect on joblessness (especially of those on income support) would arguably be a better indicator, and especially the effect on jobless families and job-poor communities. If reform can at the same time lead to a reduction in the unemployment rate that would be an added bonus.

This whole process should be viewed as having medium to long-term benefits rather than being a quick fix. A major challenge for future policy development is to determine the right blend of policy initiatives that should be taken in implementing welfare reform. In so doing, an important issue will be to estimate the economic and social returns to alternative investments in participation support processes. This will require a major ongoing agenda of research and evaluation and appropriate policy adjustments, as the welfare reform process proceeds.

Notes

1. An earlier version of this chapter was published in *Mercer - Melbourne Institute Quarterly Bulletin of Economic Trends*, 1'00, pp. 14-27. Peter Dawkins is a member of the Reference Group on Welfare Reform, but the views expressed in this chapter are those of the author and may not be shared by other members of the Reference Group.

2. In particular, the article includes a number of charts and tables drawn from the Appendices to the Interim Report. Thanks are due to the staff of the Department of Family and Community Services who produced these tables and graphs. I am particularly grateful to Jocelyn Pech for comments on an earlier draft.

Chapter 12

Examining the assumptions behind the welfare review

Michael Raper

The Australian welfare system plays a crucial role in supporting the most disadvantaged in our communities, in shaping our society, and determining our collective future. If properly handled, the current welfare review, announced recently by the federal government, presents a real opportunity to realise better outcomes for the many individual Australians who rely on income support and for our society as a whole. Unfortunately, the ability of the review to identify and develop strategies designed to enhance our already world class social security system is being undermined by some of the key assumptions that appear to be driving the reform agenda.

This chapter examines these assumptions in some detail. This is not a semantic exercise – these assumptions influence the definition and identification of the problems that need to be addressed and, consequently, the range of possible solutions to be developed. The chapter argues that key assumptions underpinning the review are not supported by evidence and could prevent us from designing real solutions. In particular we refer to the concept of 'welfare dependency' and the weight accorded it; the paternalistic view of the principle of mutual obligation; a reduction of the 'social safety net' to almost solely income support; and the meaning of 'fiscal discipline'.

Is Australia's income support system encouraging welfare dependency?

The central assumption and primary motivating force of the review is the concept of 'welfare dependency'. The Government, some members of the Opposition, and a range of public commentators have voiced growing concern about increasing levels of 'welfare dependency' among income support recipients of workforce age, although they often ascribe different causes and meanings to the term.

There is no doubt that there are increasing numbers of Australians of workforce age forced to rely on low social security payments as their main source of income for long periods of time. The Australian Council of Social Service (ACOSS), along with most other analysts, argues that this is a tragic situation which has negative consequences for both many of the individuals involved and for the broader society which is deprived of their full participation and contribution. This said, ACOSS does not accept that this situation should be characterised as one of welfare dependency because this term, and its colloquial meaning, locates the primary cause in (at best) the skill deficiencies and (at worst) the character deficiencies or personal failures of individual income support recipients.

A more accurate and ultimately useful description of the situation in Australia at the end of the 1990s is that we have: more unemployed people than jobs, and much longer average periods of unemployment; more people facing the difficult task of raising children alone; more older people living in their own homes being cared for by prime-aged family members; more people with disabilities who need care from family members and face serious workforce barriers; and more older workers, especially men, forced by economic restructuring into early retirement.

It is the combination of these factors which has led to increased numbers of people receiving unemployment benefits, disability pensions, carer and parenting payments. Even so, there has been no recent blow-out in social security expenditure. Data from the Department of Family and Community Services show that spending on all social security programs, as a proportion of GDP, has risen from around 3 per cent in 1965 to around 7 per cent in 1998, with the major period of growth being 1972 to 1978 (Figure 12.1).

Further, Australia's welfare system is structured in a way that strongly discourages unnecessary long-term reliance on social security payments. Australia has been an international leader in terms of constructing an 'active' system – one that fully embraces mechanisms which not only encourage labour market participation and skills development by social security recipients, but which requires those who can reasonably be expected to do so to take up job and training opportunities or forfeit payment.

This latter point is particularly pertinent to the welfare dependency debate. Our welfare system is not one of passive or unconditional support for people of workforce age. Contributions to public discussions which focus on a 'culture of unconditional welfare' are wide of the mark. On the contrary, there has been a steady program of cumulative reform over the past two decades to ensure exactly the opposite. The current reality is that payments are not easy to get or to keep. The system has tight eligibility and retention criteria as well as substantial waiting periods and penalties. While changing economic conditions mean that people are out of work for longer periods of time, most still manage to replace social security payments with wages within a year. Figures from the Department of Family and Community Services reveal that

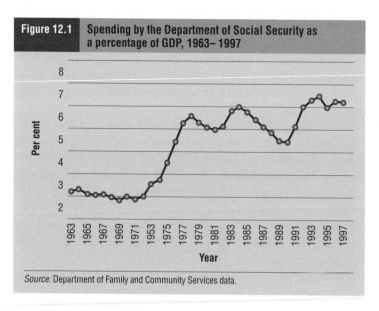

Figure 12.1 Spending by the Department of Social Security as a percentage of GDP, 1963–1997

Per cent

Year

Source: Department of Family and Community Services data.

only 38 per cent of people granted unemployment benefits in 1997 were still receiving payment by the end of that year, despite the fact that the number of unemployed people greatly exceeds available job vacancies.

Furthermore, a significant and growing proportion of other payment recipients also take up employment opportunities. For example, 26 per cent of all sole parents receiving Parenting Payment (single) currently report earnings from employment – up from 9 per cent in 1983. Most significantly, over a 12-month period, approximately 40 per cent of these people earn income. Among people receiving disability payments, the increase has been from 2 per cent in 1991 to 8 per cent in 1999. In both groups, there are significant numbers of people who desperately want to increase their earnings but are constrained from doing so, either by the restricting factors in their own lives or by external economic and social factors beyond their control.

These statistics are not proffered in an attempt to deny the reality that growing numbers of people are on unemployment benefits for very long periods, or that many people with disabilities and sole parents do not desire, or would not benefit from, increased workforce participation. They do, however, point to the causes and dimensions of the problem and where the answers are likely to lie. They are not to be found in giving currency to pejorative and inaccurate terms such as 'welfare dependency' or in overstating either the dimension of the problem or its causes. While the Minister for Family and Community Services (Newman 1999a) has said herself that 'a modern safety net is not about blaming the victim, or penalising or punishing disadvantaged people,' far too many government pronouncements and policies fuel this attitude and lead to precisely this outcome.

One of the myths fuelling the 'welfare dependency' debate is that income support payments are too high and as a consequence there is little incentive for people to enter the labour market. ACOSS argues that far from encouraging people to become dependent on the income support system, income support payments are simply keeping people alive – although in many cases living in a state of poverty.

The number of people living in poverty in Australia is increasing. In 1975, the Commission of Inquiry into Poverty headed by Professor Ronald Henderson estimated that there were around 600,000 or 6.4 per cent of Australians living in poverty. In 1996, the figure was around two million people or over 11 per cent (King 1998).

There have been a number of debates over the years about the appropriateness of the Henderson Poverty Line as a measure of deprivation. The key criticism has been that the method of indexation has increased its value relative to wages, and hence has lifted it above what the community might regard as a realistic measure of hardship. However, recent research looking at the expenditure side of the deprivation issue showed substantial similarities between the Henderson Poverty Line and calculations of the expenditures required to maintain a 'low cost' standard of living – one 'below which it becomes increasingly difficult to maintain an acceptable living standard because of the increased risk of deprivation and disadvantage' (Social Policy Research Centre 1998). The report, entitled *Development of Indicative Budget Standards for Australia*, found that payment rates for unemployed people and for sole parents were below this budget level, with housing costs being a critical factor. Another study has calculated that poverty rates among unemployed households have grown from 20 per cent in 1972–73 to over 60 per cent in 1996. This compares to age pension couple households, where the poverty rate is now 3.8 per cent (King 1998).

There are several reasons why poverty is so common among people in receipt of unemployment benefits, but less common among other groups where high proportions of people get most or all of their income from social security payments (such as those relying on the Age Pension).

First, while still lean, pensions are paid at a rate that is generally sufficient to prevent people falling below the poverty line, whereas allowances are paid at a lower rate. This gap between pensions and allowances is getting wider because, while pension payments are legislatively tied to 25 per cent of Male Total Average Weekly Earnings, the rate of allowance payments is only linked to changes in the Consumer Price

Index. The allowance payment is now $19.90 a week *less* than the single pension rate – and this disparity is increasing at an alarming rate in a low inflation environment.

Second, people who are unemployed face extra costs in looking for work, so need higher levels of income to achieve the same standard of living and participate fully in the community.

Third, some of the people in receipt of other income support payments – particularly older people – face comparatively low housing costs because they are more likely to own their own homes which reduces their general living expenses.

Poverty in Australia does not generally mean going without food or shelter (although it does for some people, whether for short or long periods of time). It does, however, always mean significant hardship comparative to the rest of the population. Equally important is the fact that poverty greatly restricts choice – choice about expenditure on items such as clothing, education, medication, heating/cooling and, most importantly, choice about participating fully in the community. Such constraints cause severe problems and social exclusion. For the individual, poverty can lead to social isolation, physical ill health, family conflict or separations, and depression or other mental health problems. For an affluent society, a growing body of research shows that poverty contributes to increased social division and disharmony.

Although not often openly articulated, there seems to be a growing body of thought amongst policy and decision makers in Australia and elsewhere that short-term poverty is not a significant problem, and that, even if not actually 'character building' and a potential plus for the individual, it is an acceptable outcome of some public policies because of its limited duration. This attitude seems to apply particularly to young adults undertaking further education or training, and to unemployed people. In relation to young people, the assumption is that students have made a choice to defer earning income in order to undertake study. The argument goes that it is acceptable for students to struggle in the short term as they can expect to enjoy financial rewards as a result of their endeavours in the future. Against this, ACOSS argues that these people should be adequately supported on a means-tested basis while participating in this worthwhile activity – upon which, as a nation, we ultimately rely.

In relation to unemployed people, the belief appears to be based on the incorrect assumption that people will be without work for only short periods of time. Although, historically, unemployment benefits were a short-term payment (in the 1950s periods of unemployment averaged around six to eight weeks), this is not the case today. At present, up to one-third of unemployed people can expect to be out of work for two years or more, and the average period is fifty-five weeks. The low rate of unemployment benefits, combined with the liquid assets test, means that unemployed people quickly find themselves living in poverty.

There is little evidence to support the view that periods in poverty are beneficial to people. Indeed, some authors argue that people who are forced to go without basic necessities for any length of time find the experience debilitating rather than strengthening (see Trethewey 1989).

In the context of the debate over 'welfare dependency', the issue of particular concern is the negative impact that poverty has on a person's capacity for both economic and social participation. The *Development of Indicative Budget Standards for Australia* report found that, for many households, social security payments are insufficient to ensure 'a standard of living which . . . would still allow social and economic participation consistent with community standards and enable the individual to fulfil community expectations in the workplace, at home and in the community' (Social Policy Research Centre 1998).

In addition, the Organisation for Economic Cooperation and Development (OECD 1997b: 87-88) has concluded that: 'The level and generosity of unemployment benefits in Australia remains below the OECD average, particularly with regard to shorter duration unemployment. Combined with ongoing measures to tighten the administration of the activity test, this means that it is unclear that the unemployment benefit system, when taken as a whole, has contributed significantly to the rise in structural and long-term unemployment.'

People in receipt of unemployment payments, in particular, are often unable to afford to fully undertake the activities required of them, such as job search. As at February 2000, the basic Newstart Allowance payment for people aged over twenty-one years was just $163 a week. Even adding in the full rate of Rent Assistance still brings the payment to only $201 a week. The situation is even worse for young people. Independent 16–20-year-olds living away from home get just $133 a week (or $171 if they are eligible for maximum rate of Rent Assistance).

In addition, people in receipt of allowance payments do not get many of the fringe benefits associated with pension payments. These include a larger income-free area (the amount of income people can earn before they start to lose a portion of their social security payment); less harsh income and assets test; access to the Pensioner Concession Card; and, in most cases, access to Pharmaceutical Allowance. Consequently, people in receipt of allowance payments often cannot afford public or private transport in order to attend interviews or undertake cold canvassing of employers; they cannot maintain the social contacts which research shows play a major role in securing employment; and they have difficulty in presenting well at interview due to their inability to maintain appropriate clothing. The extent of this problem is reflected by the fact that a service provider in Melbourne is lending clothing to people on income support to assist them to present well at interviews.

Other income support recipients particularly affected by inadequate payment rates include people who have extra non-discretionary costs associated with their disability or chronic illness, and people living in remote areas.

It is worth noting that there has been no government-sponsored inquiry into levels of poverty in Australia since the Henderson Inquiry in the early 1970s.

Despite the evidence showing that many income support payments are below or only just above the poverty line (Table 12.1), some commentators argue that the levels of payment are too high and act as a disincentive for people to participate in the labour market, thus contributing to welfare dependency. They argue that there needs to be greater differentiation between levels of income support payments and minimum award wages.

However, the evidence shows that replacement rates in Australia are not a major issue. The replacement rate is a measure of the financial incentive to enter the workforce from unemployment. It is defined as the ratio of disposable income of a person or family receiving unemployment benefits to the prospective disposable income from employment.

Replacement rates are important for two reasons. First, they describe the extent to which the income support system for unemployed people is able to maintain the income of people who become unemployed. Second, they are a key factor influencing the incentive for unemployed people to seek employment. The higher the replacement rates, the greater the relative financial attractiveness of income support relative to wages. Therefore, from the point of view of maintaining

Table 12.1	Comparison of Social Security payments with the Henderson poverty line: after housing, $ per week, September 1999		
Family/income unit	Poverty line $	Social Security payment $	Payment as % of poverty line %
Couple unemployed - no children	337.66	329.50	97
Couple unemployed - one child	405.88	391.45	96
Couple unemployed - two children	474.10	444.80	94
Single adult unemployed	252.41	200.75	80
Single under 21 unemployed	252.41	171.60	68
Sole parent - one child*	276.26	292.30	106
Sole parent - two children*	344.48	345.65	100
Single mature age allowee	252.41	214.70	85
Single aged pensioner	204.67	218.60	107
Pensioner couple - no children*	289.91	337.30	116
Pensioner couple - one child*	358.14	396.80	111
Pensioner couple - two children*	426.36	454.20	107

Notes: Assumes receipt of maximum rate of Rent Assistance. * Out of the workforce.
Sources: Poverty lines as at September Quarter 1999, Melbourne Institute of Applied Economic and Social Research, 1999. Payment rates as at September 1999, Centrelink, 1999.

work incentives, there is concern that replacement rates should not be too high.

Commentators tend to agree that replacement rates are not an issue in the Australian context. A study undertaken by the OECD (1996b) found that Australia has relatively low replacement rates. For a short spell of unemployment, Australia has the fourth lowest gross replacement rate out of twenty-one OECD countries for single people, while replacement rates for couples are consistent with the OECD average. Australian replacement rates were the equal ninth lowest out of twenty-one OECD countries against the OECD's summary measure of gross replacement rates (this measure is not restricted to short spells of unemployment), and net replacement rates (taking account of both taxation and other benefits) for Australia are also comparatively low according to the OECD. Furthermore, Ingles and Oliver (1999) suggest that the income floor set by social security benefits is sufficiently low relative to wages to have had little impact on labour supply.

It is important to note that the group with the highest replacement rates (families with children), and who therefore

Table 12.2	Replacement rates June 2000 (projected rates)		
Family type	Maximum income support payments $/wk	Minimum wage plus income support entitlement (where applicable) $/wk	Ratio
Single	168	334	0.50
Couple parents	304	411	0.74
with one child	369	461	0.80
with two children	424	516	0.82
with three children	521	650	0.80
Single parent			
with one child	276	472	0.58
with two children	331	531	0.62

Notes: These rates are for the period prior to the introduction of the Government's 'A New Tax System'. Rent Assistance has not been included in calculations.
Source: Department of Family and Community Services data, 1999.

are the group most likely to have an incentive problem, have been given increased in-work benefits over the 1980s and 1990s. In fact the major purpose in providing these in-work benefits is precisely to prevent increases in replacement rates for this group. It is equally important to note that the replacement rate is low for a single unemployed person who could expect to double their income through employment.

There is a danger that welfare reform in Australia will seek to side-step the serious problem of payment rates that are so low they directly cause poverty. ACOSS is convinced that if the question of adequacy is not confronted head-on and successfully addressed, any other reform measures will rest on shaky if not immoral foundations.

A specific characterisation of the principle of mutual obligation

The concept of mutual or reciprocal obligation has long been a central feature of the Australian social security system. In particular, receipt of unemployment payments has always been linked to requirements that the person engages in active job search and preparation and meets 'work tests'.

However, the character of these past links is being questioned by the current government – specifically, that previous procedures and programs involved too great a degree of voluntarism. The government argues that its reworked mutual obligation framework provides the greatest potential to further its objectives of preventing social problems and dependency. The most succinct expression of the government's understanding of mutual obligation came from the Prime Minister (Howard 1999a) when he defined it as 'asking people to give something back to the community in return for assistance in times of need.' The clearest program and legislative manifestation of this policy is Work for the Dole.

ACOSS does not accept this current interpretation or implementation of the principle of mutual obligation, which is a significant departure from the meaning of the concept employed by successive governments since it was first introduced in the mid-1940s.

During the 1930s, when approximately one-third of the Australian labour force was unemployed, there was no entitlement to benefits for unemployed people. Assistance in cash or kind was only provided in return for work on public projects. Underpinning this approach was the common assumption at the time that, to a substantial degree, unemployment was caused or at least prolonged by a weakening of the work ethic.

In the mid-1940s, a dramatically different approach was adopted – one which implemented a positive job generation/full-employment strategy, together with the introduction of unemployment benefits. This change was predicated on recognising the fact that unemployment was, first and foremost, a societal responsibility.

From its inception, the unemployment benefit has been based on a reciprocal obligation: on the part of government, to make a sustained effort to generate full employment and to pay an allowance to those still unable to secure work; and on the part of the unemployed person, to make a sustained effort to seek employment and take up any job opportunities – in essence, to satisfy a 'work test'. Payments were made on the condition that applicants for unemployment benefit showed they were capable and willing to undertake suitable work and had taken steps to obtain such work. The 'work test' was based on the assumption that full time work was generally available to a person seeking it regardless of background, qualifications or experience, and that if a person was unemployed, it would only be for a short period.

From 1945 to the early 1970s, there were few changes to the unemployment benefit arrangements. Subsequent variations to the work test were in part responses to changes in labour demand and growing structural unemployment, and in part reflected views about the appropriate nature of obligations within this changed labour market.

By the late 1980s, high and entrenched levels of unemployment, and the emergence of long-term unemployment, forced a re-think of the system. Consequently, the nature of the 'work test' was called into question for people severely disadvantaged in the labour market. The government considered it to be more appropriate for these job seekers to be required to undertake activities which would improve their employability in the longer term, rather than be involved in a potentially fruitless search for jobs for which they were uncompetitive.

Accordingly, in 1988, the work test was expanded to include a broader range of activities than job search, and became known as the 'activity test'. At the same time, an 'active employment strategy' was introduced for long-term unemployed people which increased places in labour market programs; improved information, counselling assistance and intensive interviews for people; introduced a more active job placement strategy; and improved incentives to take up work.

These initiatives were evidence of a change in the political philosophy of welfare. They represented a shift away from the principle of income support entitlement based on need, to a system incorporating conditional benefits for unemployed people. Unemployed people were now required to accept greater responsibility for improving their employability by responding to the increased opportunities provided to them. In addition, there was now a preparedness to withdraw benefits from people if compliance was not achieved.

In July 1991, unemployment benefit was abolished and Job Search Allowance and Newstart Allowance were introduced. Job Search Allowance incorporated an activity test for people who received the payment for three months or more. Long-term unemployed people on Newstart Allowance were required to enter into an individual Newstart Activity Agreement, outlining an agreed course of action aimed at maintaining their job search efforts and/or improving labour market competitiveness.

Other initiatives were also introduced around this time. First, the Jobs, Education and Training Program (JET) for sole parents has seen improvements in the labour market participation of sole parents by providing opportunities for education, training and work experience and other support services, most notably child care. Second, the Disability Reform Package improved workforce participation among people with disabilities and improved greatly the opportunities for rehabilitation, training and work experience. Third, there was a broadening of the ways that unemployed people could be required to, and could, satisfy the activity test to enable greater opportunities for education and training, and for voluntary work.

It is notable that these three changes involved the expansion of choice and opportunity, that they were oriented to encouraging workforce participation among social security recipients, and that – in the case of unemployed people – they included a substantial element of obligation on the part of the recipient of payments to make efforts to improve their work prospects and find work. It is also worth noting that the income tests for sole parents and people with disabilities are more relaxed than those applying to unemployed people, making it more rewarding for the former groups to take up part-time work. In other words, consideration was given to the way the provision of opportunities interacts with financial incentives in the system.

Over the 1990s, one of the more notable changes has been the progressive intensification of the activity test requirements imposed on the recipients of unemployment payments. For example, penalties for non-compliance have been expanded dramatically; there has been an increase in the requirements for employer contacts, together with increased requirements for evidence; and the introduction of compulsory work requirements for some young unemployed people under the Work for the Dole scheme, recently expanded to people aged 25–34 years. Some of these changes have been introduced in a budget context as savings measures, but they have usually been justified in terms of the 'enhancement' of obligations.

The introduction of Work for the Dole represented a crucial policy shift – the imposition of direct work obligations on some unemployed people *in exchange for receiving a payment*, rather than for undertaking activities explicitly and directly related to improving their employment prospects. As the previous potted history shows, this approach turns the clock back to the 1930s.

Work for the Dole has been cited by Minister Newman (1999a) as a successful example of mutual obligation in operation. Legislation for the Work for the Dole program was passed by the federal government in June 1997. The program initially required people aged 18–24 years who had been registered as unemployed for six months and who were in receipt of full Newstart Allowance to work in community projects for between twenty-four and thirty hours per fortnight, for a period of six months. In September 1998, the scheme was expanded to include school leavers who were not employed or in education or training three months after leaving school. The scheme was further expanded in the 1999–2000 Budget, with an increase in the target number of places from 32,000 a year to 50,000. From 1 July 1999 people aged 25–34 years who have been unemployed for twelve months are referred to a Work for the Dole project if they cannot meet their 'mutual obligation' requirements in another way.

An evaluation of the scheme was released on 26 May 1999. A large part of the evaluation focused on the popularity of the scheme among participants and community organisations which were sponsoring projects. Some data were also presented on the employment outcomes and compliance aspects of the scheme. However, the evaluation did not measure the net employment effect of Work for the Dole in relation to a comparable group who did not participate in the program. Moreover, the evaluation authors pointed out that 'employment' is not actually a formal objective of the Work for the Dole program.

ACOSS has regularly expressed opposition to this scheme on the grounds that it is both compulsory (where it should not be) and deficient in that it does not guarantee properly structured supervision or training, or any substantial mainstream employment experience.

From the outset, the government has justified the Work for the Dole program as being both a pathway to work, and a reasonable community expectation of people receiving unemployment payments under the principle of mutual obligation. ACOSS has always supported programs designed to improve the employment prospects of unemployed Australians, and has always accepted the principle of balanced, reciprocal obligations. However, ACOSS believes that the burden of obligation in the Work for the Dole program rests too heavily on the unemployed person and that the government has failed its obligation to provide participants with the opportunity to improve their prospects for achieving paid employment through the inclusion of recognised vocational training which will enable them to acquire transferable skills. As a contribution to the obligation of government within the framework of mutual obligation, the program fails, both in terms of its investment and its evaluation.

The policy behind the Work for the Dole initiative reflects the rise of a social policy movement that has been labelled as 'new paternalism'. Mead (1997a: 2) defines new paternalism as 'social policies aimed at the poor that attempt to reduce poverty and other social problems by directive and supervisory means'. Under this approach, a government takes a very direct role in the lives of poor people who depend on public support and actively seeks to change their behaviour by using sticks rather than carrots. By contrast, under a traditional social policy framework, governments fund social programs that provide benefits to people who qualify according to objective criteria of need – and only after this point, intervene to assist the individuals to reshape their lives, using carrots more often than sticks.

New paternalism ignores the underlying structural causes of unemployment by placing the 'blame' for a person's unemployed status directly on the individual. It is based on the assumption that unemployed people lack the skills, character traits, and abilities necessary for them to be able to help themselves out of their current situation. Consequently, they need to be forced to participate in welfare to work programs, and their participation needs to be closely monitored and supervised. The sentiment behind this approach was captured by Newt Gingrich when he suggested that the objective of welfare reform in the United States must be to 'correct those individual behavioural dysfunctions – such as moral laxity, inadequate work discipline – which are seen as a cause of poverty but more importantly as a consequence of the welfare system' (Peck 1998).

Another concern is that under new paternalism, control is most strongly exercised by governments over the least powerful, the most marginalised and disadvantaged groups in society, the ones who are judged as least able to be self-determining. These people have the least capacity to fight for a 'fair go' and influence government decision making.

ACOSS rejects the paternalistic overtones that the current federal government has brought to the mutual obligation concept. It is not only unhelpful but plain wrong in an environment where there are currently over six unemployed people for every single job vacancy (and the average for the past decade has been ten to one); where there is often no correlation between where the jobs are and where many unemployed people live; where there is a significant degree of mis-match between the available jobs and the skills of unemployed people (particularly long-term unemployed people); and when government expenditure on employment services has been reduced by $1.2 billion since 1995–96, so that now only around one in three long-term unemployed people are offered intensive assistance.

Given the signals that the government may be considering extending its version of mutual obligation to both more classes of unemployed people and to workforce age people on other types of benefits, it is worth exploring the objective economic environment a little further.

The figure of more than six unemployed people for every job vacancy is derived from official Australian Bureau of Statistics data for December 1999 showing 671,000 unemployed people at a time when there were approximately 100,000 job vacancies. Given the very restricted definition of 'unemployment' used by the Australian Bureau of Statistics, it is universally accepted that the actual figure is much higher. A further 588,000 people receive Disability Support Pension and another 385,000 people receive Parenting Payment Single (Department of Family and Community Services 1999). In the sticks and carrots approach, no amount of sticks can make the equation match.

The current mutual obligation push is not only out of touch with economic realities but is morally repugnant in that it has the effect, even if not the intention, of dividing those who rely on income support into the 'deserving' (those without 'activity' obligations – for example, age and carer pensioners) and 'undeserving poor' (those with increasing 'activity' obligations under the sticks approach). The debate invalidates the lives of many Australians who through no fault of their own, or through caring responsibilities which most Australians would endorse, are precluded from paid employment.

ACOSS has always supported the principle of reciprocal or mutual obligation where the requirements placed on people are reasonable and are within their capacity to meet; where the activities required to be undertaken are specifically designed and deliberately directed to enhancing the person's employment prospects; and where the government meets its side of the contract by providing security of income and adequate access to employment, training and other opportunities. In its submission to the welfare review, ACOSS urged the Reference Group on Welfare Reform to adopt this meaning of the term when developing its policy and program recommendations.

A reductionist approach to the components of the social safety net

There has also been a policy shift in the meaning attached to the 'social safety net'. Increasingly in public and political debate, the concepts of both welfare and the safety net have been reduced simply to the provision of social security payments. Where the definition is expanded at all (as it is in the Terms of Reference of the Reference Group on Welfare Reform), it is still usually limited to acknowledging the importance of employment and training services to assist low income people achieve better labour market outcomes and hence diminish the need for them to draw on income support.

While there is no doubt that social security payments and employment-related services are the most important threads in the social safety net, they do not constitute the whole weave. They need to be accompanied by other publicly-provided social supports, such as affordable child care and other family support services; services for people with disabilities and their carers; health and aged care services; and adequate and affordable housing, provided by way of a public and community housing program (as well as Rent Assistance payments for low income people in the private housing market). With the exception of the public health and aged care systems, these other areas of public policy should be central to any review of the welfare system.

Consideration also needs to be given to the crucial role played by community social welfare organisations in the actual operation of the safety net. For most of this decade, community service agencies in Australia have been the subject of a 'reform agenda' resulting in new or altered arrangements for planning, financing and delivering community services.

In any review of the welfare system, attention needs to be paid to the impact of these reforms. This is a complex issue, with the pace and direction of change differing in the various government jurisdictions, as well as within and between government agencies in the same jurisdiction. However, there is no doubt that while some of these changes have been beneficial, others are having a negative impact on community organisations and the services they provide, and contributing to an erosion of the social safety net (ACOSS and the State and Territory Councils of Social Service 1999).

The welfare review provides the government with an opportunity to prove itself in relation to the development and implementation of sound social policy. Since coming to office, its achievements in this area have been few and far between. As a result, it is considered to be lightweight by many in the community. The review is a major test for the government and many are waiting expectantly to see if it will pass.

ACOSS will be watching to ensure that the government does not shirk its responsibilities in this area by hiding behind talk of a 'social coalition'. We acknowledge that there are aspects of this concept that are sound and should be strongly supported. It is clearly true that government alone cannot fix complex social problems, and that the skills, expertise and knowledge of other sectors must be harnessed into creative partnerships to tackle them. At the end of the day, however, there are some things that rest squarely with government. Foremost among these uniquely government functions is income support policy and determining the level of public expenditure on essential services such as employment services, housing assistance and child care. These are critical areas of public policy that government alone has responsibility for and control over.

The meaning of fiscal discipline

The Terms of Reference of the Reference Group on Welfare Reform specify one of the review's guiding principles as 'maintaining the government's disciplined approach to fiscal discipline'. There is always a risk that this will be interpreted as requiring reform proposals to be revenue neutral. However, fiscal discipline is not synonymous with fiscal neutrality (at best) nor with cost cutting (at worst), and the government itself has often explicitly stated this when pursuing reform agendas in a range of public policy areas.

Implementing fiscal discipline does not imply that no extra funds should be spent; but rather that any increased expenditure is warranted, is effectively used, and represents 'value for money' by producing good and necessary ends.

As with any nation, Australia faces a range of policy and expenditure choices in both the short and the long term. ACOSS acknowledges and supports strategic vision and planning for the future, and the careful husbanding of national resources. At the same time, we are also alive to the research on inter-generational reliance on income support that highlights the importance of immediate investment in people (particularly in the areas of education and training) so that they can produce better futures for themselves and their families (ABC 1999). It is not a matter of either/or. The quality of the immediate lives of people and the quality of their futures are inter-related, and we need strategies which address both aspects.

In recent policy debates around welfare reform, there are some who argue that 'point-in-time' or 'here and now' inequality measures are the product of a range of factors connected with post-industrial labour markets and must be accepted as a fact of life (Myles 1997). The focus of this argument lies in the popular idea that the solution is only to be found in more productive investment in education and training, and that any other measures are wasted resources. This view is based on an observation that those with the lowest skill levels in society are suffering most from the effects of globalisation and technological change – a view supported by recent Australian Bureau of Statistics (1999a) data on job churning.

While always acknowledging the critical importance of education and training, ACOSS argues that this approach is a stark manifestation of the dangers of taking a good idea too far. Governments cannot *only* focus on the future and ignore the realities of their citizens' present lives. Further, governments should not focus on investment in the future *at the cost of* investment now. If they do, they imperil our collective future in another way. Research shows that what erodes people's sense of well being and trust in their society is perceived inequality – the size of the gap between the rich and the poor. This gap is growing in Australia, and must be addressed in the short term if the sort of societal disruption it produces is not to become a permanent feature of our society. Government alone cannot do this, but it can make important contributions. In fact, as previously argued, some of the remedial actions required, such as decisions about income support payment rates and the provision of supportive social and community services, can *only* be taken by government.

Governments must also be concerned with inequality for economic as well as social imperatives. While some still argue that there is a trade-off between social equity and economic efficiency, recent research suggests that this may be a false premise. In fact, the opposite may be true. According to Myles (1997): 'The new endogenous growth models argue that, *ceteris paribus*, more equal economies will expand more quickly than less equal ones.'

Seen in this context, the difficult question facing the welfare review and the government is: how much is too much to invest in a stable, more equal, more economically productive society?

References

Albert, M. (1993), *Capitalism Against Capitalism*, Whurr Publishers, London.

Allard, T. & Murphy, D. (1999), 'Billions down the drain in a nation hooked on gambling,' *The Sydney Morning Herald*, 20 July, pp. 1; 6.

Annie E. Casey Foundation (1999), *Kids Count Data Book 1999*, Annie E. Casey Foundation, Baltimore.

Atkinson, A. (1993), 'Participation income', *Citizen's Income Research Group Bulletin*, no. 16, July, pp. 7-10.

ABC (1999), 'Reversing the real brain drain', *Background Briefing*, 3 October, Radio National, Australian Broadcasting Corporation, Sydney.

ABC (2000), 'Welfare trap', *Lateline*, TV Program Transcript, 21 March, Australian Broadcasting Corporation, Sydney.

ABS (1994), *Focus on Families: Education and Employment*, Australian Bureau of Statistics, Catalogue No. 4421.0, Canberra.

ABS (1997a), *Labour Force Status and Other Characteristics of Families, June 1997*, Australian Bureau of Statistics, Catalogue No. 6224.0, Canberra.

ABS (1997b), *Australians' Employment and Unemployment Patterns 1994-1996*, Australian Bureau of Statistics, Catalogue No. 6286.0, Canberra.

ABS (1998a), *Australian Social Trends*, Australian Bureau of Statistics, Catalogue No. 4102.0, Canberra.

ABS (1998b), *Persons Not in the Labour Force, Australia*, Australian Bureau of Statistics, Catalogue No. 6220.0, Canberra.

ABS (1999a), *Job Quality and the Churning of the Pool of the Unemployed*, Occasional paper, Australian Bureau of Statistics, Catalogue No. 6293.0.00.003, Canberra.

ABS (1999b), *Labour Force Experience Australia, February 1999*, Australian Bureau of Statistics, Catalogue No. 6206.0l, Canberra.

ABS (2000), *Labour Force Australia*, Australian Bureau of Statistics, Catalogue No. 6203.0, Canberra.

Australian Council of Social Service (ACOSS) and the State and Territory Councils of Social Service (1999), *Common Cause:*

Relationships and Reforms in Community, ACOSS Paper 102, Australian Council of Social Services, Sydney.

Bagnall, D. (1999), 'The state of welfare', *The Bulletin,* 13 July, pp. 47-49.

Bardach, E. (1997), 'Implementing a paternalist welfare-to-work program', in L. Mead (ed.) *The New Paternalism: Supervisory Approaches to Poverty,* Brookings Institute Press, Washington DC.

Barnett, W. (1992), 'Benefits of compulsory preschool education', *Journal of Human Resources,* vol. 27, pp. 279-312.

Bejerot, N. (1978), *Missbruk av Alkohol, Narkotika och Frihet,* Ordfront, Stockholm.

Bellah, R. (1995), 'The quest for self", in A. Etzioni (ed.) *Rights and the Common Good: A Communitarian Perspective,* St Martin's Press, New York.

Besharov, D. & Gardiner, K. (1996), 'Paternalism and welfare reform', *The Public Interest,* no. 122, pp. 70-84.

Birrell, B. & Rapson, V. (1998), *A Not So Perfect Match,* Centre for Population and Urban Research, Monash University, Victoria.

Blundell, R. Duncan, A., McCrae, J. & Meghir, C. (2000), 'The labour market impact of the Working Families' Tax Credit', *Fiscal Studies,* vol. 21, no. 1.

Bond, K. & Whiteford, P. (2000), 'Trends in income support receipt 1965-1999, Mimeo, Department of Family and Community Services, Canberra.

Bos, J., Huston, A., Granger, R., Duncan, G., Brock, T. & McLoyd, V. (1999), *New Hope for People With Low Incomes: Two-Year Results of a Program to Reduce Poverty and Reform Welfare,* Manpower Demonstration Research Corporation, New York.

Brotherhood of St Laurence (1999), 'The children come first: paid work for single parents with children at school', *Changing Pressures Project Bulletin,* no. 8, November.

Brown, J. (1990), 'The focus on single mothers', in D. Green (ed.) *The Emerging British Underclass,* Institute of Economic Affairs, London.

Brown, M. & Madge, N. (1982), *Despite the Welfare State,* Heinemann, London.

Buckingham, A. (1999), 'Is there an underclass in Britain?', *British Journal of Sociology,* vol. 50, pp. 49-75.

Castles, F. & Mitchell, D. (1991), 'Three worlds of welfare capitalism or four?' *Discussion Paper Number 21,* Australian National University, Canberra.

Caughy, M., DiPietro, J. & Strobino, D. (1994), 'Day care participation as a protective factor in the cognitive development of low-income children', *Child Development,* vol. 65, pp. 457-471.

Centrelink (1999), *A Guide to Commonwealth Government Payments: July to September,* Centrelink, Canberra.

Chapman, B. (1992), *Austudy: Towards a More Flexible Approach,* Australian Government Publishing Service, Canberra.

Corcoran, M. & Chaudry, A. (1997), 'The dynamics of childhood poverty', *Children and Poverty,* vol. 7, pp. 40-54.

Curtain, R. (1999), 'Mutual obligations: intention and practice in Australia compared with the UK and the US', *Submission to the Reference Group on the Review of the Welfare System,* Commonwealth Department of Family and Community Services, Canberra.

Danziger, S., Haveman, R. & Plotnick, R. (1981), 'How income transfers affect work, savings and income distribution', *Journal of Economic Literature,* vol. 19, pp. 975-1028.

Danziger, S., Sandefur, G. & Weinberg, D. (1994), *Confronting Poverty: Prescriptions for Change,* Harvard University Press, Cambridge.

Dawkins, P. (1996), 'The distribution of work in Australia', *Economic Record,* vol. 72, no. 218, pp. 272-286.

Dawkins, P. (1999), 'A plan to cut unemployment in Australia: an elaboration on the Five Economists' letter to the Prime Minister, 28 October 1998', *Mercer-Melbourne Quarterly Bulletin of Economic Trends,* pp. 48-57.

Dawkins, P., Beer, G., Harding, A., Johnson, D., & Scutella, R. (1998), 'Towards a negative income tax system for Australia', *Australian Economic Review,* vol. 31. pp. 237-57, September.

Deacon, A. (ed.) (1997), *From Welfare to Work: Lessons from America,* Institute of Economic Affairs, London.

Deacon, A. (2000), 'Learning from the US?: The influence of American ideas upon "new labour" thinking on welfare reform', *Policy and Politics,* vol. 28, pp. 5-18.

Dean, H. & Taylor-Gooby, P. (1992), *Dependency Culture: The Explosion of a Myth,* Harvester Wheatsheaf, Hemel Hempstead.

DeParle, J. (1999), 'Life after welfare', *New York Times,* 10 October.

Department for Employment and Education (DEE) (1999), *Education and Training Statistics for the United Kingdom,* The Stationary Office, London.

Department of Eduction and Employment Training (DEET) (1996), *'Working Nation': Evaluation of the Employment, Education and Training Elements,* EMB Report 2/96, Canberra.

Department of Family and Community Services (FaCS) (1999a), *Fact Sheet: What is the Welfare System and Who Uses it?,* Commonwealth Government, Canberra.

Department of Family and Community Services (FaCS) (1999b) *Research FaCS Sheet,* Number 3, November, Commonwealth Government, Canberra.

Department of Social Security (DSS) (1981), *Work Incentive Experiments in the United States and Canada,* Research and Statistics Branch, Development Division, Canberra.

Department of Social Security (DSS) (1998), *New Ambitions for Our Country,* HMSO, London.

Department of Social Security (DSS) (1999), *Social Security Statistics,* HMSO, London.

Duncan, G. (1984), *Years of Poverty, Years of Plenty: The Changing Economic Fortunes of American Workers and Families,* University of Michigan, Ann Arbor.

Durkheim, E. (1933), *The Division of Labor in Society,* MacMillan, Toronto.

Eardley, T. (1998), 'Working but poor: low pay and poverty in Australia', Discussion Paper no. 91, Social Policy Research Centre, University of New South Wales, Sydney.

Eardley, T. (1999), 'A fair go or a hard line? Australian attitudes to unemployed people and activity testing', Paper presented at the Social Policy Research Centre Seminar, Sydney, 5 October.

Ellwood, M. & Bane, D. (1994), *Welfare Realities,* Harvard University Press, London.

Ellwood, M. & Summers, R. (1986), 'Is welfare really the problem?', *The Public Interest,* vol. 83, pp. 57-78.

Erikson, R. & Goldthorpe, J. (1992), *The Constant Flux: A Study of Class Mobility in Industrial Societies,* Clarendon Press, Oxford.

Ermisch, J. (1986), *The Economics of the Family,* Discussion Paper, no. 40, CEPR, London.

Esping-Andersen, G. (1977), 'Welfare states at the end of the century: the impact of labour market, family and demographic change', in *Family, Market and Community,* OECD, Paris.

Esping-Andersen, G. (1990), *The Three Worlds of Welfare Capitalism,* Polity Press, Cambridge.

Etzioni, A. (1995), 'The responsive communitarian platform: rights and responsibilities', in A. Etzioni (ed.) *Rights and the Common Good: A Communitarian Perspective,* St Martin's Press, New York.

Fegan, M. & Bowes, J. (1999), 'Isolation in rural, remote and urban communities', in J. Bowes & A. Hayes *Children, Families and Communities: Contexts and Consequences,* Oxford University Press, Melbourne.

Field, F. (1995), *Making Welfare Work,* Institute of Community Studies, London.

Field, F. (1996), *How to Pay for the Future,* Institute of Community Studies, London.

Field, F. & Owen, M. (1994), *Beyond Punishment,* Institute of Community Studies, London.

Finch, H., O'Connor W., Millar J., Hales J., Shaw A. & Roth W. (1999), *'New Deal' for Lone Parents: Learning From the Prototype Areas,* Department of Social Security Research Report 92, HMSO, London.

Finn, D. (1999), 'Job guarantees for the unemployed: lessons from Australian welfare reform', *Journal of Social Policy,* vol. 28, pp. 53-71.

Ford, R. (1997), 'The role of child care in lone mothers' decisions whether or not to work', in *DSS Research Yearbook 1996–97,* HMSO, London.

Fraser, N. & Gordon, L. (1997), 'A genealogy of "dependency": tracing a keyword of the US welfare state', in N. Fraser (ed.) *Justice Interruptus: Critical Reflections on the 'Post-Socialist Condition',* Routledge, New York and London.

Freebairn, J. (2000), 'Evaluating effects of social security and taxation reform on employment and unemployment', *Mercer-Melbourne Quarterly Bulletin of Economic Trends,* 1'00, pp. 28-29.

Gallie, D. (1994), 'Are the unemployed an underclass? Some evidence from the social change in economic life initiative', *Sociology,* vol. 28, pp. 737-757.

Giddens, A. (1984), *The Constitution of Society,* Polity Press, Cambridge.

Giddens, A. (1998), *The Third Way: The Renewal of Social Democracy,* Polity Press, Cambridge.

Gilder, G. (1980), *Wealth and Poverty,* Basic Books, New York.

Goodin, R. (1995), 'In defence of the nanny state', in A. Etzioni (ed.) *Rights and the Common Good: A Communitarian Perspective,* St Martin's Press, New York.

Gottschalk, P. (1992), 'The inter-generational transmission of welfare participation: facts and possible causes', *Journal of Policy Analysis and Management,* vol 11, pp. 254-272.

Gottschalk, P., McLanahan, S. & Sandefur, G. (1994), 'Dynamics of poverty and welfare participation', in S. Danziger, G. Sandefur & D. Weinberg (eds) *Confronting Poverty: Prescriptions for Change,* Harvard University Press, Cambridge.

Government Statistical Service (GSS) (1989), *Education Statistics for the United Kingdom,* HMSO, London.

Gregory, R. (1999), 'Children and the changing labour market: joblessness in families with children', Paper presented at the *Labour Market and Family Policies: Implications for Children* Conference, Canberra, July.

Gregory, R. & Hunter, B. (1998), 'The macro economy and the growth of ghettos and urban poverty in Australia: the National Press Club Telecom address', Discussion Paper no. 325, Centre for Policy Research, Australian National University, Canberra.

Hakim, C. (1995), 'Five feminist myths about women's employment', *British Journal of Sociology,* vol. 46, pp. 429-447.

Hardin, G. (1977), 'The tragedy of the commons', in G. Hardin & J. Baden (eds) *Managing the Commons,* WH Freeman & Co, San Francisco.

Harding, A. & Loundes, J. (1999), 'Policy watch: employment initiatives' *Mercer-Melbourne Institute Quarterly Bulletin of Economic Trends,* 1'99, pp. 35-47.

Harding, A. & Percival, R. (1999), 'The private costs of children in 1993–94', *Family Matters,* no. 54, Spring/Summer, pp. 82-87.

Harding, A. & Szukalska, A. (1999), 'Trends in child poverty: 1982 to 1995–96', Paper presented to *the Australian Association for Social Research Conference,* Sydney, February.

Haskey, J. (1998), 'Families: their historical context, and recent trends in the factors influencing their formation and dissolution', in D. Green (ed.) *The Fragmenting Family: Does it Matter?,* Institute of Economic Affairs, London.

Hayek, F. (1967), 'The moral element in free enterprise', in F. Hayek, *Studies in Philosophy, Politics and Economics,* Routledge & Kegan Paul, London.

Henman, P. (1999), *What is Welfare Dependency and What are its Causes?,* Submission to the Reference Group on Welfare Reform, Department of Family and Community Services, Commonwealth of Australia, Canberra.

Hobcraft, J. (1998), *Intergenerational and Life-Course Transmission of Social Exclusion: Influences of Childhood Poverty, Family Disruption and Contact with the Police,* CASE paper 15, Centre for Analysis of Social Exclusion, London.

Howard, J. (1999a), *The Australian Way,* Federation Address presented to the Queensland Chamber of Commerce and Industry, Brisbane, 28 January.

Howard, J. (1999b), Address to the 'Australia Unlimited Roundtable' Transcript, 4 May.

Ingles, D. & Oliver, K. (1999), 'Options for assisting low wage earners,' Paper presented at the *National Policy Research Conference,* University of New South Wales, Sydney, July.

Jackson, S. (1996), *The Way Forward,* Brotherhood of St Laurence, Melbourne.

Jackson, S. & Crooks, M. (1993), *Existing but not Living: A Research Project Canvassing the Aspirations and Views of Long-Term Unemployed Australians,* Brotherhood of St Laurence, Melbourne.

Jencks, C. (ed.) (1990), *The Urban Underclass,* Brookings Institute, Washington DC.

Jencks, C. & Swingle, J. (2000), 'Without a net: whom the new welfare law helps and hurts', *The American Prospect,* 3 January, pp. 37-42.

Johnson, P. & Reed, H. (1996), 'Intergenerational mobility among the rich and poor: results from the National Child Development Study', *Oxford Review of Economic Policy,* vol. 12, pp. 127-142.

Kalisch, D. (2000), 'Welfare to work: a review of international practices and outcomes', Paper delivered to the seminar on welfare reform, Melbourne Institute, 25 January.

Kant, I. (1798), *Der Streit der Facultäten in drey Abschnitten,* Königsberg.

Kelly, G., Kelly, D. & Gamble, A. (eds) (1997), *Stakeholder Capitalism,* Macmillan, Basingstoke, UK.

Kewley, T. (1973), *Social Security in Australia: 1900–72,* Sydney University Press, Sydney.

Kewley, T. (1980), *Australian Social Security Today: Major Developments from 1900 to 1978,* Sydney University Press, Sydney.

Kiernan, K. (1997), *The Legacy of Parental Divorce: Social, Economic and Demographic Experiences in Adulthood,* Paper 1, Centre for Analysis of Social Exclusion, London.

King, A. (1998), 'Income poverty since the 1970s', in R. Fincher & J. Nieuwenhuysen (eds) *Australian Poverty: Then and Now,* Melbourne University Press, Melbourne.

Lasch, C. (1995), 'Communitarianism or populism?' in A. Etzioni (ed.) *Rights and the Common Good: A Communitarian Perspective,* St Martin's Press, New York.

Latham, M. (1998), *Civilising Global Capital: New Thinking for Australian Labor,* Allen and Unwin, Sydney.

Layard, R., Nickell, S. & Jackman, R. (1994), *The Unemployment Crisis,* Oxford University Press, Oxford.

Laydon, R. (1979), *Managers and Workers at the Crossroads,* Sentry Holdings, Sydney.

Lewis, O. (1961), *The Children of Sanchez,* Random House, New York.

Loprest, P. (1999), 'How families that left welfare are doing', *NewFederalism,* Series B, Number B-1, August, Urban Institute, Washington.

Loprest, P. & Brauner, S. (1999), 'Where are they now?', *NewFederalism,* Issue 6, July, Urban Institute, Washington.

Lown, J. (1990), *Women and Industrialisation: Gender at Work in Nineteenth Century England,* Polity Press, Cambridge.

McAllister, I. (1991), 'Political attitudes of voters and candidates', *Australian Journal of Social Issues,* vol. 26, pp. 163-190.

McClelland, A. (2000), '*No child . . . ' Child Poverty in Australia,* Brotherhood of St Laurence, Fitzroy.

MacDonald, F. (2000), *Uncertain Work, Unsettled Lives: The Work Opportunities and Experiences of Some Families Over the 1990s ,* Brotherhood of St Laurence, Fitzroy.

MacFarlane, A. (1978), *The Origins of English Individualism,* Blackwell, Oxford.

McLanahan, S. (1988), 'Family structure and dependency: early transitions to female household headship', *Demography,* vol. 25, pp. 1-16.

McLean, D. (1987), *Public Choice,* Basil Blackwell, Oxford.

Marsh, A. (1997), 'Lowering barriers to work in Britain', *Social Policy Journal of New Zealand,* vol. 8, pp. 111-135.

Marshall, G., Roberts, S. & Burgoyne, C. (1996), 'Social class and the underclass in Britain and the USA', *British Journal of Sociology,* vol. 47, pp. 22-44.

Marshall, T. (1950), *Citizenship and Social Class and Other Essays,* Routledge and Kegan Paul, London.

Martin, J. (1998), 'What works among active labour market policies: evidence from OECD countries' experiences', in Borland, J. & Vickery, P. (eds) *Unemployment and the Australian Labour Market,* Proceedings of a Conference, Reserve Bank of Australia and the ANU, pp. 276-302.

Martin, J. (2000), 'Making active labour market policies more effective: key lessons and experiences', The OECD Perspective, OECD Conference on Jobs, Helsinki.

Mead, L. (1986), *Beyond Entitlement: The Social Obligations of Citizenship,* Free Press, New York.

Mead, L. (1992), *The New Politics of Poverty: The Nonworking Poor in America,* Basic Books, New York.

Mead, L. (1996), 'Welfare reform and children', in E. Zigler, S. Kagan, and N. Hall (eds) *Children, Families and Government: Preparing for the Twenty-First Century,* Cambridge University Press, Cambridge.

Mead, L. (1997a), 'The rise of paternalism', in L. Mead (ed.) *The New Paternalism: Supervisory Approaches to Poverty,* Brookings Institute Press, Washington DC.

Mead, L. (1997b), 'Welfare employment', in L. Mead (ed.) *The New Paternalism: Supervisory Approaches to Poverty,* Brookings Institute Press, Washington DC.

Mead, L. (Ed.) (1997c), *The New Paternalism: Supervisory Approaches to Poverty,* Brookings Institute Press, Washington DC.

Mead, L. & Wilson, W. (1987), 'The obligation to work and the availability of jobs: a dialogue between Lawrence M. Mead and William Julius Wilson', *Focus,* vol. 10, pp. 11-19.

Melbourne Institute of Applied Economic and Social Research (1999), *Poverty Lines: Australia,* September Quarter, University of Melbourne, Melbourne.

Miller, P. (1998), 'The burden of unemployment on family units: an overview', *Australian Economic Review,* vol. 30, pp. 16-30.

Miller, W. (1962), 'Lower class culture as a generating milieu of gang delinquency', in M. Wolfgang, L. Savitz & N. Johnston (eds) *The Sociology of Crime and Delinquency,* Wiley and Sons, New York.

Morris, L. & Irwin, S. (1992), 'Employment histories and the concept of the underclass', *Sociology,* vol. 26, pp. 402-20.

Murray, C. (1988), *In Pursuit of Happiness and Good Government,* Simon Schuster, New York.

Murray, C. (1994), *Losing Ground: American Social Policy, 1950–1980,* 2nd edn, Basic Books, New York.

Murray, C. (1995), 'The partial restoration of traditional society', *The Public Interest,* no. 121, pp. 122-134.

Murray, C. (1996), 'The emerging British underclass', in Lister, R. (ed.) *Charles Murray and the Underclass: The Developing Debate,* Institute of Economic Affairs, London.

Murray, C. (1999), 'The underclass hasn't gone away', *The Sunday Times,* News Review Supplement, 5 September.

Murray, C. (2000), 'Baby beware', *The Sunday Times,* News Review Supplement, 6 February.

Murray, C. & Herrnstein. R. (1994), *The Bell Curve: Intelligence and Class Structure in American Life,* Free Press, New York.

Myles, J. (1997), 'When markets fail: social policy at the turn of the century', Paper to the National Social Policy Conference – States, Markets, Communities: Remapping the Boundaries.

Newman, J. (1999a), 'The future of welfare in the 21st century', Speech to the National Press Club, Canberra, 29 September.

Newman, J (1999b), 'The challenge of welfare dependency in the 21st century', Discussion Paper, Department of Family and Community Services, Canberra.

Newman, K. (1999), *No Shame in My Game: The Working Poor in the Inner City,* Knopf and Russell Sage Foundation, New York.

Nickell, S. & Bell, B. (1995), 'The collapse in demand for the unskilled and unemployed across the OECD', *Oxford Review of Economics,* vol. 11, pp. 40-62.

Office of National Statistics (ONS) (1998), *Social Trends 28,* HMSO, London.

Office of National Statistics (ONS) (2000), *Social Trends 30,* HMSO, London.

Olsen, M. (1965), *The Logic of Collective Action,* Harvard University Press, Cambridge, Mass.

OECD (1996a),*Employment Outlook,* Organisation for Economic Cooperation and Development, Paris.

OECD (1996b), *OECD Country Economic Surveys: Australia 1996–97,* Organisation for Economic Cooperation and Development, Paris.

OECD (1997a), *Family, Market and Community: Equity and Efficiency in Social Policy,* Organisation for Economic Cooperation and Development, Paris.

OECD (1997b), *OECD Country Economic Surveys: Australia,* Organisation for Economic Cooperation and Development, Paris.

OECD (1998a), *The Battle Against Exclusion,* Organisation for Economic Cooperation and Development, Paris.

OECD (1998b), 'Low income dynamics in four OECD countries', *OECD Economic Outlook,* Organisation for Economic Cooperation and Development, Paris.

Paugam, S. (1995), 'The spiral of precariousness', in G.Room (ed.) *Beyond the Threshold: The Measurement and Analysis of Social Exclusion,* Policy Press, Bristol.

Pearson, N. (1999), 'Positive and negative welfare and Australia's indigenous communities', *Family Matters,* no. 54, Spring/Summer, pp. 30-35.

Peck, J. (1998), 'Workfare: a geopolitical etymology,' in *Environment and Planning D: Society and Space.*, vol. 16, pp. 133-161.

Perry, J. (1995), *A Common Payment? Simplifying Income Support for People of Workforce Age,* Policy Discussion Paper No. 7, Department of Social Security, AGPS, Canberra.

Probert, B. & Macdonald, F. (1999), 'Young women: poles of experience in work and parenting', in Dusseldorp Skills Forum, *Australia's Young Adults: Reality and Risk,* Dusseldorp Skills Forum, Sydney.

Probert, B. with Macdonald, F. (1996), *The Work Generation,* Brotherhood of St Laurence, Fitzroy

Productivity Commission (1999), *Productivity and the Structure of Employment,* Productivity Commission, Melbourne.

Quinlan, M. (1998), 'Labour market restructuring in industrialised societies: an overview', *The Economic and Labour Relations Review,* vol. 9, June, pp. 1-30.

Rainwater, L. (1987), *Class, Culture, Poverty and Welfare,* Center for Human Resources, Heller Graduate School, Brandeis University, Waltham Mass.

Reference Group on Welfare Reform (2000), *Participation Support for a More Equitable Society: The Interim Report of the Reference Group on Welfare Reform,* Department of Family and Community Services, Canberra.

Review of Higher Education Financing and Policy (RHEFP) (1998), *Learning for Life: Final Report,* AGPS, Canberra.

Room, G. (1995), 'Poverty and social exclusion,' in G. Room (ed.) *Beyond the Threshold: The Measurement and Analysis of Social Exclusion,* Policy Press, Bristol.

Saunders, P. (1993), 'Citizenship in a liberal society', in B. Turner (ed.) *Citizenship and Social Theory,* Sage, London.

Saunders, P. (1996), *Capitalism: A Social Audit,* Open University Press, Buckingham.

Saunders, P. (1996), 'Poverty and deprivation in Australia', *1996 Year Book Australia,* Australian Bureau of Statistics, Catalogue no. 1301.0, Canberra.

Smith, P. & Bond, M. (1993), *Social Psychology Across Cultures,* Prentice Hall, London.

Social Exclusion Unit (1999), 'Bridging the gap: new opportunities for 16-18 year olds not in education, employment or training', http://www.cabinet-office.gov.uk/seu/1999/16-18yearolds/index.htm/

Social Policy Research Centre (1998), *Development of Indicative Budget Standards for Australia,* Research Paper No. 74, Department of Social Security Policy, University of New South Wales, Sydney.

Swan, W. (1999), 'Two-way street to end poverty rraps', *The Sydney Morning Herald,* 6 May, p. 17.

Tasker, G. & Siemon, D. (1998), *Is Child Care Affordable? Pressures on Families and Their Use of Formal Long Day Care,* Brotherhood of St Laurence, Fitzroy.

Taylor, J. & Macdonald, F. (1998), *Life at Six: Life Chances and Beginning School,* Brotherhood of St Laurence, Fitzroy.

Travers, P. (1998), 'Welfare dependence, welfare poverty and welfare labels', *Social Security Journal,* vol. 1998, no. 2, pp. 117-128.

Travers, P. & Richardson, S. (1993), *Living Decently: Material Wellbeing in Australia,* Oxford University Press, Melbourne.

Trethewey, J. (1989), *Aussie Battlers: Families and Children in Poverty,* Collins Dove and Brotherhood of St Laurence, Melbourne.

Turok, I. & Edge, N. (1999), *The Jobs Gap in Britain's Cities*, Polity Press, Cambridge.

Urban Institute (1999), *National Survey of America's Families*, Urban Institute, Washington DC.

US Department of Commerce, Bureau of the Census (1994-1999), Unpublished data from the March Current Population Survey, Washington DC.

US Department of Commerce, Bureau of the Census (1999), *Poverty in the United States 1998*, Series P-60, No. 207, Government Printing Office, Washington DC.

Warby, M. & Nahan, M. (1998), 'From workfare state to transfer state', *IPA Backgrounder*, vol. 10/3 (Institute of Public Affairs).

Weber, M. (1968), *Economy and Society*, Volume Three, Bedminster Press, New York.

Webster, E. (1999), 'Job Network: What can it offer?', *Just Policy*, vol. 17, December, pp. 32-42.

Wilson, K., Bates, K. & Pech, J. (1998), 'Parents, the labour force and social security', Background paper for the Family and Community Services and Centre for Public Policy Research Conference, *Income Support, Labour Markets and Behaviour: A Research Agenda*, 24-25 November, Australian National University, Canberra.

Wilson, W. (1987), *The Truly Disadvantaged*, University of Chicago Press, Chicago.

Winter, I. (ed.) (2000), *Social Capital and Public Policy in Australia*, Australian Institute of Family Studies, Melbourne.

Wooden, M. (1996), 'Hidden unemployment and underemployment: their nature and possible impact on future labour force participation and unemployment', *National Institute of Labour Studies Working Paper Series*, no. 140, Flinders University of South Australia, Adelaide.

Wooden, M. (1998), 'The changing nature of employment arrangements', *The Transformation of Australian Industrial Relations Project, Discussion Paper no. 5*, National Institute of Labor Studies, Flinders University of South Australia, Adelaide.

Wooden, M. & Hawke, A. (1998), 'Factors associated with casual employment: evidence from the AWIRS', *The Economic and Labour Relations Review*, vol. 9, pp. 92-107.

Yeatman, A. (1997), 'Contract, status and personhood', in G. Davis, B. Sullivan & A. Yeatman (eds) *The New Contractualism?*, Macmillan Education, Melbourne.

Index

clients 142
see also: claimants

coalition, social – *see:* partnership, social

collectivism 5
collectivistic cultures 11-12, 13, 42n
problems of 9, 11, 13

colonialism – *see:* Aboriginal people, dispossession

commodification 10, 11, 162

communitarianism 156, 164, 176n

community
disintegration 70, 136-7, 146, 148-9, 155, 222
ideology of 165-6, 176n
networks 118, 142-3, 211, 257
sector – *see:* voluntary activity, organisations
self-regulation 12, 163
strengthening 5, 7, 153-4, 222, 248
weakened by welfare state 30, 139, 143, 146, 151-2, 155
see also: social capital; social cohesion

competence – *see:* poverty, competence of the poor

compulsion – *see:* work, voluntary participation by unemployed

constraints on action – *see:* structural influences on behaviour

contract
social 72, 157, 163-4, 174-5
see also: mutual obligation, contracts; welfare state, contract agencies

contracting out of government services 216 *see also:* welfare state, contract agencies

Corcoran, M. and Chaudry, A. 94

counselling 39, 40, 81, 230, 262
see also: job search

crime
exacerbated by welfare state 150, 177
participation in 118
rates of 77, 113, 150
reduced by welfare state 5
see also: law enforcement

criticism in social science xi, 3

culture
Aboriginal 30, 116, 137, 142-3, 144, 149, 152
American 13
Australian 5, 6, 13, 179
British 5, 13
capitalist 13
collectivistic – *see:* collectivism
explanation for behaviour 23, 59
individualistic - *see:* individualism
national 13
see also: Anglo countries, common culture; dependency culture; poverty, culture of

Curtain, R. 220

Danziger, S. 42n

Dawkins, P. x, xii, 2, 4, 16, 20, 26, 34, 41, 134, 174, 226, 238, 239

Deacon, A. 42n, 65

Dean, H. and Taylor-Gooby, P. 115

DeParle, J. 37, 40

Department for Employment and Education 81, 90n

Department of Education and Employment Training 84

Department of Family and Community Services 14-15, 251, 266

Department of Social Security 42n, 72, 74, 78, 79, 87, 205n

dependency – *see:* welfare dependency

dependency culture 4, 23-5, 27-32, 112-8, 125-32
  attitudes to education 91, 113, 127-8
  attitudes to employment 91, 113, 114, 117, 124-7
  attitudes to money 144
  attitudes to welfare reliance 91, 126-7, 130, 131
  causes of 23, 28, 29-32, 130-2, 132-3, 151
  defined 116-8, 135n
  existence of 25, 28-9, 91-2, 114-5, 119, 125, 130, 132, 206, 209, 221, 252
  family patterns 118, 128
  irrationality of 141, 144
  solutions to 24, 25, 33, 133-4
  transmission of - *see:* welfare dependency, intergenerational transmission
  see also: poverty, culture of; welfare state, passive welfare

deprivation
  cultural 38, 113
  economic – *see:* poverty; social exclusion

disabled people
  compulsory work requirements 19, 39, 52, 163, 229, 234, 242
  desire to work 33
  employment 253, 262-3
  nature of disabilities 42n-43n
  numbers of 18, 19, 251
  provisions for 267
  see also: income support, disability

divorce 21, 44, 57, 96, 185-6, 196, 214

drug abuse 29, 47, 56, 66, 113, 118, 127, 129-30, 131, 134, 144-6, 148

Duncan, G. 95

Durkheim, E. 29, 132, 160, 163, 176n

duty, social – *see:* citizenship; reciprocity

Eardley, T. 39, 215

economy
  affected by welfare spending 187, 270
  subsistence 140, 147

education
  commitment to 117, 120
  condition of dole 2, 56
  early leaving/retention 117, 127, 128, 171, 193, 202, 226, 231
  experience of 120, 123, 127-8
  higher/further 90n, 255
  moral 160, 163
  parenting skills 56
  performance 55, 96, 113, 136
  provision by government 7, 137, 222, 270
  raising standards of 51, 70
  see also: training

equal pay legislation 30, 141
fairness 158
family 70, 98-9, 188-93, 203,
260
influence on life chances 94,
101, 144
see also: work, low-paid
income support
age pension 10, 67, 180-1, 183,
188, 196, 225, 254, 267
'bludging' 121-2, 125, 185,
221 see also: free rider
problem
categories of 197, 204-5,
227, 234
complexity of system 227,
237, 243, 247, 248
cost of – see: expenditure,
welfare
dependency – see: welfare
dependency
disability support pension 2,
15, 16, 19, 26, 27, 42n, 66,
107-9, 110, 180, 181-3, 188,
196-7, 199, 226, 227, 228,
229, 230, 236, 253, 266
distinction between benefits
and pensions 183, 188,
203, 204, 243, 254-5, 257
eligibility rules 10, 11, 14, 18,
40, 57, 66, 70, 176n, 181,
183, 188, 189, 221, 242,
252, 261-3 see also: means
testing
extent of 14-16, 93, 109
family allowance/child
endowment 98, 111n,
188-9, 193, 197, 204, 205
increasing numbers on –
see: claimants, increasing
numbers
in-work benefits 16, 88, 99-
100, 166, 197, 201, 230, 232,
238, 260 see also: taxation,

Working Families Tax Credit
Parenting Payment 15, 16,
19, 26, 89, 99, 107, 110,
177, 183, 185-7, 188, 189,
194, 197, 199, 203, 204,
206, 219, 228, 229, 236,
253, 266 see also: lone
parents, receipt of Parenting
Payment
rent assistance 257, 268
repayable 204
return to work benefits
239-40
sickness benefits 10, 66, 107,
227
take-up rates 16
turnover in claimants 26-7,
84, 86-7, 252-3 see also:
welfare dependency,
duration of
unemployment benefits
(Newstart /JobSeekers'
Allowance) 2, 10, 15, 27,
63, 182, 183-5, 188, 191,
194, 196, 197-8, 203, 204,
206, 210, 225, 228, 229,
235-6, 254, 257, 258, 261
value/adequacy of 7, 10, 121-2,
124, 181, 183, 184, 187-8,
189, 191, 193, 197, 209,
210, 212, 225, 253-5, 256
Widows' Pensions 182, 183,
187, 189
Youth Allowance 2, 126, 204,
241
see also: claimants; expenditure, welfare; welfare
dependency
individualism
concept of 'individual' 163-4,
165
individualised casework 40,
133, 165, 167-71, 176n, 248,
262 see also: counselling

individualised welfare solutions 72, 139, 160, 163, 165, 234, 248

individualistic cultures 5, 11-14

self-interested behaviour 9 *see also:* - free-rider problem

see also: paternalism; structural influences on behaviour

industrial relations 13, 138, 158, 179

inequality – *see:* equality; income, distribution of; work, polarisation of households

Ingles, D. and Oliver, K. 259

intelligence 28

interests, objective 35, 138, 171

Jackson, S. 211
and Crooks. M. 210, 211

Jencks, C. 80
and Swingle, J. 173

job availability - *see:* work, opportunities

job creation 25, 47, 68, 212, 222, 231, 261

job search
active commitment by unemployed 72 *see also:* unemployment, desire to find work
compulsion 75, 77-8, 84, 86, 197
costs of 236-7, 255, 257
government help with 37, 67-8, 78, 230, 234 *see also:* counselling
success of 81, 230-1, 245
tests 242, 260

Johnson, P. and Reed, H. 95

Kalisch, D. 37, 134

Kant, E. 141, 144

Keating, Paul 6, 79, 138

Kelly, G. 77

Kewley, T. 205n

Kiernan, K. 96

King, A. 254

labour market
demand for labour 22, 24, 30, 34, 63, 64, 70, 214, 217, 226, 244-5, 247
demand side policies 68, 71, 245-6
job availability - *see:* work, opportunities
participation in – *see:* participation, economic
power in 138, 175
regulation 158 *see also:* industrial relations
supply side policies 231-43, 246
see also: job creation; unemployment

Lasch, S. 166

Latham, M. 116

law enforcement 51, 56, 136
see also: crime

Layard, R. 80

Laydon, R. 179

Lewis, O. 112, 116

liberalism 10-14, 61n, 157, 162

liberal welfare regimes – *see:* welfare regimes

literacy 1, 178, 240

lone parents
compulsory work requirements 35, 36-7, 39, 52,

Urban Institute 54

underclass 8, 74, 76, 82-3, 87, 115, 117, 140, 148, 177

underemployment 25, 214, 233

unemployment
Aboriginal - *see under:* Aboriginal people
causes of 24, 30, 46, 63, 79, 83, 113, 128, 177, 185, 256, 265
desire to find work 24, 32, 53, 78, 79-83, 121-2, 124-7, 129, 133, 158, 169, 171-2, 176n, 209, 219, 232, 233, 253 *see also:* lone parents, desire to work
duration 214, 244-5, 251, 252-3, 256, 261 *see also:* income support, turnover; welfare dependency, duration
experience of 207, 210-12, 221
hidden 214, 232
Jobs Education and Training scheme 218, 262
patterns of 92-3, 197, 213, 225, 261
poverty 209, 254-7
vacancy rate 26, 43n, 80, 243-5, 249, 251, 253, 266 *see also:* work, opportunities
young people 1-2, 28-9, 31-2, 77, 88, 94, 95, 96-7, 107, 109-10, 113, 124-30, 185
see also: income support, unemployment benefit; job creation; welfare dependency

U.S. Department of Commerce 46, 53

victim, self-identification as 30, 48, 118, 142

violence 136, 150
domestic 143, 148

voluntary activity 6, 81, 162, 174, 176n, 263
organisations 6, 41, 187, 268
see also: participation, social work, voluntary participation by unemployed

vote-buying 8, 58

wage subsidies 240-1, 246 *see also:* income support, in-work benefits; job creation

Warby, M. and Nahan, M. 15

Weber, M. 174

Webster, E. 244

welfare dependency
causes of 18, 24, 29, 30-1, 53, 61, 62, 65, 68, 72, 74, 114, 115-6, 132, 140, 141-6, 150-2, 154, 174, 183, 196, 251, 257-8, 265
concern about 54, 156, 161-2, 179, 250-1
duration of 26-7, 38, 74, 82, 86-7, 109-10, 155, 206, 216, 229-30, 252
extent of 1, 8, 16, 18, 187, 193, 233, 251 *see also:* claimants, increasing numbers; welfare reform, effects of
explains worklessness 14, 17, 65, 116, 151 *see also:* work, incentives
inter-generational 27-9, 51, 91, 94-8, 106-9, 110-11, 112, 130-2, 135n, 222, 269
lack of personal control 31, 61, 83, 141-2, 154
meaning of 206, 208-9, 217, 250, 253

by welfare system; social cohesion; welfare dependency; welfare reform; welfare regimes

Whitlam, Gough 155

Wilson, K. 219

Wilson, W. 24, 76, 116

Winter, I. 5

Wisconsin 37, 39, 40, 53-4, 55, 56-7, 75, 177

women
dependency on men 162, 175n
see also: patrimonial authority
employment 64-5, 66, 199-201, 214-5, 225
work 162
see also: lone parents

Wooden, M. 216, 232
and Hawke, A. 216

work
casual 25, 82, 83, 92, 207, 213-4, 216, 217, 241
ethic 28, 29, 82-3, 115, 117, 120, 123-4, 131, 132, 134, 221, 261 *see also:* unemployment, desire to find work
habit of work 25, 33, 50, 65
hierarchy 126
impact on family life 25, 44, 45, 57
improves quality of life 38, 54, 161-2
incentives 9, 16, 18, 19, 20, 22, 47, 48, 58, 60, 69-70, 80, 85, 126, 166, 175n, 184-5, 190, 194, 203, 213, 235-42, 243, 247, 248, 253, 257-60, 262
low-paid 24, 36, 38, 46, 126, 175, 207-8, 215-6, 217 *see also:* income, distribution

opportunities 14, 18, 24, 25, 26, 28, 34, 35, 46-7, 53, 63, 65, 66, 80, 113, 114, 115, 121, 123, 125, 144, 149, 209, 213-5, 217, 226, 243-5, 249, 266
participation rates – *see:* participation, economic
part-time 16, 25, 39, 64-5, 66, 92, 122, 173, 197, 201, 208, 213-4, 215, 225, 229, 232-3, 239, 241, 242, 263
polarisation of households 19, 93, 214-5, 225-7, 231
self-employment 217
source of identity 212, 223n
voluntary participation by unemployed 33, 47, 48, 52, 68, 86, 116, 124-7, 129, 158, 167, 171-2, 175n, 230, 234, 242, 260, 265 *see also:* disabled people, compulsory work requirements; lone parents, compulsory work requirements; mutual obligation, compulsion; Work for the Dole, compulsory participation; youth, compulsory work requirements
see also: income support, eligibility rules; job search; labour market

workfare 41, 51, 73
see also: welfare state, American system

Work for the Dole policy 1-2, 54, 73, 78, 84, 220, 260, 263-4
compulsory participation 33, 34-5, 36, 43n, 84, 126-7, 221, 263, 264 *see also:* mutual obligation, compulsion; work, voluntary participation by unemployed